Natives of Sarawak

Natives of Sarawak

Survival in Borneo's Vanishing Forest

Evelyne Hong

Institut Masyarakat, Malaysia. 1987

Published by
Institut Masyarakat
9 Lorong Kuching
10350 Pulau Pinang
Malaysia

Second Edition
© Evelyne Hong, 1987
ISBN 967-9966-03-8

The Institut Masyarakat is an independent
non-profit institute involved in research on
economic and cultural developments in the
Third World in general and Malaysia in
particular.

Printed by
Jutaprint
54 Kajang Road
10150 Penang
Malaysia

CONTENTS

TABLES

GLOSSARY

The apostrophe (') after a word refers to a glottal stop.

Adat/Adet: A world view. A moral and religious system involving customs, rules, sanctions, and a system of rights and obligations acknowledged by the whole community. It applied in all areas of Dayak life, economic, political, spiritual and social.

Anak biak: Iban term for the people of a longhouse under one headman or leader.

Apau: Refers to the top of the plateau. The *Usun Apau* was the original homeland of the Kayan and Kenyah.

Batang: A big river.

Belian: Eusideroxylon zwageri. Also known as the iron wood tree of Borneo.

Council Negeri: Literally the 'Council of State' or State Assembly in Sarawak.

Damar: Several species of Dipterocarpaceae (Shorea and Hopea) yield several kinds of resin which are used as medicine, torches and pitch. Resin from these trees are obtained from cuts made in the bark.

Durian: Durio zibethinus. The fruit is highly prized among the Dayak. The spiky round or oval shaped fruits contain seeds with creamy pulp which are a favourite with the locals.

Engkabang: Iban word for species of shorea which produce illepe (illipe) nuts. These nuts are valued for their edible oil which is exported for chocolate manufacture. It is also used in the cosmetic and pharmaceutical industry.

Gantang: A unit of weight measure or the Malay gallon which is equivalent to 3.6 kilogrammes or 7.92 pounds. Padi and rice is measured in *gantang*.

Jelutong: Dyera costulata. The latex from this tree was used in chewing gum manufacture.

Jeramie: Iban word for swidden in the first year of fallow. Although padi has already been harvested, *tanah jeramie* or *jeramie* land still contain many other crops which have not been harvested by Iban swiddeners. These include the sacred plant (*indu padi*) in the swidden after the rice harvest. Thus *ngambi jeramie* means to fetch home the *indu padi* for safe-keeping.

Kati: A Malay unit of weight measure which is equivalent to 0.60 kilogrammes or 1⅓ pounds.

Kerangas: Iban term for lowland forest with infertile soils which are unsuitable for hill rice cultivation. However *Kerangas* forest is very rich in tree species.

Long: Confluence of two or more rivers. Kenyah and Kayan take their present identity from the river confluences at which they first settled after leaving their original homeland on the *Usun Apau*. Usually the place or settlement is named after the smaller river.

Lepo'/Lepu': Kenyah term which refers to a particular group, settlement or village of longhouses.

Orang Ulu: Refers to the 'peoples of the interior'. They include the Kayan, Kenyah, Punan Bah, Tanjong, Sekapan, Kejaman, Lahanan and Penan.

Penghulu: A government appointed native chief who is in charge of a few communities covering an area or a region.

Pikul: A Malay unit of weight measure which is equivalent to 100 *kati* or 60 kilogrammes.

Rotan: Rattan. They are palms which are climbers valued for their vines.

Sago: Eugeissona utilis. A spiny palm tree from which *sago* starch is obtained from the pith of a mature tree. *Sago* is the staple of the Penan. In times of rice shortages, it is eaten by the Kenyah and Kayan.

SOCSO: Acronym for 'Social Security Organisation', the government department which operates a social security scheme for all employees earning a monthly salary of M$1000 and below.

Sungai: A smaller river.

Temuda: Iban word for fields in fallow.

Tuba: Derris elliptica. The roots of this liane is pounded and used to poison fish in streams and rivers.

Tuai rumah: Iban word for headman.

Tua kampong: Malay word for headman.

Ulu: The word for head or upriver. Hence *orang ulu* refers to upriver or interior peoples.

Uma': Refers to a settlement or longhouse community.

MAP OF SARAWAK

Bintulu District became the Ninth Division on 31 August 1986. Samarahan will be declared the Eighth Division in 1987.

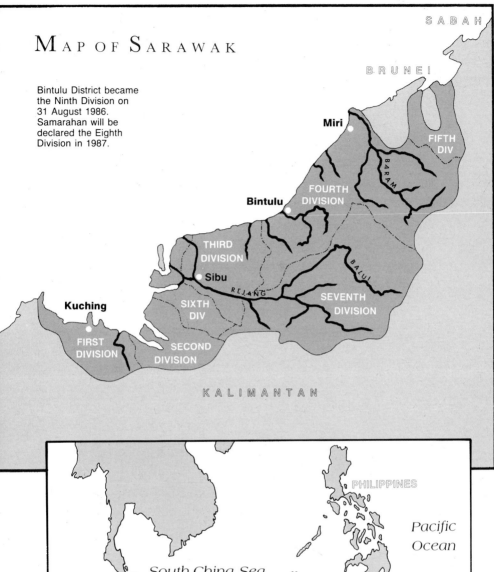

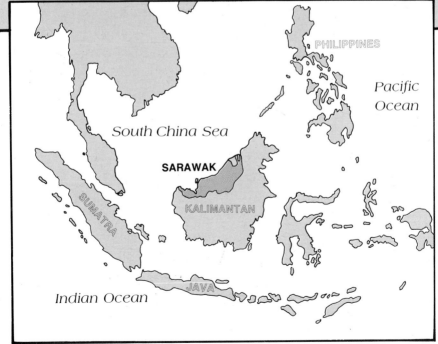

CHAPTER ONE

Sarawak and Its People

This book is about the Dayak natives of Sarawak and how their lives have been affected by the processes of modernisation and development.

Sarawak, located in the western part of Borneo, is geographically the largest State in Malaysia. Its land area of 124,449 sq. km.(48,612 sq. miles) is roughly 38 per cent of the total land area of Malaysia. In terms of its concentration of natural resources, Sarawak is also probably the richest State. It has abundant petroleum, liquified natural gas and forests, three of the most important export resources of the country.

Sarawak joined the Federation of Malaysia in 1963. Before that, it had been under the colonial rule of the British for over a century. Beginning in 1841, the British adventurer, James Brooke, and his descendants, took control of increasing amounts of land on which Sarawak now stands, often with the help of British gunboats. In 1946, Vyner Brooke ceded Sarawak to the British Government. In 1963, Sarawak gained independence from the British and joined the Malaysian Federation. Although defence, security, financial affairs such as collection of income tax, and petroleum resources come under the direct jurisdiction of the Federal Government, the Sarawak State Government holds overwhelming powers in matters related to land tenure, alienation and utilisation, and to forest resources.

Administratively, the State of Sarawak is divided into seven Divisions, the First to the Seventh Divisions.[1] Within each Division there are a number of Districts. Each Division is under the charge of a Resident who is assisted by a District Officer in each of the Districts. Under the District Officer are a number of Sarawak Administrative Officers who manage the day to day affairs within the District and the sub-Districts. District Officers in Sarawak also sit as Magistrates and preside over court cases on matters pertaining to civil, criminal and customary law in the District. Similarly, Sarawak Administrative Officers are empowered to hear cases at the level of the Native Officer's

1. Bintulu District became the Ninth Division on 31 August 1986. Samarahan will be declared the Eighth Division in 1987.

or Chief's Court and the Penghulu's Superior Court. Below the Resident, there is also a Divisional Development Officer (DDO) who is appointed to deal with matters concerning development projects in each Division.

The population of Sarawak in 1985 was 1,542,800, of which 1,246,400 (or 81 per cent) lived in the rural areas. By comparison, 59 per cent of the people in Peninsular Malaysia were in rural areas in the same year (Fifth Malaysia Plan:129, 134-35).

The native peoples are numerically the largest grouping in Sarawak. According to the Malaysian Constitution, the native peoples of Sarawak are the Bidayuh (Land Dayak), Bukitan, Bisayah, Dusun, Iban, Kedayan, Kelabit, Kayan, Kenyah (including Sabup and Sipeng), Kajang (including Sekapan, Kejaman, Lahanan, Punan, Tanjong and Kanowit), Lugat, Lisum, Malay, Melanau, Murut, Penan, Sian, Tagal, Tabun and Ukit. Under the law these are the natives of Sarawak who are citizens of Malaysia. The indigenous peoples can be broadly classified into two groups; those who live on the coastal areas of Sarawak (namely the Malay and the Melanau) and the interior peoples or Dayak.

The Dayak peoples is a collective name for a vastly diverse ethnic group inhabiting the island of Borneo. However, they share some important features. They are largely shifting cultivators of hill rice; they live in longhouses usually along the rivers and tributaries in the interior; and they all observe native customary law or *adat*.

The latest available data on the population size of various ethnic groups are in the 1980 population census. According to the State Population Report Sarawak (221-222), the total Sarawak population in 1980 was 1,233,103. The Dayak peoples comprised 539,824 or some 44 per cent of the population. They included the Iban (368,208), Bidayuh (104,885), Kenyah (15,557), Kayan (13,368), Kedayan (10,669), Murut (9,473), Punan (5,600), Bisayah (3,837), Kelabit (3,672) and other Dayak groups (4,555). The Dayak were therefore the largest broad ethnic grouping in Sarawak. The population of the other two indigenous groups were the Malay (247,972 or 20 per cent of the total population) and Melanau (69,578 or 6 per cent). The non-indigenous groups comprised the Chinese (359,884 or 29 per cent), Indians (3,293), Indonesians (7,040), other Asians and Europeans.

This book is confined to an examination of the Dayak natives of Sarawak. Although the term 'native' may carry a colonial connotation to some, the Dayak refer to themselves by this term, and most of them are proud to be called 'natives'. In this book we therefore retain the term when referring to the Dayak.

Another term which is often used in this book is '*orang ulu*' or 'peoples of the interior'. '*Orang ulu*' is a term used by most Dayak ethnic groups to describe themselves, as peoples who inhabit the interior forests of Sarawak which are inaccessible except by boat and on foot. However, on rare occasions (such as a visit by important politicians), helicopters land on clearings near some longhouses. All Dayak groups[2], except the Iban, Bidayuh and Dusun, call themselves '*orang ulu*'. The '*orang ulu*' mainly inhabit the headwaters of the major river systems of Sarawak, namely the Balui, (Seventh Division), Baram and Tatau (Fourth Division), and Limbang and Trusan (Fifth Division).

Most of the Dayak in Sarawak practise shifting cultivation in the hilly inland areas of the State and some 36,000 households are presently engaged in this activity. For them, the land and forest is the basis for their livelihood and their life. Their most cherished traditions and spiritual beliefs are centred on their relationships to the land. The Dayak communities based on longhouses are scattered along the riverine areas in the inaccessible remote interior. For most natives, their only means of communication is the river. In many ways the river is the lifestream of the people, providing them fish, water for their domestic needs, toilet and bathing facilities, and transport using boats to get to their farms. Apart from the agriculturalists, there are the forest peoples who depend to a large extent on hunting and gathering activities for a livelihood. These groups include the Penan, Ukit, Bukitan (Baketan) and Sian (Sihan) peoples. To them, especially the Penan who are largely nomadic, the forests is the only home they know. To all these Dayak peoples, the land, the waters, and the forests have provided them their livelihood and daily needs ever since they can remember. Their communities have thrived on a complex system of rights and obligations towards the land, the forests and resources of nature which were observed by all its members.

The shifting agriculturalists of Sarawak had inherited a sophisticated social system centred on the longhouse. The longhouse represents the village community. Each family has a 'house' or 'room' in this village. Each family cultivates its own land and each member of the community observes *adat*, the set and system of customary laws and practices.

These peoples possess a profound knowledge of growing hill padi, an economic activity which has deep social, spiritual and religious significance for them. The myriad of rituals and ceremonies attached to growing hill padi and the traditions and customs tied to the use of land and its resources have made shifting cultivation central to their way of life. It has not only provided them with food, it has also given them an identity and a rich cultural heritage which they are proud of. When asked 'What is *adat?*' a Dayak would say: 'It is the Dayak way of life, how we live and become farmers. It is our *adat* to plant hill rice and live in the longhouse'. Their deep respect for the land and its resources is reflected in the rich and dynamic *adat* or system of customary law. This system of legal values and principles existed long before Colonial rule or the advent of the modern State. The natives' system of rights to land and its resources had already been long recognised

---

2. The Kedayan are also shifting cultivators who live on small streams inland in the Fourth and Fifth Divisions. They are Muslims and no longer live in longhouses. They were originally from Brunei.

and observed by the peoples who have long inhabited the area. This indigenous system ensured that access to land and forest resources was available to all families. Land or other economic and personal disputes were settled by native courts using the principles of *adat*. The native way of life was integral, combining economic, cultural, spiritual and legal aspects, bound together in shifting agriculture, longhouse social organisation and the all pervading *adat*.

This traditional system is now fast disintegrating. Many of the natives now find their way of life threatened by the profound and drastic changes that are taking place as a result of the modern process of 'development' imposed on them by the larger society or the State. Powerful economic and social forces are competing with the natives for the wealth and resources existing in the areas in which they live, namely the commercially valuable timber in the forests, and their ancestral lands.

This 'development' has caused the imposition of an alien legal system which the natives cannot comprehend, the forfeiture of their traditional lands, and the progressive destruction of their livelihood and way of life. These cultural minorities who know of no other life except the life of the forests and growing hill padi are being thrust into modern society, often against their own will, and ironically, in the name of 'development'. It is generally agreed that genuine development must bring about an improvement of the human condition. By this we would include the satisfaction of basic needs, reduction of inequalities, elimination of poverty and the attainment of material and human or spiritual well being. Very often when development is translated into policy and action it achieves just the opposite. This is especially true when developmental concepts are superimposed on societies and structures without first examining and understanding how these new forces can work against the interests of the people concerned, how it can destroy traditional or indigenous social, economic and cultural structures without offering better alternative systems and mechanisms.

This process is often triggered by the penetration of the modern market economy into traditional subsistence communities. The influence of the market transforms the indigenous land tenure system, agricultural production, labour organisation and sociocultural system with adverse consequences. This encroachment is accompanied by the propagation by the State of ideas and attitudes to prove the economic, social and cultural superiority of the new systems over the traditional systems. Very often this is done with the creation of a legal system which is alien to indigenous concepts of law and justice; and the use of modern economic, social and cultural arguments, often garbed in 'scientific' language, which indigenous people are ill equipped to counter, even though they often feel 'in their bones' that something is wrong.

Sarawak is abundantly rich in forest products, oil and natural gas. This wealth has brought great benefits to the country but the natives who should have gained most from this wealth have found that many aspects of the development process that have accompanied the exploitation of these vast natural resources have led to the disintegration of their societies and threatened their very existence. Many of their ancestral lands have been taken away from them very often without even their knowledge. Outsiders and non-natives have come to log their forests and leave behind a trail of destruction to the environment on which the natives depend.

Not only are the native communities threatened by the profitable timber that others have come to take, large tracts of native lands will also be submerged under water by the construction of multibillion dollar dams now on the drawing board. These dams will generate hydro-electric power, most of which will be piped to Peninsular Malaysia, and the neighbouring countries.

With their land area increasingly restricted; with many thousands of them being 'resettled' from the interior to more accessible areas to make way for timber or dams; and with many of their children, schooled in modern ways, unwilling to work on the land; the native longhouse way of life is rapidly breaking down.

This unfolding drama of the disappearance of the social, cultural and economic system of important ethnic groups is little seen or known by the outside world. By and large, the native peoples of Sarawak have been unable to adequately articulate their problems or to seek proper redress for the immense tribulation and misery being inflicted upon them.

This book is a small attempt to contribute to an understanding of the world of the Sarawak natives: their traditional systems; the mechanisms through which these systems have been disrupted; and also how the natives have fought back.

Firstly, we describe the central features of the traditional Dayak swidden society (Chapter Two), in terms of social organisation, customary land tenure and shifting agriculture. Since the latter is a much misunderstood economic activity, blamed mistakenly for deforesting Sarawak, we examine the rationality of swidden as a form of agriculture which is ecologically suitable under tropical forest conditions (Chapter Three).

Following this, Chapters Four to Eleven examine how the traditional Dayak system has come under threat by various laws, policies and practices. Chapter Four examines how the natives' land rights have been gradually encroached upon through changes in the State's land laws and system through the decades. Native communities have been increasingly restricted in terms of access to land, and even existing land rights have been 'extinguished' to make way for timber concessions or 'development projects'. Natives who are asked to make way for such projects are usually put into agricultural resettlement schemes producing cash crops such as rubber and oil palm. These land development programmes themselves impinge upon native lands. They are examined in Chapter Five.

The biggest threat to the natives has so far come from the timber industry, and this is next discussed in detail. Chapter Six looks at Sarawak's forest law and policies, which have complemented the land laws in restricting the natives' access to forest resources, to pave the way for these resources to be freely exploited by the timber industry. Logging activities have expanded tremendously in Sarawak in the past ten years (especially since 1979) and led to the mushrooming of timber camps in areas long considered the province of native communities. This has led to several clashes between the natives and timber companies, with the natives almost invariably at the losing end, since the companies have State backing. The dramatic fight for the forest between natives and the timber industry is documented in Chapter Seven.

The next two Chapters address the issue who is to blame for the rapid destruction of Sarawak's vast tropical forests: the natives' practice of swidden agriculture, or the logging of the timber industry. Chapter Eight provides estimates on the extent of logging in Sarawak and how it has depleted and is depleting a very large part of the State's forests. Chapter Nine on the other hand examines the case put forward against the swiddeners by proponents of the logging industry, who have maligned swidden as a primitive, inappropriate and environmentally destructive system that has to be rooted out of existence. To quote J.E. Spencer in his comprehensive study of *Shifting Cultivation in Southeastern Asia*: 'It is popular in many quarters to express concern, distress, and even horror over the destruction and waste resulting from shifting cultivation. Almost *a priori* the modern forester uses a standard vocabulary on the subject, whether he is a commercial timberman, a government civil servant, or a member of an international organization' (Spencer 1966:3).

Ironically, this attack on swidden is led by planners, policy makers and bureaucrats who are the very people responsible for the wholesale logging of tropical forests, causing massive erosion, depletion of precious top-soil, ecological disruption and climatic imbalances in the environment. The social and environmental impact of the timber industry is documented in Chapter Ten.

Meanwhile, a new threat to the natives' land has loomed large in the form of hydro-electric dam projects. The first project, at Batang Ai, has already resettled 3,000 natives. Other dams on the drawing board could affect another 20,000 natives and flood huge areas of tropical forest. The dams, and native opposition to them, are discussed in Chapter Eleven.

Chapter Twelve examines the consequences that have resulted from development for the natives. Apart from wanton ecological destruction of their environment, increasing land scarcity has resulted. Natives find it more and more difficult to fell forest to build new farms. As a result, the period of fallow in shifting agriculture had to be shortened or else less hill rice was grown. This has led to a drop in food output, and malnutrition among the natives has risen to very high proportions. To make things worse, the young are weaned from the traditional way of life when they go to live in boarding schools in the urban centres. School and the urban lifestyle and culture alienate them from their own society. They are not equipped with the skills and knowledge of a farmer. Their hands will not touch the soil. Many young natives have migrated to towns. Some have found good jobs but others crowd the squatter colonies and look out for contract work. As increasingly the younger generation of natives become more urbanised, they will lose their roots in the community and the longhouse will become a thing of the past.

In Chapter Thirteen, the problems of Sarawak's natives are placed within the context of the increasing world recognition of the rights of native and indigenous peoples and cultural minorities to retain their lands, to have their cultural and economic systems respected, and not be forced to change their lifestyle or their place of settlement. The concept of 'development' is also critically examined. It is argued that the natives have the right to retain their cultural and economic identity, and the right to benefit from development, not to become its victims.

Finally, Chapter Fourteen provides some brief suggestions on steps which should be taken to prevent further erosion of the rights of the natives, and to instead enhance their status, particularly in relation to land and forest resources.

This book has, in a sense, been many years in the making. My interest in Borneo was first kindled when as a child my maternal grandparents would show me old photographs of themselves, our relatives, and the native peoples of Borneo, and tell me stories of the place and its people. My grandparents were the fourth generation in our family who had settled in Borneo, and so my attachment to the island had its roots in family history. This initial interest was further deepened when I was a student reading anthropology at Universiti Sains Malaysia in the early 1970s. Subsequently I made three visits to various parts of the Sarawak interior, including a nine-month stay in a longhouse community in the Baram District. In 1977, I completed a thesis for the degree of Master of Social Science on the process of economic, social and political transformation of a Kenyah longhouse community under the impact of Colonial rule and post-Colonial modernisation. My latest visit to Sarawak was for a month in 1985 when I visited several longhouse communities in the Seventh Division.

During my visits to Sarawak, I stayed with and enjoyed the hospitality and friendship of many Sarawakians, natives as well as non-natives. I listened to many stories told to me by natives. These peoples are extremely gifted in the art of story telling and are most eloquent in relating their experiences and in expressing their feelings, especially in relation to their land, their culture and their *adat*. I was most touched by the warmth and humanity of longhouse social relationships, and I personally witnessed, listened to and took down notes of the experiences these natives are undergoing in the painful transition of their lives from an integral self-subsistent community to the traumas of fighting against the powerful forces of the modern economic and political system. It was their plight, and their expectation that those who understand should do something to make others in the outside world understand, that spurred me on to complete this book.

I thus worked on this book in the hope of setting out the dilemmas, experiences, problems and traumas of the Sarawak Dayak natives, as I perceived them from the many natives I met. I have done this in all sincerity. Yet in a book dealing with such complex issues, I could not have covered them all in a satisfactory or adequate manner. Thus I hope the reader will excuse any shortcomings that may be present in this book.

This book would not have been possible without the friendship and support of many people. Firstly, I would like to thank the many Sarawakian friends who have rendered their kind assistance and hospitality during my visits to that beautiful and blessed land. Most of all, to all those natives young and old who have taken such good care of me and made my stay there very memorable. I shall always recall their friendship, love and concern with deep gratitude, respect and even pain. I am greatly indebted to Khor Kok Peng for his comments and suggestions and for making available to me data for this book especially in Chapter Eight, as well as for reading the final drafts of the book. I am also grateful to Chuah Siew Lean for typing the manuscripts. I would also like to thank Dennis Lau, Philip Hii, Richard Gerster, S.C. Chin, Wong Meng Chuo and the Royal Tropical Institute, Amsterdam, for kindly allowing me access to their photographs. And to Martin, for your kind understanding towards my attachment to a land and its people, and for your encouragement, support and patience in this exercise.

Above: Kenyah craftsman making decorative shields in Lioh Matoh longhouse, Baram.

Below: Kelabit women sharing a story inside a family room in their longhouse in Bario in the Kelabit Highlands.

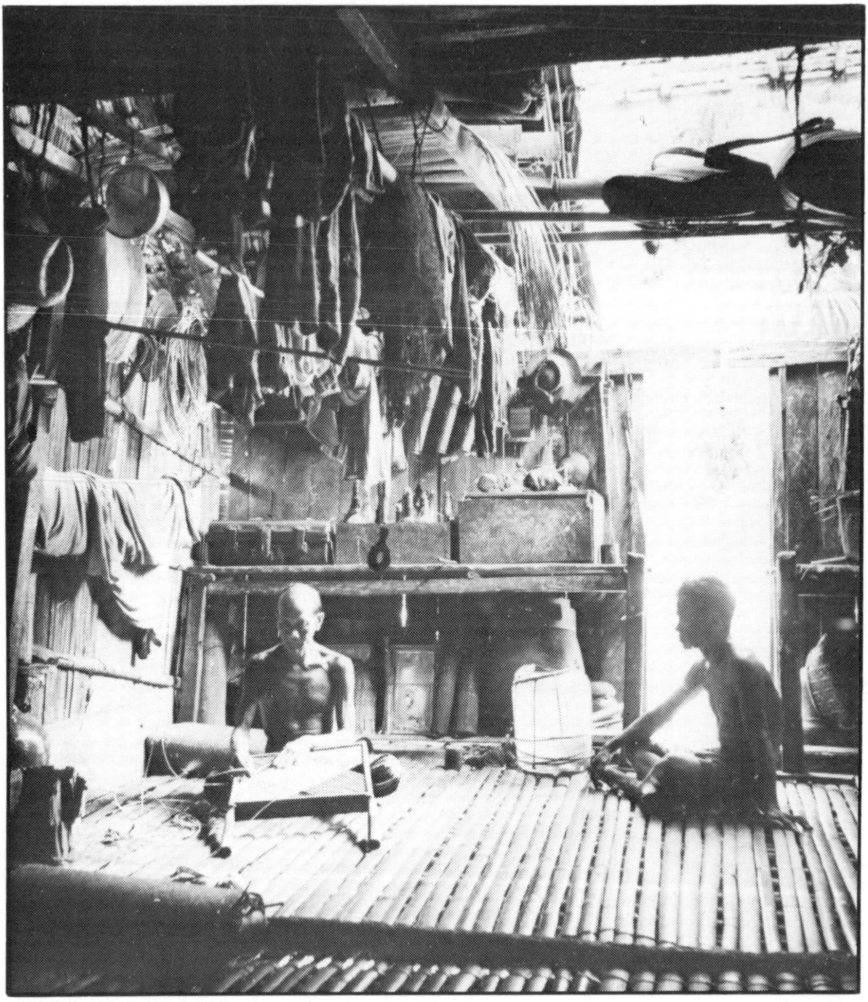

Kon Inst. v d Tropen

CHAPTER TWO

Traditional Dayak Swidden Society

The Dayak of Sarawak have traditionally lived in longhouses built along the banks of rivers or navigable streams. Families lived in rooms within the longhouse structure. Using dug-out boats, the people used the waterways to reach their farms and move from place to place.

The major economic activity was shifting agriculture, in which hill padi is grown as the staple crop. The padi is grown on steep hillsides and slopes, which is the characteristic landscape of the inland regions of Sarawak. Under these conditions and given the simplicity of the tools they used, planting hill rice was hard work. They therefore required each other's help to work the land together. In such a society, the important values were cooperation, harmony and the community above the self. Apart from planting crops, they also fished, hunted wild animals and collected jungle products from the forest. But these activities remained secondary to shifting cultivation.

The three main features in traditional swidden society were: i) Longhouse social organisation; ii) Customary land tenure; and iii) Shifting cultivation. All swidden communities shared these three features. This chapter will examine these three major aspects of traditional Dayak society.

Longhouse Social Organisation

In traditional swidden society in Sarawak, the centre of social organisation was the longhouse, in which members of the community resided. The basic social and economic unit was the family which occupied a wooden 'apartment' within the longhouse. The longhouse itself was thus made up of a long row of these apartments. Each apartment was called a 'room' or a 'door'. These terms also referred to the family or all the people living within the room. Thus in swidden society, the terms 'family',[1] 'door' and 'room' were interchangeable and mean the same thing.

---

1.   There are different terms for the word 'room' among the different longhouse communities. The Iban *bilek* refers to the family of a room or members of the room. The Kenyah equivalent is *lamin* while the Kayan use *amin*.

Between families there was a complex system of relationships, under-
lying which were the principles of reciprocity and cooperation. Although
the various Dayak communities all lived in longhouses and practised
shifting cultivation, there were differences among them where social
stratification is concerned. Traditionally, the Iban (which is the largest
Dayak community) and Bidayuh had a basically egalitarian social
structure. Access to land was equally distributed amongst families and
rights and obligations between members in the community were based
on equal status. In these relatively classless societies, the families
cooperated in work, in some activities working the land collectively
(e.g. firing the forests), and in other cases practising a system of
reciprocal labour (helping in one another's farms). Members of the
community enjoyed the same privileges and shared the same social
standing.

However the Dayak communities or *orang ulu* who lived in the interior
(such as the Kenyah, Kayan, Kajang and Kelabit) maintained a ranked
social order. In the pre Colonial period, these swidden societies were
divided into three main classes: aristocrats, commoners and slaves. By
virtue of their control over slave labour and a portion of the labour
time of commoners, the aristocrats were able to accumulate more wealth
than the other classes. In return they were expected to provide aid to
commoner families, such as food in the event of a poor harvest. Among
the commoner families, a system of reciprocal relationships was
practiced, helping one another in sowing, harvesting and other activities,
as well as frequent exchanges of gifts.

In all Dayak communities, the family unit exercised rights over its
own living conditions within the longhouse 'room'. It also had rights
over its own plots of land, allocated tasks among family members, controlled its own labour process and obtained the fruits of its labour.
However, in those societies with a clearly defined aristocracy, the
commoner families had to contribute a portion of their labour to the
aristocrats. This was known as tribute or corvee labour. Each member
of the family had well defined roles which encompassed economic,
household, religious and communal chores. Parents combined the roles
of head in production and household activities, and the younger
generation followed the orders and wishes of the elders.

The rights and the obligations and the chain of command within
a family and between families (including families of different classes)
were sanctioned by *adat*, the all-encompassing customary system of
beliefs and values that guided behaviour in traditional society. *Adat*
was the unwritten body of rules and principles which was extended
to all things and all relationships in both the physical and supernatural
world. It included the living and the dead, the evil and the good, sacred
and profane. There was a proper way to conduct oneself in one's
relationship with these elements. Hence it was important to maintain
the balance and harmony with these elements in the conduct of one's
affairs. Each of these elements had a soul. Thus the forests, hills, the
padi, earth, living things, the house and its structures have a 'soul'

or life of its own. If there is any disturbance in this balance, this will adversely affect the family or the community. Balance must be restored so that the group can continue its affairs normally and preserve its harmonious relationship with these elements. Thus *adat* provided the individual and his community a coherent world view in both secular and spiritual terms. It was a belief system covering all spheres of life. It was the integrative mechanism for all social interaction within the community.

All longhouse communities had a council of elders. These comprised men who were well versed in *adat* and its rituals, and those who commanded great respect in the longhouse because of their outstanding qualities like bravery, wisdom or oratory. These individuals made the collective decisions on all matters that affected the members of the longhouse. Among the *orang ulu*, an important part of *adat* was the acceptance of the aristocracy or chiefs in the longhouse as the leaders, and the role of the village elders (made up mainly of aristocrats) which made major decisions in matters such as moving house and agriculture. The village elders also formed the traditional court where they performed the roles of arbitrators and mediators responsible for settling disputes and imposing sanctions on longhouse members.

Adat was also deeply embedded in the system of swidden agriculture which had deep spiritual and religious significance for the people. The wealth of ceremony and rituals linked to swiddening reinforced the importance of the longhouse community. An old Dayak described it thus: 'You see for yourself that our *adat* is bound up with our work. Our worship goes with our work. We don't worship unless it has something to do with our work. . . . I need help on my farm, for planting, weeding, harvesting, and to get help I must give it in return. I can only get it and give it if I farm with others, and observe the same periods of work and rest as they do' (Howes, Peter 1960:488-95).

Among the egalitarian Dayak longhouse communities, the system of longhouse elders has continued. The additional feature is the existence of a village headman who is a candidate nominated by the State. Today village meetings are still conducted by the village council of elders in the presence of a *tua kampong* or village headman. Similarly among the *orang ulu* communities, although the feudal system of slaves was abolished in the colonial period, the basic components of traditional social organisation have remained to the present: the longhouse, the 'rooms', the basic rights of individual families to land, the village councils and dispute settlement systems. Nevertheless, modern political, economic and cultural forces have significantly penetrated and influenced the traditional system. Thus, Sarawak longhouse community today can be said to combine the traditional with the modern in various spheres of life: in the economy (where the swidden system is being challenged by the modern economy), in political organisation (where traditional leadership and judicial patterns co-exist with the State structures of state assemblymen, district office and courts), and in culture and lifestyle where community values, traditional beliefs, music and dance compete with the increasing influence of 'modern' individualistic attitudes, pop music and western dancing on the youth.

Customary Land Tenure

Land has always been the most crucial of all resources in traditional swidden society in Sarawak. It provided the natives with food and other materials to satisfy their basic needs. It has held deep significance in the spiritual life of the people, since it held their ancestral graves, and was a link between present and past generations. The rights of natives to the use of the land were enshrined in the community *adat*, and the system of land tenure was the bedrock upon which the social, economic and cultural system rested.

Sarawak swidden society practised a customary land tenure system. Under customary law or *adat*, the concept of private ownership of land did not exist. *Customary land tenure provided and entitled anyone who cultivated the land with rights to the use of land.* These usufructary rights did not amount to permanent ownership rights. Thus rights over land were created by an individual and his family who cleared the forest and observed native *adat* with regards to land, the required rituals and religious beliefs.

So long as the land was cultivated, or there was still some sign of cultivation on it (usually the presence of fruit trees), claims to land would not be challenged. Hence under *adat* or customary law, the rights to land rested on felling the forest and the occupation of the land thereby cleared; the planting of fruit trees on land; and the occupation or cultivation of land. Once derived, rights to the use and disposal of the land belonged jointly to the family of the original feller. In this manner any family or members of a room and their descendents could attain rights to the use of land, simply by clearing the forests, showing proof that the land was being used and observing the *adat* of the longhouse community. Every female and male member living in the longhouse family 'room' was entitled to rights of use and inheritance to the land vested in the family, provided he or she did not leave his or her natal family apartment.

Rights to land which had been earlier cleared by a family room were lost upon 'abandonment' of the house, or when no sign of cultivation or mark of 'ownership' was shown. These rights were weakened if the land was not used for the period longer than the fallow cycle. In all these instances, rights would revert to the community as a whole and the unused land felled anew. Hence the traditional land system enabled each family and community to gain access to the abundant forests, land and water, as well as providing for cleared but unused land (or old forest) to be the property of the community.

This land could also be loaned to individuals or their families with the permission of the community. Rights to land could also be passed on from generation to generation, the children inheriting their parents' rights to the same plot. However if the land is left idle upon the death of parents, it could also be claimed by the community.

Members of the community possessed rights for the use not only of all cultivated plots but also the surrounding forest to the extent of half a day's journey from the longhouse, as well as all the water running through this area (Richards 1961: Part IV para 10). A family had right to the forest immediately contiguous to his clearing as it formed his area of extension. Exclusive right to certain wild trees especially *durian* and *engkabang* could be created in the forest outside a family room's 'sphere of influence' if these were marked on discovery (Richards 1961: Part V para 9) However, all fallen crop or fruit could be freely appropriated by anyone who found it.

There are variations of this system of customary land tenure and land rights among the various native groups in Sarawak. However, the basic principles of this system were the same for all the groups.

Shifting Agriculture and Other Economic Activities

Traditional swidden society in Sarawak was and is still characterised by shifting agriculture, by far the most important economic activity. In this system, rice is cultivated on the hill slopes with the help of simple tools. After making use of a plot of land for one season (or a few seasons), the farmers move on to another plot of land, and then to another. After a number of years, they return to the original plot when the soil has regained its fertility.

There were basically five stages in the swidden cycle: felling the forest, firing the dead vegetation, planting or sowing the seeds, weeding the farms, and harvesting. When the fertility of the soil diminished, the gardens were 'abandoned' and new lands were sought to begin cultivation. This was repeated until the original plot was returned to. Then the rotation of the gardens started all over again. Similarly the longhouse community will move together with the rotation of the land.

The natives were also traditionally involved in other economic activities, besides swidden farming. These included hunting, fishing, the rearing of pigs and poultry, planting subsidiary crops, and collecting other food and resources from the jungle. In terms of the division of labour, all family members had their own roles. The men hunted, fished and gathered jungle products. In hill (or dry rice) cultivation, the men were mainly responsible for felling and burning, whilst the women took charge of decision-making in sowing and both contributed to the harvesting. The children and old people performed odd jobs in the rooms and simpler economic tasks, such as gathering fire wood and carrying water from the river.

Although these other economic activities were not unimportant, shifting agriculture was undoubtedly central to the whole tempo of community life. The swidden cycle determined the main allocation of economic tasks, the major rituals and spiritual beliefs of the community were tied to swidden agriculture, and the need to rotate the land led to the shifting also of the longhouse itself.

Since swidden was and is still so central to the life of the natives, the next Chapter will examine the rationality of this traditional form of agriculture, which has been so misunderstood by so many people.

Above: Long Busang, the furthest Kenyah-Badang longhouse settlement on the Balui river in Ulu Belaga.

Below: Long Busang natives returning from the farm along the Balui.

CHAPTER THREE

Swidden as a Rational Agricultural System

In recent years, swidden farming has been accused of being ecologically destructive, and is blamed for removing the tropical forest. This view is however most misleading, for swidden is in fact very suited to the tropical forest ecology.

Swiddening or shifting cultivation was basically a system of agriculture in which the land cultivated was rotated: land on which rice had been grown for one season (or a few seasons) would be vacated and allowed to lie fallow while the cultivator opened another plot for the next season's planting.

This pattern of farming is carried out until the original piece of land is returned to when its fertility has been restored. This technique by shifting cultivators to safeguard the once cultivated land for future use (including its use by descendents and the return of the land to fallow or the regenerative process) is an integral concept of shifting cultivation (Spencer 1966:10). This type of cultivation has also been called 'slash and burn' because the opening up of new land involved chopping down trees or bush cover and firing the fallen vegetation.

Shifting Agriculture:
Complex and Ecologically Sound

Shifting cultivation is a complex system of land use and cultivation requiring sophisticated knowledge of the stability of soil types to crops grown, climatic variations and soil fertility. Referring to swidden farmers, Erik Eckholm of the Worldwatch Institute writes that 'few of the men and women who practise it have been educated in primary schools, let alone universities. Yet they usually carry in their heads an extraordinary fund of scientifically sound knowledge about plant species and soil qualities' (Eckholm 1976:138). According to Spencer, soil studies clearly indicate that shifting cultivation does not in itself ruin soils and produce destructive erosion. In fact many shifting cultivator peoples develop a fine sense of the regional and qualitative variations in the soils they cultivate. According to him: 'Such awareness is indicative of a people who are far advanced

technologically from the very beginnings of crop-growing practice'
(Spencer 1966:167).

Shifting agriculture is a highly suitable and viable form of agriculture
in the tropics where soils are poor. Tropical vegetation grows very
quickly during fallow and enables the soil to regenerate. Increasingly,
studies have shown that swidden agriculture is in many ways 'imitative'
of the tropical forest ecosystem and more ecologically conservative than
permanent field cultivation (Grandstaff 1980:8). 'Swidden cultivation
comes closer to simulating the structure, functional dynamics and
equilibrium of the natural ecosystem than any other agricultural systems
man has devised' (Harris 1969:6). It is also acknowledged that in many
marginal farming areas of the world there is as yet no suitable substitute
for swidden farming (Grandstaff 1980:23).

In Sarawak, about 80 per cent of the total land area comprises
moderate to steep, dissected hilly and mountainous country where most
shifting agriculture is practised. Soils are also generally infertile and
low in plant nutrients (Hatch 1980:485). In these areas where soils are
poor, shifting cultivation is a suitable form of agriculture.

The following sections give a detailed account of the characteristics
of swidden, demonstrating how it blends the shifting agriculturalists
with the natural environment and ecology and forms a scientific and
rational form of agriculture. In this analysis, we will review the research
on various swidden communities in Southeast Asia as well as Sarawak.

Multiple Cropping

The most outstanding feature in shifting cultivation is the variety of
crops grown. These are planted at various times in the swidden cycle
and they mature or ripen at different periods, thus providing the farmer
and his family with a steady supply of food. This also means that the
ground cover is protected and the soil is shielded from water and wind
erosion. This practice enables the swiddener to get the most use in one
single plot with the minimal effort. Multiple cropping discourages pests
and diseases unlike monoculture or single crop cultivation. The diversity
of crops grown also helps to keep down the weed growth which is a
major problem in swiddening. Most crucial, multiple cropping means
that the continuous and varied supply of foods from the swidden gardens
will enable the swiddener to fulfill most of his nutritional needs.

For example the Karen swiddener in Northern Thailand can provide
for almost all his essential needs except salt and iron (Hinton 1970:4).
Among the Lua' hill farmers in Northwestern Thailand, 84 plant
varieties are cultivated in the swidden gardens of which 70 are food
species and at least 13 are grown for their medicinal purposes
(Kunstadter 1978:130; Table 6.19).

In the Philippines, Harold Conklin listed some 77 types of plants
among the Hanunoo shifting cultivators (Spencer 1966:110 footnote).
In another study of Tiruray shifting cultivators of Southwestern
Mindanao, Stuart Schlegel documented 107 plant types which are

regularly planted in Tiruray swiddens. Seventy eight of these yield some form of food and 30 are grown for medicine (Schlegel 1979:39).

Among the Kantu[1] in Kalimantan, Michael Dove found that each year the average Kantu household grows twenty to twenty-one different plants in its swiddens. In doing so, each household can ensure that at least several different types will be available for consumption during every month of the year (Dove 1985:173).

Among the Sarawak Land Dayak, Geddes noted that the most important supplementary crops in the swidden farms were cucumbers, pumpkins, beans, maize, cassava (grown after the rice harvest) sugarcane and Job's tears (*Inyok*). These crops depend upon the cultivation of sufficient dry padi to provide cleared areas for them. Many of the crops are important to the diet of the people, while others are part of their cultural life. For example, the grain from the Job's tears plant is used to make wine which is an essential part of all religious offerings (Geddes 1954:65).

Freeman mentions that the Iban of Sarawak cultivate a wide range of edibles in the swidden plots, some of which are sown separately (e.g. mustard or *ensabi*) after the burn. Others are planted simultaneously with the padi (e.g. cucumber, pumpkin, luffa and gourd). All these crops ripen before the rice and are eaten as supplement to the diet. He adds that around the edges of the swidden hut, cassava, maize, pineapples and *changkok* (*Sauropus albicans*) are also grown (Freeman 1970:191-2).

Among the Kenyah in Baram District, Sarawak, Chin records that the swidden is planted with a variety of crops like maize, cucumber, pumpkin, sweet potato, tapioca, sesame, brinjal, sugarcane, ginger, bananas whilst tobacco, chillies and betel leaf are grown around partially burnt tree stumps (S.C. Chin 1981:7-8).

The Bidayuh communities in Sarawak's First Division plant mustard, maize, cucumber, pumpkin, brinjal, ginger, sweet potatoes, chillies, betel leaves and sugar cane when hill rice is grown; whilst during the weeding season, tapioca and bananas are planted. Tapioca is always used as a substitute for rice should the latter run out before the next harvest. The variety of food crops ensures a continuous supply of food to the people until the next planting season (Gumis 1981:113).

According to Grandstaff, multiple cropping is both ecologically sound and promotes forest regeneration (Grandstaff 1980:8). Different crops continue to be grown at different stages of the rice cycle. Even after the rice harvest and during the fallow period, swidden gardens continue to yield a variety of crops and wild plants. Among the Lua' and Skaw Karen hill farmers in Northwestern Thailand, women still go to the fallow swiddens in their daily search for firewood, and gather a variety

1.   The Kantu Dayak inhabit the Upper Kapuas river in West Kalimantan, Indonesia. They are closely related to the Iban ethnic group. They are actually part of the Ibanic peoples in the Kapuas river from which the present-day Iban of Sarawak originated in the sixteenth century (Dove 1985:11).

of edible and otherwise useful plants. The Lua' recognise and use some 482 varieties of plants in the fallow swiddens for use as food, animal food, medicine, construction, weaving dyeing materials, decoration, fuel, poison, fencing and insect repellent among others (Kunstadter 1978:99; Table 6.19).

Self Sufficiency in Rice

Although researchers have arrived at different estimates in determining self sufficiency among swidden cultivators, the general conclusion is that they are able to feed themselves adequately. In the case of Sarawak, Freeman maintains that an Iban household of 5.7 members would require some 1203 kilograms (kgs) or (501 gantang[2]) of padi for its yearly subsistence. Chin's estimate is about 1935 kgs (806 gantang) for a Kenyah household of 9 persons. From the above results, one can say that a swidden household (depending on its size) would require between 1203 kgs (501 gantang) to 1935 kgs (806 gantang) of padi to meet its yearly padi consumption.

Although shifting cultivation requires large tracts of land, it makes use of a small labour force and simple tools. Thus to measure the efficiency of shifting cultivation, it is important to take into account the total yield per unit of labour and not per unit of area (Conklin 1969:231). Based on 1949 data from Freeman among the Baleh Iban, it has been found that an average shifting cultivator family of 5.7 members would require about 501.6 gantang (1203.8 kgs) of padi a year for subsistence (Freeman 1970:249, 261).

In a detailed survey of four farms with varying sizes and yields, Freeman found that the total yields were 620 gantang; 639 gantang; 710 gantang and 960 gantang. In other words, all the farms produced enough padi to far exceed the requirements of the family. These outputs were achieved in the 1949-50 planting season which was an unusually bad year (Idem 1970:253-4, 259). According to him, '. . . yields of 13 to 16 bushels per acre is typical of the sort of return generally achieved under worse than average conditions. In the best of years on the other hand, remarkably heavy crops are sometimes produced . . . There can be little doubt that with fully favourable weather conditions, and particularly when working virgin land of good quality, Iban farmers are sometimes able to achieve crops ranging from 30 to 40 bushels per acre' (Idem 1970:254-5). Freeman's study also showed that the average family farm size was 4.5 acres in 1949 (Idem 1970:249).

In his study of 26 separate Kantu rice swiddens between 1975-76, Dove concluded that the average yield from each hectare was 928 kgs of threshed and winnowed (but unhusked) grain (Dove 1985:289). Taking 4.6 hectares as the average size of each household swidden, the average yield for each household would amount to 4268.8 kgs. This amount far exceeds the average yearly requirement of 2820 kgs for each

2.   One gantang of unhusked rice = 2.4 kilograms.

Kantu household (*Idem* 1985:94-5). According to Dove, the consumption and seed requirements (the rice set aside for the next planting season) of a household constitutes the minimal level of self sufficiency. Kantu households attain or surpass this measure one out of every three years. The shortfalls in the other years are supplemented with stored grain. Any household with surplus rice is obliged to assist any other household that is in need. This aids as an important levelling mechanism among swidden cultivators against excessive surpluses and shortages. In fact he observed that the total rice resources of the longhouse usually exceeds the total rice requirements of all its households (*Idem* 1985:295).

Among the Long Selatong Kenyah in the Baram, Chin found that the average yield of unhusked rice from one hectare of swidden was 833 kgs. This is considered sufficient for the needs of a household. Given that the average household swidden size is about 2.76 hectares for each season, the amount of unhusked rice each household can produce is 2299 kgs. The average requirement of unhusked rice of each individual is 215 kgs. With an average household size of nine persons, the total consumption of unhusked rice for each household would be 1935 kgs. This leaves a surplus of 364 kgs. When the harvest is very good, the output from half of the swidden is more than sufficient to meet the subsistence needs of the household (Chin 1984:265; 351-3).

According to Hatch of the Sarawak Agriculture Department, swidden farms from primary forest can attain yields of over 1000 kgs. per hectare (kg/ha) or 583.3 *gantang* per acre. In exceptional cases where disease and pest attack are low, as high as 2000 kg/ha (1166.6 *gantang* per acre) have been recorded (Hatch 1980:488). With families having an average farm size of four to five acres, the yields are more than sufficient to fulfil the family's needs.

Hatch's study was carried out in primary forest, where we can expect yields to be higher than on secondary forest. On the latter type of forest, trials were conducted by the Sarawak Department of Agriculture on hill padi varieties. Trials carried out for three seasons beginning from the 1965/66 season revealed that the hill padi varieties can yield in excess of 2000 pounds per acre (378.7 *gantang* per acre) on soil which have been under long fallow. This was a sufficient yield to fulfil a normal family's needs. 'With minimal input for such a system of agriculture the varieties currently used by the hill padi farmers are the most adaptable and best suited for the environment', the research concluded (Dept. of Agriculture 1982). Even with the introduction of cash crops, Iban in the Undup river (Second Division) have been found to grow enough rice for their own needs (Jensen 1966).

The low input of labour required in shifting agriculture has been shown in a number of studies (See Appendix I). Speaking of the Kantu, Dove states: 'If the labour that is incidentally devoted to the cultivation of the nonrice crops is factored out or if their harvests are added in, then the return on labour is still higher, increasing by about 50 per cent in each case' (Dove 1985:379).

Thus it can be seen that shifting cultivators can grow enough to feed themselves with minimal input of labour. This is also true of the Lua' and Karen who have shown that they can produce enough for their subsistence needs as long as population is stable and land is sufficient (Kunstadter 1978:109-122). As noted by Spencer (1966:43): 'Shifting cultivation is still practised in sections of the Asian tropics because there has been developed no other system of greater efficiency, effectively suited to the rather poor physical environments and specific ecologic situations in which shifting cultivation is still employed'.

Economic Use of Land

Since shifting cultivation involves a rotation of fields, forest regeneration is integral to the system. This recycling of land use is a form of conservation practice which prevents land wastage. A swidden farm comprises several scattered plots. This helps to cut down damage from pest attack if the farm had been concentrated on one site. The dispersal of the sites also enables seeds from the surrounding forest belts to germinate there, hence hastening forest regeneration (Grandstaff 1980:24). The forest belt also serve as windbreaks to reduce evaporation and protect the soil when the land is cleared for farming (Watters 1960:19). It has been argued that although swidden farms in virgin forests can give higher yields, swiddeners in fact prefer secondary forest cultivation. This is because clearing primary forest is an arduous and dangerous task which requires more manpower for a given area. It also demands a longer drying period before the fields can be burnt and thus more time is taken (Conklin 1969:225).

A study of the Lua' Karen system in Northeastern Thailand showed that the same swidden fields had been used for at least 150 years (Kunstadter 1967:652). And Conklin has suggested that the Hanunoo system of shifting cultivation in the Philippines has been stable for at least nearly a century (Spencer 1966:146 footnote). Christine Padoch has stated that the Iban in Sarawak have continuously farmed their areas of settlement for over three centuries. This 'immediately indicates that land use among all Iban groups is not predicated on constant abandonment of devasted lands and migration into new forests. The further observation that no extensive area of Sarawak colonized by Iban in the past has been completely abandoned voluntarily and that all such areas continue to be exploited by shifting cultivation points to the fact that the natural resources of these areas have not been exhausted' (Padoch 1982:13). This further demonstrates the rational use of land among swidden agriculturalists.

It also shows that swiddening can be a stable system with minimal cutting of new forests. In one Hanunoo community in the Philippines, a study revealed that out of a total of 48 new swiddens cleared, only four were cut partly from primary forest. This amounted to less than ten per cent of the total area cleared (Conklin 1969:224). Similarly in

Sarawak, Leach found in his 1950 study that in 'most normal circumstances the total amount of virgin jungle cleared in any one year is almost infinitesimal' (Leach 1950:89). Chin also found that the Baram Kenyah confine most of their swiddens in secondary forests (Chin 1984:389). Hence swidden is not as destructive of primary forest and as wasteful as it is made out to be.

Conservation of Soils:
Retention of Nutrients

It is an established fact that the long-term success of a shifting cultivation system depends on the maintenance of soil fertility. If the nutrients lost or displaced during the cultivation phase of the cycle are approximately balanced by those replaced during fallow, the system may continue in practice indefinitely (Zinke, Sanga Sabhasri & Kunstadter 1978:134). Many researchers have found that shifting cultivators have a profound knowledge of soil types and they make use of this knowledge to grow different crops that will utilise the varying qualities of soil. 'Sometimes what looks like an unplanned garden may be quite precisely planted' (Spencer 1966:35). Conklin has pointed out that the Hanunoo have great skill and knowledge of soils. They have their own method of rating the fertility of soil types. This rating was found to correlate with both modern scientific pH ratings (measure of alkalinity or acidity in the soil) and chemical analyses for mineral constituents[3] (*Ibid*).

The Kantu evaluate the quality of soil according to seven criteria which are crucial to swidden cultivation. These soil types are identified according to the structure of the soil, friability of the soil, moisture content in soils, soil temperature, soil colour, 'taste' of the soil and smell of the soil. The Kantu also gauge the soil features of a swidden by observing the character of the vegetarian growing on it. For example land covered with *madang* (a densely growing fern common in younger secondary forest which is used to make fish traps *bubu*) is considered 'dry', 'hot' and likely to be composed of 'clays' (*tanah Kelilit*). They will be reluctant to make swiddens on such soil. When swampland is covered with *purun* (*Fimbristylis globulosa*), a sedge (a type of grass found in swamps commonly used for plaiting), they know the soil underneath is 'sour' or highly acidic and avoid it. *Kerapa* and *Kerangas* vegetation in heath forest reflect the existence of 'sour' and sandy soils (Dove 1985:47-8). The Iban also recognise poor soils which they call *Kerangas*. It means soils on which hillrice cannot be grown. *Kerangas* forest is

---

3. Soil properties considered of greatest importance to fertility were the quantity of nitrogen, carbon and phosphorus; exchangeable calcium, magnesium, potassium, sodium; soil reaction or pH; and the cation exchange capacity (c.e.c.) and composition. Cation exchange capacity is the measure of the ability of the potential of that soil to bind the minerals in the soil so that it will be absorbed by the plants. Generally, minerals are not bonded so they get leached off by water.

characterised by highly leached, podzolised sand which are very poor in nutrients. According to Watters:

'The close dependence of shifting cultivation on soil fertility is clearly evident in analyses of changes in the soil following burning[4]. Burning leads to an accumulation of potash (probably the most prized by-product of burning) and valuable phosphates are often released at just the right time — immediately prior to planting the crops that will need them. Burning produces, moreover, a marked decrease in potential acidity, which is especially important in the more senile lateritic soils; . . . it often performs a function . . . that is often ideal for the germination of seeds. In view of these facts, it can be seen that burning is not only part of the shifting cultivator's technology — a device for clearing away vegetation — but also leads to an improvement in certain properties of the soil which in some areas makes cultivation possible and generally leads to increased yields during the period of cultivation' (Watters 1960:81-2).

As soils are impoverished in the humid tropics, the main source of nutrients are found in the living vegetation[5]. Swiddening makes use of this resource as firing the vegetation releases the nutrients into the soil from the ash formed. The low technology involved in swiddening limits the type of clearing and weeding done. This means that the soils will be less disturbed and erosion is minimized. In fact, Sutlive has observed that the Iban practise incomplete clearing of hill farms which is a deliberate measure. According to the Iban, thorough removal of the vegetation, especially on steep slopes only accelerates the rate of erosion (Sutlive 1978:74). With partial clearing, forest regeneration will be faster and fuller when the farm is abandoned. This will be good for the soil when swiddening is ready to be carried out again.

In a Thai study of the Lua' forest fallow system of shifting cultivation on forest production and soil, it was shown that 'the practice of cutting and burning the forest before cultivation increases the available nutrients

4.   Burning is the only method in shifting cultivation to clear the forest since allowing the felled vegetation to decay does not promote the rapid turnover of nutrients within this system. Unburnt plant material is low in ash. Decaying slowly, waters percolating through it would leach the elements released in the humificating process thus resulting in the soil becoming highly acidic. In addition the unburnt vegetation exposed to the sun would be reduced of microbial activity. Burns are usually completed in one to two hours. Rapid burning does not produce extreme heat deeper than 2 or 3 cm beneath the surface and allows some termites to survive and to loosen the compact soil structure caused by burning. The relatively shallow effect of the fire is attributed to the high soil moisture content in the burnt-over area. Researchers have also observed that many trees survive the fire. This is indicated by the heavy coppice growth in the fallow fields (Sanga Sabhasri 1978:173).

5.   The greatest concentration of nutrients in forest soils planted with crops is found in the top 7½ centimeters layer of soil (Chin 1981:3).

in the cultivation seasons' and 'secondary succession (regrowth) suggests that rejuvenation of the site is completed in eight to ten years after each period of cultivation under the Lua' forest fallow system' (Sanga Sabhasri 1978:172-4). This means that the fertility of the soil is restored to almost the same level before clearing ever took place as a result of the long fallow period[6].

In a separate study of five cultivation sites for different years of the Lua' forest fallow cycle, it was shown that in the forest fallow cycle, calcium, phosphorus and potassium are returned to the soil mainly in the ash from burnt cover-crop forests and nitrogen is added to the soil mainly during the growth phase of the forest cover-crop (Zinke, Sanga Sabhasri & Kunstadter 1978:158). The study further added that if the system is to be sustained, these amounts must be available in the form of trees (for firewood) or returned to the soil surface in the ash, at the time of the burn, for use by the growing rice crop (*Idem* 1978:159).

In Sarawak, Andriesse also showed that the level of nutrients in the soil increases greatly immediately after the burn, but virtually drops to the initial preburn levels after the harvest, thus confirming that burning is an essential part of the cultivation system and a prerequisite for a good harvest (Andriesse 1977:487).

Conservation of Soils:
Minimal Soil Erosion

Because the soil is not disturbed to a depth beyond a few centimeters in planting and weeding, erosion is minimal. In Sarawak it has been found that soil erosion is of little importance under traditional shifting cultivation. According to Hatch and Tie 'erosion and run-off occurring during the hill padi cropping cycle is very low and does not differ significantly from that under either primary or well grown secondary jungle . . . provided the organic matter content of the soil is high (i.e. after a long fallow) soil erosion and run-off will usually not be serious under a shifting cultivation system . . . Even when the bush/fallow period declines in response to land and population pressure, the early stages of this trend may not significantly increase the rate of soil erosion' (Hatch & Tie 1979:14-5).

Soil erosion trials recently conducted by the Sarawak Agriculture Department of swidden farms on steep land of more than 25 degree gradient have confirmed that soil erosion and run-off is insignificant under this system of agriculture. However when pepper was grown on these steep inadequately terraced slopes, very serious soil erosion and gullying occurred (Hatch 1980:490; Padoch 1980:479). Thus the growing of some cash crops in modern agriculture resulted in far more soil erosion than the traditional swidden system.

6.   In fact the Lua' avoid cutting trees on ridge tops and along water courses in a conscious effort to preserve the watersheds and reduce erosion (Peter Kunstadter 1978:83).

Nye and Greenland concluded from studies on shifting cultivation in Africa that these 'traditional systems of cultivation in the forest admirably protects the soil from erosion in spite of steep slopes and heavy rainfall' (Nye & Greenland 1960).

It can be seen from the above discussion that under conditions of low population density, low technology, poor humid soils and availability of land, swidden agriculture is a highly adaptive form of agriculture. It 'implies the almost complete molding of human practices to fit the environment as it is', according to Eckholm. In comparison to other forms of tropical agriculture he further adds: 'The unpleasant truth is that, for many tropical areas of Africa, Latin America, and SouthEast Asia, no alternative food production system to shifting cultivation has yet proven both biologically and economically workable' (Eckholm 1976:139).

The Forest as An Important Source of
Animal and Plant Resources

Although it is seldom realised, hunting, fishing and gathering play a significant role in the economy and life of shifting cultivators. These activities provide an important source of protein to their diet. Wild animals, birds, fish and shellfish are important complementary items in the diet of these peoples. Jungle products are also a source of sustenance, providing 'tool materials, fibres, medicines, ritual materials, insecticides, and poisons from the wild plant world of the surrounding forest'; and 'many groups also draw cash-sale products from this reservoir' (Spencer 1966:125).

Kunstadter has mentioned that fishing yields an important source of protein for the diet among the Lua' and Karen hill farmers and is carried out by several methods; while the hunting of game like wildboar, deer and birds employs the use of guns, traps and snares (Kunstadter 1978:107).

Among the Tiruray of Southwestern Mindanao, Schlegel records that hunting and fishing comprise the two primary activities after the major work of clearing the swiddens is complete. He has also noted a wide range of methods of hunting, namely 28 in all. In the case of fishing, which is carried out by both men and women, the Tiruray employ 28 methods which include the use of poison, hook and line, fish spears and fish traps. They also have several methods of preserving fish. Although fishing and hunting is primarily an individual activity, the game or catch is very often distributed to other members in the village as well. For example when a pig or deer is caught, it has to be equally divided among the entire neighbourhood. Although there is no mandatory sharing of the catch in fishing, in the event of a good harvest, each family in the village will receive a portion from it (Schlegel 1979:71-99). In this manner food resources are distributed and shared in the community.

Plants and animals play an important role in the life of the Kantu of West Kalimantan. Dove observed that fishing is an important daily occupation in which some 14 techniques are employed by the Kantu. A variety of animals are also hunted and trapped. They include the deer family, the primates, civets, leopard, squirrel, porcupine, monitor lizard, python, larvae of cetain insects, honey, pangolin, birds and the flying fox. In fact Dove has estimated that the mere consumption of venison and the wild pig by a Kantu household amounts to 90 kgs a year (Dove 1985:33; 51-2; 257).

In the case of Sarawak, Freeman observed that hunting and fishing among the Iban extended over the whole of the longhouse territory and sometimes into the territories of neighbouring communities which is allowed under Iban *adat* (Freeman 1955:108-9). He also noted that *tuba* fishing (poisoning fish with *tuba* roots) was an important activity involving a large number of Iban families. Among the Baram Kenyah, fishing and hunting are important supplementary activities. Both these activities which are carried out by the menfolk contribute to the community's daily food requirements (Hong 1977:104). Various lift nets, traps and spears are used in fishing and hunting. Whenever a person catches more fish than he needs or has more meat or venison than his *lamin* family can consume, he will distribute what remains to *lamin* families on both sides of his own *lamin* until all is exhausted (*Idem* 1977:126). The redistribution of the food surplus through collective consumption or sharing is a kind of 'insurance policy' for an individual in lean times as one can always expect a share of meat and fish from one's neighbour who has a surplus of these items. Chin also found that fishing, hunting and gathering accounted for a substantial portion of the food requirements of the Kenyah in the Baram. He noted that 11 methods were employed in fishing, which provided up to one-third of the food. Animals which were hunted and trapped also contributed more than 20 percent of the food intake (Chin 1984: 180, 195).

Gathering of plant products from the forest is another important activity in the life of shifting cultivators. Gathering among the Lua' and Karen usually occurs when vegetable supplies from the swiddens and house gardens are at their lowest ebb. Gathering is usually done by small groups of women. The most important food items, gathered in the largest quantities, are ferns, bamboo shoots and mushrooms and these foods comprise the major vegetable component of the diet from April (when the village gardens are almost dried up) through June (when the swiddens begin to produce). Lua' and Karen also gather jungle products for sale (Kunstadter 1978:105-7).

According to Schlegel, traditional Tiruray people depend on the wild flora of the forests as a major source of food and other necessities. Plant supplies are gathered mostly from the surrounding forest, and some 223 basic plant types are regularly exploited. Starch staples, side dishes, supplementary ingredients and snack foods are supplied from the wild yams, vegetables, seeds, nuts, pods, and a multitude of wild fruit trees.

Apart from food, the jungle provides firewood, construction materials, weaving materials, fencing, lashing, tool handles, weapon and trap preparation, musical instruments, starches, soaps and medicine through gathering. Products like rattan and vines from the forest are also collected and sold to raise cash. Hence the dense tropical rain forest is not merely the scene for shifting cultivation, it is itself, like the river, regularly and richly harvested (Schlegel 1978:99-101).

Among the Kenyah, women and children contribute largely to gathering activities which include tubers, shoots, mushrooms, fruits, vegetables and edible greens. These are often obtained from the fallow swidden fields and the surrounding forest. In recent years, chronic rice shortage has become increasingly frequent and wild tubers and sago are a major source of food (Hong 1977).

Chin observed that the gathering of food items, the most important of which are the mushrooms (*kulat*), ferns (*paku*), and the 'hearts' of various plants (*ubot*) which include bamboo shoots, wild palms and wild bananas also provide for ten to 25 per cent of the food consumption. The Kenyah also collect forest products of prime economic importance which are sold for cash. They include *garu* (eaglewood), illipenut (*a'bang*), and *damar* or resin (Chin 1984:209, 225). However these resources are becoming scarce as a result of the rapid deforestation taking place in the Baram.

It can be seen from the above examples that the forest is an important source of nutrition and materials to shifting cultivators. The forest environment plays a crucial role in their existence as most of their subsistence and livelihood is derived from it. It also goes to show that swidden is by far a more complex agricultural system than it is commonly believed. To quote Kunstadter: 'swidden agriculture is a far more complex and diverse system of production than is irrigated agriculture, . . . fallow swiddens make important contributions to the economy . . . In addition to their role in restoring soil fertility for the next cycle of cultivation, and the uncultivated portions of the environment are of major economic importance' (Kunstadter 1978:130). Swidden cultivation may well be the oldest system devised by man for use of his ecosystem that involves the combination of systematic cultivation of tree, root, and/or seed crops, and the primeval practices of hunting, fishing and gathering (Pelzer 1978:271).

The Increasing Marginalisation of Shifting Cultivators

From the above discussion of shifting cultivation practices among the swidden communities of Southeast Asia, it can be seen that these peoples have managed very successfully to carve a niche in the harsh tropical forest environment which is both ecologically viable and self sustaining. Shifting cultivators thus lived in harmony with the forest and maintained an intimate relationship with its environment. Today these self contained communities are threatened by the larger society and powerful forces of the State which they cannot avoid or control. The despoilation of their physical environment and the negative attitudes borne of ignorance and arrogance (often reflected in official policy) towards these shifting cultivators have threatened their existence and very survival. In many regions of Southeast Asia, shifting cultivators have been displaced from their natural environments, deprived of their livelihood and suffer extreme deprivation and cultural alienation.

Stereotype images of shifting cultivators continue to be projected as despoilers of forest and land resources. To what extent is this true? Spencer who had spent some 18 years of his life observing and studying shifting cultivators in Southeastern Asia has mentioned that a large share of the blame must rest with the lumbermen 'who often leave behind them a torn and bared earth in which local drainage is disturbed and erosion channels are created by log transport' (Spencer 1966:34).

According to Schlegel, the single most devastating change on the Tiruray world has been the systematic clearing of the forest cover. By 1966, the Philippines government had divided up all forest areas in their vicinity into concessions for logging operations. In doing this, the government took no notice whatsoever of the existence of the traditional Tiruray population residing in scattered hamlets throughout these forests. When Tiruray were encountered living in a section of the forest they intended to cut, they were callously harrassed into evacuating or threatened with arrest as 'squatters' on the logging company's franchised land. In the process of this rapid extension of logging, hundreds upon hundreds of Tiruray families had been unfeelingly displaced and forced either to retreat further into the mountains beyond the penetration of the loggers or to find work as tenants somewhere upon the cleared land. They experienced profound acculturation with their forest now gone, shifting cultivation was impossible, and most of them become plow farmer tenants on another person's land. Unable to cope with Philippine municipal law, their traditional system withered and the once authoritative role of *kefeduwan* (legal leader) faded from social importance (Schlegel 1979:15-6).

Moreover, Kunstadter speaking of the Lua' and Karen hillfarmers add that 'meanwhile the resources of the swidden areas (lumber, minerals, some agricultural products) are siphoned off to the benefit of an external economy, with little or no effect on the development of the local area nor improvement in the life of the local people' (Kunstadter 1978:291).

It would appear that shifting cultivators in Southeast Asia have not only been left out of the main-stream of the national consciousness, they also have obtained little benefits from the national economy. 'Because European administration reinforced and extended the systems of private ownership of land and state control of the public domain, the incompatibilities between the loosely administered pre-European land systems and shifting cultivator land systems were greatly increased and made more emphatic. The result has often been the restriction of territorial ranges of shifting cultivator societies to the point where maladjustments have become severe and shifting cultivation has begun to exhibit all the faults that commonly are ascribed to it as a system' (Spencer 1966:168).

As the above shows, shifting cultivators in Southeast Asia have been increasingly marginalised, displaced or severely restricted, due to the encroachment of the 'modern sector', its various forms of logging companies, dams and other 'development projects'. In Sarawak, the story is no different. Increasingly the natives have had their lands being taken away from them, often without their even knowing it, (with or without the backing of law) and through the implementation of government policies. When the loggers came to their forest, the natives suffered the shock and bitterness of seeing their forests farms, ancestral lands and sacred places destroyed and defiled before their very eyes. When the dams were built, they were ordered to pack their belongings and leave, never to return or ever glimpse their homes, their lands, their fruit trees, and the graves of their beloved ancestors which will all be flooded out of existence. They have been herded into resettlement schemes heartsick and broken in spirit, yearning for the old life that has come to an end and wondering why. In these 'reservations' they are made to grow cash crops (on individual plots alloted to them) exposing them to the vagaries of commodity prices in the modern market economy. When prices are extremely low, there is no income and there is not enough to eat. When the children grow up, there is not enough land to go around, so they pack their belongings once again and head for the towns ending up as poor, forgotten, and dispossessed urban squatters.

In the following Chapters, we will discuss the various aspects of this marginalisation as it happened, and is still happening, to the natives of Sarawak.

Above: Swidden rice farms cultivated on rolling hills.

Below: Natives on the way to their swidden farms.

Above: Natives harvesting some greens for a meal. This swidden plot is systematically cultivated with rice (foreground), banana, tapioca, sugar cane, chilli and various vegetables.

Below: This photo shows a wide range of crops in a small swidden patch, including tomato, bitter gourd, peanuts, vegetables and edible mushrooms on the fallen tree trunk.

Right:
Kenyah
woman
collecting
peanuts
from her
swidden.

Hong

Below:
Harvested
rice from
the swidden
being
sieved.

Wong

CHAPTER FOUR

Changes in Sarawak's Land Laws: Impact on Natives

Land has been the Sarawak natives' most important economic resource, and the relationship between land and the community has been the cornerstone of native society. Land has both spiritual and social significance to native people. The community is closely bound to the soil and the land. This is understandable as the land is the source of their livelihood. It gives them food and provides them with their material needs. Similarly when they die, they return to the land which receives them. It houses the ghosts and memories of their departed ancestors. It is also the dwelling place of the benevolent spirits that protect them, their crops and their land. Land is their sweat, blood and life. To the natives, rights to land also involves a complex of responsibilities towards both kith and kin and departed ancestors who had similarly worked and farmed on these lands. According to Leach, land to the natives involved 'a host of obligations towards abstrusely connected relatives not to mention their ancestral spirits' (Leach 1947:151-2). This was reflected in the preservation of genealogies sometimes to a depth of up to thirty generations among the Iban (Sutlive 1978:150) and in the oral history of the migrations of their villages for example among the Kenyah communities. The preservation of this oral tradition among these preliterate communities served as a means of establishing their rights to land as well.

The Significance of Land to the Natives

Thus the land is a living entity which is dear and precious and holds a very deep and spiritual meaning for them. In traditional society this reverence for the land also meant that it could not be bought or sold. Land was inalienable and no one had the power to alienate it. This principle was couched in *adat* law which has legal, moral and religious aspects. *Adat* defined an individual's right to land. When an individual works a piece of land, he is in effect creating a personal identity with the soil. He thus establishes a legal relation to it and this is recognised by the community whose rights to it are diminished (Ter Haar 1962:90). 'Ownership' and rights to land also encompassed a system of obligations. These rights and obligations involving land extended between

individuals and the community. Under *adat* the community as a group
exercises rights to land. The group controls and regulates the rights
and claims among its own members to the extent that each member
obtains his or her share of common benefits to be derived from the
land (*Idem* 1962:89). This concept of native justice and morality *vis-a-
vis* land is a living concept among native peoples.

The Encroachment of the Modern State on
Native Land

The land system of the natives, and their very rights to the use of the
land, have been disturbed and threatened by the intervention of the
modern State into the resources and life of native communities in
Sarawak.

Contact with an economically more sophisticated and powerful
society is often accompanied by the imposition of an external authority
and culture system on a traditional society. In Sarawak, the larger
State and its machinery was able to impose itself over wide spheres
of community life. This was done with the help of a system of laws
and administrative policies enforced through administrators and law
enforcement personnel. This was bound to result in ramifying changes
in traditional society. The opening of the society to the modern
economic, political and cultural system (which began under Brooke
and Colonial rule) and Sarawak's subsequent entry into Malaysia,
and the effects and changes brought about in the process, are still
being felt. James Brooke, an English adventurer, became the first
Rajah of Sarawak in 1841. Before he took over control of Sarawak,
the natives of Borneo practised a form of customary law commonly
known as *adat*. *Adat* is commonly shared by societies of insular Southeast
Asia especially those of the Malay-Indonesian world. Sarawak was
ruled by the Brooke family for 105 years, until it was ceded to the
British Crown in 1946. Sarawak became a British Colony for the next
17 years until 1963 when it joined with the former British territories
of Malaya, North Borneo and Singapore to form the Federation of
Malaysia.

This chapter will deal with some of the major events and changes
related to land laws, policies and systems in Sarawak which have led
to far reaching consequences on the native peoples.

Under the impact of Colonial rule and, later, the entry into Malaysia,
the land system in Sarawak underwent a drastic change. Natives found
that their traditional rights to land use and expansion were severely
curtailed. They became more and more 'restricted' in terms of their
access to land. To the natives, land was the most important asset and
still is crucial to their survival. Land in traditional society was free for
the taking subject to customary law. About the first thing that Colonial
rule brought under its purview was land. Beginning from the first land
enactments under the Brooke Raj to the modern period, natives were

progressively isolated and their rights to land curtailed by boundaries
which defined their access to land. The rest of the country was exploited
under a *laissez faire* policy. As the pace of modernisation stepped up
and land and the resources on it fetched a high market value, native
lands were increasingly encroached upon.

As earlier discussed, the indigenous land tenure system under *adat*
practised by the natives gave the right to cultivation to all members
of the community. Priority to the right to cleared jungle land was vested
in the heirs of the original feller. This right was again exercised in
accordance with a cycle or rotation of land use which preserved the
maximum fertility of the land. No individual may hold more land than
he can use. The exercise of this right over land was not simply an
economic or individual right. It was part and parcel of a moral and
religious system or philosophy. Within this belief system, land had
economic, social and religious significance. This was at variance with
a market economy where private ownership of land was the prerequisite
to the establishment of western capitalistic enterprises. The indigenous
system of land tenure has been gradually and systematically eroded
as a result of new laws related to land and the forests introduced at
various political and administrative periods in Sarawak's history. We
shall now trace some of the key laws enacted and their consequences
on the people.

The 1863 Land Order

When he took over control of Sarawak, James Brooke realised the
importance of native customary tenure and rights among the people.
In fact: 'From the beginning, Brooke's assumption of sovereignity
and presumption of proprietorship in land was burdened by the
recognition of customary rights' (Porter 1967:12). He recognised the
traditional domain of the natives and their customs within this domain,
in which:

> 'The fruit trees about the Kampong, and as far as the jungle
> round, are private property, and all other trees which are in
> any way useful, such as bamboo, various kinds for making
> bark-cloth, the bitter kony, . . . and many others. Land,
> likewise is individual property, and descends from father to son,
> so, likewise, is the fishing of particular rivers, and indeed most
> other things . . .' (Mundy 1848:210).

Thus, the official policy was one of non-interference in native customary
rights as manifested in the 1842 Code of Laws permitting immigrant
races (especially Chinese) to settle only on land not already occupied
by the natives (Porter 1967:12,26).

In 1863 the first land law known as The Land Regulations, 1863,
was promulgated. The most important effect of this Order was the
creation of government rights and proprietorship to land in the State:
'all unoccupied and waste lands' were to be 'the property of the

government'. The Rajah's administration could now lease out land to private individuals or companies. Hence:

'All unoccupied and waste lands, the property of Government, required for agricultural purposes, with the exception of such tracts, as may be reserved or disposed of by public sale, shall be granted at the pleasure of the Government to applicants on lease of 900 years at the rate of 50 cents per acre, with an annual quit rent of 10 cents per acre exclusive of a survey fee of 25 cents per acre' and 'Persons taking land on lease for 900 years to have the option at the expiration of 3 years of purchasing the land in fee simple upon the payment of the additional sum of $1 per acre' (*Idem* 1967:32).

The significance of the 1863 Land Order was that although natives could continue to practise customary tenure within their domain, they could no longer automatically claim rights to land outside their existing domain, which now belonged to the State. Natives wanting to open new land outside their domain had, according to the Order, to obtain government permission. Hence the natives' freedom of land use and access became restricted. At the same time private ownership of land was now instituted in the form of leases supplied by the government.

The 1875 Land Order

Under the second Rajah, Charles Brooke, the Land Regulations, 1863, was revised in 1871. Regulation 5 gave recognition to squatters who 'could be dealt with leniently' or 'to take out title' for the land they occupied. In 1875, a major addition to the Land Order appeared. Under this Order, squatters were allowed to occupy without interference land cleared and abandoned by others. According to Porter's *Land Administration In Sarawak*, 'the order seems to be directed at land which was occupied and cultivated in accordance with native customary laws and then abandoned; . . . It suggests a curious misunderstanding on the part of Government, not simply of the practices permitted under native customary law but also of the biological demands the practices made on the land'. The author was referring to the practice of long term fallow in shifting cultivation. 'The Order is taken further beyond comprehension by the imposition of a fine in respect of land cleared and abandoned' (*Idem* 1967:37).

It would appear from the above that the 1875 Order was the first deliberate attempt to curtail shifting cultivation and customary land tenure.

Fruit Trees Order I, 1899

The next important legislation which had a major bearing on customary law was the Fruit Trees Order of 1899 issued by the Rajah to Dayak removing (migrating) from one river or district to another. Section 2 of this Order says that:

'Any Dayak removing from a river or district may not claim, sell or transfer any farming ground in such river or district, nor may he prevent others farming thereon, unless he holds such land under a grant' (*Idem* 1967:13).

This Order curtailed the power of natives to establish customary rights and to dispose of these rights within the community. Further, it served to control the movement of natives from one area to another.

Land Order No. VIII and No. IX, 1920

The pace of the commercialisation of agriculture accelerated with the introduction of gambier and pepper in the late 1870s, and rubber in the second decade of the twentieth century (*Idem* 1967:38,45). After 1915, an attempt was made to introduce a more comprehensive attitude to land administration for the whole state.

In 1920 all the previous Orders and Regulations were consolidated under Order No. VIII. This order decreed State land as 'all lands which are not leased or granted or lawfully occupied by any person and includes all lands which hereafter may become forfeited or may be surrendered to the State by the lawful owner thereof' (*Idem* 1967:47). It also defined two important land concepts, namely:

• Grant which 'means a grant of State land issued by or on behalf of his Highness the Rajah and includes a lease of State land in perpetuity' and

• Lease which 'means any lease of State land given by or on behalf of his Highness the Rajah for a term of less than 99 years'.

Land was now classified into Town and Suburban Lands, Country Lands and Native Holdings. The provisions concerning Native Holdings allowed the free occupation of land for the cultivation of fruit trees, padi, vegetables, pineapples, sugarcane, bananas, yams and similar cultures 'in accordance with the customary laws'. It also mentions that claims to fruit groves and farm lands should be registered 'where possible' and introduced a form of registration certificate for the purpose of Native Holdings (*Idem* 1967:48).

Order No. IX, which was a Supplementary Order to Order No. VIII, provided the necessary regulations to implement the latter. Order No. IX made provisions for the creation of 'Native Land Reserves'. These were to be divided into three acre lots for occupation by any 'native born subject'[1] whilst natives were permitted to obtain one such lot free of all charges (*Ibid*).

---

1. The Land Order No. VIII defined any 'natural born subject of his Highness the Rajah' as a native. This would include all persons both indigenous and non indigenous.

The Land orders were an attempt to introduce a more uniform and coherent policy towards land administration in the State. This was necessary for the development of commercial agriculture which was in line with the Rajah's policy. With the registration of land, under Native Land Reserves, natives were encouraged to make claims to private ownership of land.

The Land Order (Order L-2), 1931; and Land Settlement Order, 1933

With increased settlement and commercial land development, land became a scarcer and more valuable commodity. Land laws were accordingly refined and consolidated. The Land Order of 1931 divided land into 'Native Areas' to be inhabited by natives under customary law, and 'Mixed Zones' which could be owned and occupied by Chinese and other non natives. Under this Order, State Land was further defined to mean 'all lands for which no document of title has been issued but includes all lands which may become forfeited or may be surrendered to the State by the lawful owner thereof' (*Idem* 1967:50). The Superintendent of Lands was empowered to declare any defined area to be town, village or suburban land, or any other category (*Ibid*). The importance of land registration was emphasized under this Order. Rights to land were registered under title in the Land Office with the help of accurate land surveys. Provisions enabling the creation of native land reserves were also more clearly defined. The definition of 'Natives' was now confined to members of the indigenous 'race' (*Idem* 1967:51 footnote). However, the Order stipulates that these reserves were not to be divided and the issue of individual titles were no longer permitted (*Ibid*).

In 1933, the Land Settlement Order came into force. This Order was meant to clear up grants which had been made since the beginning of the Rajah's administration (*Report of the Land Committee 1962*: para 125). It 'provides for the settlement of rights to land and the creation of a new Land Register based on an accurate and fully verified cadastral survey. It closely resembles the many forms of the Torrens system in use throughout the British Commonwealth' (Porter 1967:51). This Order provided for the first time a system by which settlement could take place. Settlement Officers appointed by the Superintendent of Lands and Surveys[2] were empowered to determine all rights, whether

2.   In 1933, the functions of the Land Department and the Survey Department were again combined until the present day. Before 1915 land matters had been handled by various officials acting in the name of the 'Land Office' whilst all survey work was handled by the Public Works Deparmtment. In 1915 all land and survey functions were transferred to the Director of Agriculture whose principal responsibility was the alienation of land. The Department of Agriculture was renamed the Land and Survey Department in 1919 and the Director was appointed to be the first Superintendent of Lands and Surveys. The Lands and Surveys Department was administratively split in 1925 with the creation of a Superintendent of Lands and a Superintendent of Surveys.

customary or held under a previous title, claimed within the gazetted settlement area. Hence in these declared settlement areas, customary rights to land could be settled and the registration of title in respect of such rights were effected (*Idem* 1967:52-53).

The significance of this was that the State could now exercise compulsory acquisition of native customary lands by a notification. Thus under the Settlement Order, native customary rights could be extinguished.

Boundaries were drawn around longhouse communities to define settlement and cultivation between communities, and rights to land use were restricted within these boundaries. Hence the rights to land use and to the movement of settlements were now physically defined and restricted in the 1931 and 1933 Land Orders. The State was now able to exercise firmer control and ownership over lands in the State. Thus 'by 1933 every aspect of land administration under the Rajah's authority was covered by legislation or an administrative procedure' (*Idem* 1967:53).

Secretariat Circular No. 12/1939, Native Customary Tenure

Despite the attempts by the Brooke administration to curtail and limit natives from practising customary tenure and shifting cultivation, the government still considered it a serious problem which was a major encumbrance to land administration and policy. In 1939, the government published a Memorandum Secretariat Circular No. 12/1939 on Native Customary Tenure to tackle the issue.

This memorandum was highly significant for a number of reasons. Firstly, it was an attempt to formalise the position of native customary law. Section 9 of the circular instructed officials on the appointment of village councils in each community. 'The council will be concerned with native land tenure and inheritance only' (*Report of the Land Committee 1962*: Appendix A).

More important, this document instructed that all claims to farming land held by individuals should not be allowed although under customary law this principle is recognised. Section 4 specifically points out that 'when it is necessary to build up a communal area from the claims of individuals it will be better for the time being not to record those individual claims as such, but to regard them merely as stepping stones to definition of the communal claim' (*Ibid*).

In fact officers were told that they 'will endeavour as far as possible to circumvent attempts by individuals to dispose of rights in which the community can claim an interest by *adat*' (*Ibid*).

This can be seen as a deliberate attempt by the administration to acknowledge and recognise certain features of native customary law which were in line with its policy. Native customary law was thus *selectively* applied and administered by the officers of the Rajah. Officials could now decide what particular aspects would be considered 'legal and binding'. This also had the effect of narrowing the interpretation of native customary law. Eventually, this would lead to many features of native customary law being reduced to mere rules in writing.

Although the Land Orders 1931 and 1933 provided for the registration of village boundaries, the absence of accurate triangulation surveys in the remote areas made this a problem. The Secretariat Circular 12/1939 made the demarcation of village boundaries possible in the local areas by the setting up of the village councils. These councils or committees were formed to assist the officers of the government to deal with native customary rights and land tenure. The primary objective of these councils was to define and demarcate village or community boundaries. By this exercise, the extent and limit of a village community's land could be established and controlled.

Section 14 of the circular instructs that: 'The area so described is that over which the community has acquired or may acquire customary rights in accordance with native *adat* . . . and they will become Native Communal Reserves under the Land Orders. Additions to such areas will be permitted only on application and on proof to the satisfaction of the District Officer that additional farming land is necessary because of increase in the population or for other good reasons' (*Ibid*). This policy limited once and for all the extent of land claimed by each community for its farming needs.

Government policy towards the forests was also strongly influenced by swidden cultivation. The official thinking towards swidden cultivation had always been negative and that this wasteful method of cultivation should be seriously controlled. Prior to the Second World War, no specific legislation had been enacted to restrict natives from swidden cultivation. The demarcation of forest reserves did not effectively control swidden farming. In 1934, the government introduced the concept of the protected forest. In these areas natives had to observe two restrictions: they were not allowed to open up new land for farming or settlement, and they were prohibited from extracting forest products from these areas for commercial purposes. The Forest Department retained the right to *close* (i.e. to prohibit natives from using) not more than 0.1 hectare of the area for technical purposes. According to official estimates in the first three years since this ruling was introduced, 1,072 sq. km. of commercial forest was saved from shifting cultivation (Spurway 1937:128).

In the Appendix to Secretariat Circular 12/1939, Forestry and the Use of the Land, it was revealed that the government was working towards a more rational Forest Policy which would mean that 'the evils of shifting cultivation should . . . be gradually eliminated'.

The 1948 Land Classification Ordinance

In 1946 Sarawak was ceded to the British Crown. The most important legislation introduced by the Colonial Government was the 1948 Land

Classification Ordinance. This Ordinance classified all land in Sarawak into one of five categories:

i) Mixed Zone Land;
ii) Native Area Land;
iii) Native Customary Land;
iv) Reserved Land; and
v) Interior Area Land

This was largely a consolidation of previous legislation, which was later revised and formed the basis of the 1958 Land Code.

In 1952, an amendment was made to the 1948 Land Classification Ordinance pertaining to the lawful occupation of the different classes of land created. With this amendment 'natives who were in lawful occupation of Native Customary Land were declared to be licensees of Crown Land' (Porter 1967:61). In effect what this meant was that the Crown now assumed total proprietorship over *all* land in the State. More crucial, the amendment revealed that the government was preparing for the eventual extinguishment of customary rights. This policy was also supported by administrative procedure in matters regarding land. In 1951 an official paper entitled 'Sarawak Land Policy with Particular Reference to Native Claims to Customary Rights and Settlement of Non-natives' was issued to all government officers dealing with land questions. This paper 'admitted to foreseeing a remote future in which customary tenure would disappear entirely' (*Ibid*).

This policy towards the natives was taken a step further in 1955 with another amendment to the Land Classification Ordinance. With this amendment 'a total prohibition on the spontaneous creation of further customary rights was applied' (*Idem* 1967:68). Natives were now forbidden to open up new forests and exercise customary rights or operate under customary tenure in these new areas. More important, this amendment meant that native communities could no longer move freely to establish new swiddens and new settlements in new areas as they did in the past.

The Land Classification Amendment Ordinance of 1955 was enacted as a result of a court decision in 1954. In *Sepid anak Selir v. R.*, the native appellants were convicted in the Police Court at Serian in June 1954 of the offence of unlawful occupation of Crown Land, contrary to Section 108 of the Land Ordinance. They were fined and ordered to vacate the land. They appealed against the conviction, fine and order. The appeal was upheld and the judge Lascelles, J., in his judgement said:

'In a prosecution under Section 108 of the Land Ordinance it is essential that it be proved that the accused was in "unlawful occupation of Crown Land or land reserved for a public purpose . . ."

. . . . Section 3(1) of the Land (Classification) Ordinance, No. 19 of 1948, as amended by Ordinances No. 10 of 1952 and

No. 3 of 1954 states that all land in Sarawak belongs to one of
the following five classes:
(a) Mixed Zone Land; (b) Native Area Land; (c) Native
Customary Land; (d) Reserved Land; (e) Interior Area Land.

Section 7(3) of the same Ordinance states that land which is not
Mixed Zone Land or Native Area Land or Native Customary
Land or Reserved Land is *Interior Area Land.*

By Section 8 of the Land (Classification) Ordinance natives may
occupy such land for the purpose of creating customary rights,
which is clearly what the appellants were doing here. Powers
exist for converting Interior Area Land into Mixed Zone,
Native Area, Native Communal Reserve or Reserved Land,
but it is clear that *no* such powers have yet been exercised in
respect of this land and the appellants were clearly acting within
their legal rights in doing what they did ...' (*Idem* 1967:76).

This judgement revealed a major loophole in the law by which new
customary rights could be created by natives. The Government took
immediate action to draft legislation. The Land (Classification) Rules
1954 and the Land Classification (Amendment) Ordinance 1955 which
were enacted effectively prohibited any further widespread creation of
new customary rights over land (*Idem* 1967:77).

The 1958 Land Code

The Colony embarked on its first five year Development Plan in
1955-60. Large scale rural development began and it was increasingly
realised that a more streamlined land administration could only come
about with the consolidation of the various existing land legislations
in the State. This was vital for the implementation of the State's
economic planning. In 1957, the most unified Land Code to date was
promulgated. This piece of legislation came into force on 1st January
1958. It repealed the Land Ordinance, 1931; the Land Settlement
Ordinance, 1933; the Land (Classification) Ordinance, 1948; and the
Dealings in Land (Validation) Ordinance, 1952 (Report of the Land
Committee 1962: para 27). The Land Code was based on several
sources of Land Legislation which includes the Land Act, 1948, of New
Zealand; the Finance Act (No. 2) 1953 of New Zealand; the Land Code
(Cap. 138) of the Federated Malay States; the Land Transfer Act 1952
of New Zealand; the Property Law Act 1952 of New Zealand; the Land
Acquisition Ordinance of Brunei and the Transfer of Land Act of the
State of Victoria, Australia (*Idem* 1967:78).

One of the major objectives of the Land Code was to clarify and
strengthen the law relating to native customary rights. 'The Land Code
enacted provisions which continue to effectively restrict the creation
of further customary rights' (*Idem* 1967:83). In fact one of the objectives
of the Land Code Bill was to introduce 'a new system of land settlement

in the expectation that it would enable most land in Sarawak to be brought on to the new Land Register within seven years' (*Idem* 1967:79). With this Ordinance customary rights to tenure were now restricted under Part II section 5(2) to six methods. These were:

i) the felling of virgin jungle and the occupation of the land thereby cleared;
ii) the planting of land with fruit trees;
iii) the occupation or cultivation of land;
iv) the use of land for a burial ground or shrine;
v) the use of land of any class for rights of way; or
vi) any other lawful method.

In order to enjoy rights to land, the natives now had to make applications for permits issued by the District Officer, and these may or may not be granted.

Under this Land Code, all land in the State was classified into five categories: i) Mixed Zone Land; ii) Native Area Land; iii) Native Customary Land; iv) Interior Area Land; v) Reserved Land. Recently the Deputy Director, Lands and Surveys Department Zaidi Khaldin Zainie has given figures showing how these different classifications are broken down. His figures are reproduced in Table I. According to these figures, Mixed Zone Land and Native Area Land comprise 7.9 per cent and 7.3 per cent of the total land area in Sarawak respectively. Both these categories of land are found mainly in the town and coastal areas of Sarawak. Most of these lands are held under titles. Reserved Land represents 15.7 per cent of the total land area in the State, most of which is located in the Fourth Division; these lands are reserved for government use. Native Customary Land and Interior Area Land cover over 21 million acres (eight and half million hectares) or over 68 per cent of the total land area in Sarawak. These two categories of land lie mainly in the Seventh and Fourth Divisions. Most of the Native Customary Land and Interior Area Land have not been surveyed or adjudicated. Land policy and administration in Sarawak has since been based on these classifications.

Mixed Zone Land

This land may be held under title. Anyone can hold title to this category of land which can also be occupied by indigenous peoples under customary tenure. It is the only category that Chinese and other non-natives may own or occupy. Part II section 4 of the Code reads that the Minister may 'declare any area of land to be Mixed Zone Land by notification in the *Gazette*'.

Native Area Land

This land may be held by natives under title. Part II section 4(2) and 4(3) says that this land can be created by the Minister by notification

Table 1: Sarawak Land Area
According to Land Tenure Categories, 1985

Division	Mixed Zone Land in Sq. Kilometres	Native Area Land in Sq. Kilometres	Reserved Land in Sq. Kilometres	Native Customary Right and Interior Area Land in Sq. Kilometres
First	1,387.08	525.80	1,908.05	5,081.02
Second	4,219.33	2,393.53	1,098.38	2,560.82
Third	1,890.31	651.61	3,456.43	6,888.77
Fourth	982.42	3,187.08	9,733.66	25,040.15
Fifth	396.77	983.86	861.29	5,548.12
Sixth	841.93	1,459.67	1,367.74	3,051.75
Seventh	146.78	—	1,118.46	37,668.73
Total	9,864.62	9,201.55	19,544.01	85,839.36
Percentage to Total State Area	7.927%	7.394%	15.704%	68.979%

Source: Zaidi Khaldin Zainie, 'Land Tenure System in Sarawak', *Sarawak Gazette*, July 1985, p15.

in the *Gazette*. A non-native can also acquire rights over Native Area Land in the following manner. Firstly if he is prospecting for minerals or taking forest produce. Secondly when he becomes a 'native' by identifying with and subjecting to any native system of personal law. Thirdly, the Governor can issue a permit or an order under the Land Rules, section 213 of the Code that will allow him to occupy this land. Fourthly, when a registered native proprietor executes a dealing in favour of such a person. In such a case the person shall be deemed to be a native for the purpose relating to the dealing (Part II, section 9(1) provisio (a)(b)(c)(d)). This institutionalised or corporate 'native' includes certain statutory bodies and agencies which are defined as a native of Sarawak. Two such agencies are the Sarawak Land Consolidation and Rehabilitation Authority (SALCRA) and the Sarawak Timber Industry Development Corporation (STIDC).

Native Customary Land

This is defined as 'land in which native customary rights whether communal or otherwise have lawfully been created prior to the 1st of January 1958'. After this date, Native Customary Land can be created only if a permit is obtained on Interior Land. Anyone practising native customary rights over any land after this date will be committing an offence for unlawful occupation of State land. Thus native customary land is land recognised as such only *before* 1st January 1958. Native Customary Land can also be created by the Minister who declares by notification in the *Gazette* any area of State land a Native Communal Reserve. Native Customary laws in or over such land can be applied (Part II section 6(1)). Hence if land is designated Native Communal Reserve, then the land is for all intents and purposes Native Customary Land.

However the Minister can simply declare by order in the Gazette that such Native Communal Reserve will cease to be one and the government is free to dispose of the land. Although in degazetting a Native Communal Reserve, the Minister must be satisfied that it will not cause 'in justice or oppression', there is nothing in the provision that allows for an appeal to the courts against his decision.

Native Customary Land can also be extinguished when the Minister declares by notification in the *Gazette* that the land has become Mixed Zone Land or Native Area Land. Once this happens, Native Customary Land ceases to be so.

Although the status of Native Customary Land was preserved whether it fell within an area gazetted as Mixed Zone Land, Native Area Land or in Interior Area Land; Native Customary Land could be reclassified as stated in section 4(4). This in effect means that Native Customary Land can cease to exist. Penalties were also imposed for any attempt 'to transfer or confer any such rights or privileges over Native Area Land, Native Customary Land or Interior Area Land' as this would constitute an offence (Part II section 8).

Another provision empowers the Superintendent of Lands and Surveys to replace a valid claim in respect of land held under customary tenure by title. This was amended in 1963 whereby ownership of title was replaced by a lease for 99 years, free of charge. This land shall be used for agricultural purposes only (Part II section 18). Thus native rights to land can be surrendered in exchange for a lease. 'This can scarcely be considered fair exchange for what may hitherto have amounted virtually to full ownership' commented the *Report of the Land Committee 1962* (para 124).

However, there was a new development with another amendment in 1974 of section 18, which empowers the Superintendent to issue a native a grant in perpetuity on unalienated State land which he/she has occupied and used 'in accordance with rights acquired by customary tenure'. This in effect means that full private ownership of land can be granted to individual or selected natives on what is native customary land. It opens the way to private accumulation of land by individual natives. With this development, natives who have communal customary rights to these lands would have lost these rights to individual natives, eventually resulting in landlessness among them.

Another development detrimental to native interests were amendments to the Code enabling Native Customary Land to be also acquired by *non-natives*. In Part IX section 213 (1)(c) it is stated that the Governor can make rules to provide for 'the conditions under which Native Customary Land may be occupied under permit *by persons other than those entitled to the customary rights'* Part I section 19 of the Land Rules says that a non-native can apply for a permit to the District Officer. Thus, native customary land was no longer wholly reserved for natives.

Part V which deals with the Settlement of State Lands also contain provisions *whereby native customary rights can be extinguished.* Section 94(2) specifically states that 'in the case of native customary rights, the Settlement Officer may provide for the extinguishment thereof by the payment of compensation or shall show the same in the Settlement Order, and, if the rights are such as would enable a lease to be issued to the persons entitled, shall enter also all the particulars to enable a lease to be issued'. This implies that the Settlement Officer is empowered to overrule any decision made or recognised by a native court. Section 94(1) clearly states that the Settlement Officer is empowered to investigate all claims to State land whether based upon documentary evidence, native customary tenure or otherwise and he shall have the power to determine in whose favour the rights to such land shall be shown in the Settlement Order. Every Settlement Order is then published in the *Gazette* and copies of it will be exhibited for one month at the Superintendent's office and the District Office in whose Division and District respectively the land is situated and any other place prescribed (section 95(2)). If rights to the land in any 'settlement area' are not claimed or established, then the land 'shall belong absolutely to the government and shall be entered as such in the Register' (section 99). Clearly, the Settlement Officer is vested with very wide powers in determining all claims to rights to land. Under the Settlement operation, natives have been known to lose their rights to lands they had held under customary tenure. Since the issue of titles is subject to the discretion of the Superintendent on the advice of the Settlement Officer, not all natives who make a claim to the land are assured of the titles to this land. In some instances large areas of native customary land have been alloted to certain individuals when titles are issued, depriving the rest of the community, some of whom may have valid claims to the same land (Bahrin Adeng 1975:40). This development has led to the accumulation of land under title by some individual natives and the concomitant creation of a group of landless natives (*Ibid*).

More important, the powers accorded to the Settlement Officer under section 94 of the Land Code means that he is given the authority to decide on rights of ownership in any land dispute, not unlike the functions of a judge in the court of law. This also means that the Settlement Officer in carrying out his functions can overrule or reverse any decision made by the native court. Section 102(1) states that: 'any person, aggrieved by any act or decision of the Settlement Officer . . . may . . . appeal to the court of a Magistrate of the First Class . . . and, for the purpose of any further appeal, any such decision made by a Settlement Officer . . . as is mentioned in this section shall be deemed to have been made in civil proceedings'. This would mean that a magistrate without any understanding of native customary rights to land would have the power to determine the rights of natives.

Native customary law which relies on hearsay evidence and unsworn testimony is diametrically opposed to rules of evidence which forms the basis of the Western judicial process. Therefore if a land dispute comes before a magistrate's court, where a native has to rely on native customary law for his case, there could be a miscarriage of justice to the native. It can be seen from the above that decisions of the native courts concerning rights to customary land do not have the force of law. Native customary law appears to be afforded little recognition under the Land Code.

Interior Area Land

This land is defined as all land not falling within any of the other classifications of Reserved Land, Native Customary Land, Native Area Land or Mixed Zone Land. Much of this land lies in the deep interior, is under primary forest and cannot be held under title, but native customary rights may be created subject to a permit. Under the Land Code, if customary rights are granted on a piece of Interior Area Land, the status of the land changes to that of Native Customary Land. Thus new Native Customary Land can be created from Interior Area Land.

Part II section 10(3) of the Land Code declares that: 'any native who, without a prior permit in writing from a District Officer, occupies any Interior Area Land or fells or attempts to fell virgin jungle upon any such land or attempts to create customary rights upon any such land shall be guilty of an offence'. The penalty for a first offence is a fine of five hundred dollars and in the case of a subsequent offence would include imprisonment for three months and a five hundred dollars fine.

Section 10(3) further states that: 'the occupation of Interior Land by a native or native community without a permit in writing from a District Officer shall not, notwithstanding any law or custom to the contrary, confer any right or privilege on such native or native community and, in any such case, such native or community shall be deemed to be in unlawful occupation of State land'. Section 10(5) says that the District Officer shall not give a permit 'if he considers either that he would thereby prejudice the individual or communal rights of others or that he would thereby prejudice the interests of Sarawak or its inhabitants in the area . . .'.

It can be seen that very wide discretionary powers are vested in the District Officer in giving permits to natives. According to Porter: 'whilst the creation of new rights recognised by law through the clearing of jungle or the occupation of Interior Area Land is at the discretion of individual District Officers there have, nevertheless, been introduced administrative procedures whereby his discretion is not exercised without the prior approval of certain other officials concerned with land matters' (Porter 1967:83). These are the officials who comprise the Working Sub-Committees of Divisional Development Committees. They are the ones who are now consulted before permits are issued (*Ibid*). Apart from these obstacles, natives have not been adequately informed about the provisions relating to creation of customary rights in the Land Code. Most natives cannot read or write and live away from the town centres where the District Offices are situated. In the words of a native law student: 'There is little use discussing the effective enforcement of the law in enlightened academic circles in the offices, legislatives and institutions of learning if the people who will be directly affected by such discussions are inadequately informed and in the dark as to what is going on. There is a danger that the people may look upon the laws passed as tools of oppression by the Government — as they have not taken part in the shaping of the laws, nor have they been informed of the existence and significance of the laws which directly and intimately affect their lives' (Gumis 1981:50).

Interior Area Land can be converted into Mixed Zone Land and Native Area Land. By notification in the *Gazette*, the Director of Lands and Surveys can with the approval of the Resident of the Division in which the land is situated declare the area to be Native Area Land. Similarly, the Minister can by order in the *Gazette* declare any area of land to be Mixed Zone Land (Part II section 4(1) and (3)). Under Mixed Zone Land or Native Area Land no person can occupy or exercise any rights or privileges in these lands except under a title (Part II section 10(1)).

From the above discussion it can be seen that Interior Area Land, Native Customary Land and Native Communal Reserve belong to the State. In the interpretation section of the Land Code '"State land" means all land for which no document of title has been issued and all land which subsequent to the issue of a document of title may have been or may be forfeited or surrendered to or resumed by the Government.'

Part II section 5(2) proviso (i) states that: 'any native lawfully in occupation' of State land 'shall be deemed to hold (such land by) licence from the Government . . . until a document of title is issued to him'.

According to Porter this 'suggests that native customary rights have a legal standing no greater than a bare licence' (Porter 1967:84). Although Part II section 15 states that State land shall not be alienated until all customary rights therein have been surrendered or extinguished or provision has been made for compensating the persons entitled to such rights, *it is not provided that the Director of Lands and Surveys who may extinguish these rights on the direction of the Minister should publish this order in the Gazette. Natives who are affected under this provision, may not even realise that they have lost their customary rights.*

According to the *Report of the Land Committee*, both the Interpretation of State land and section 12 of the Land Code is 'unwise and unfair'.

The Report states:

> 'There would be a considerable outcry in England if it were to be decreed that the entire property in and control of all land not held under a registered title should be vested solely in the Crown, . . .
> . . . we consider it wrong to make no saving mention in this section of the rights of those who are in customary occupation of land and the fact that section 15 provides that Crown land shall not be alienated until these rights have been surrendered or extinguished is but cold comfort. It seems to us essential that section 12 should make it clear that customary rights are to be respected and will not merely be eliminated. . . . the law must make it clear that the Crown (ie. the Director of Lands and Surveys in this context) may not dispose of land unless it is free of rights and so available for disposition . . . We believe this to be a vital principal in land administration which must be enshrined in the law' (sections 63 and 64).

Reserved Land

This includes State Land which is used by and reserved for the government for various purposes. It includes forest reserves, protected forests, national parks, wildlife sanctuaries, nature monuments etc.

Part II section 7 states that 'where an area of State land is required for a Federal or State public purpose . . . the Director may by notification in the *Gazette* declare such an area to be a Government Reserve . . .' Thus if native customary rights subsist in State land which has been declared to be a Government Reserve, native customary rights to these lands will be extinguished as well.

The 1962 Land Committee

Despite the 1957 Land Code, the Colonial government was of the opinion that sound agricultural development was still being hindered by the system of native land tenure, which it felt did not sufficiently discourage shifting cultivation (*Sarawak Year Book* 1963:52). In 1962 a Land Committee was set up, to draft a proposal for land administration reform. One of its main aims was 'to induce the native to abandon this present method of cultivation and to develop his land productivity in the national interest' (*Sarawak Report of the Land Committee* 1962:para 3). In 1963, the Committee published a report with recommendations for major changes in land tenure. Most important, it advocated the abolition of the 1958 Land Classification system. It was recommended that classification be reduced from the present five to only two categories, namely Registered and Unregistered Land. All lands under customary rights should now be registered, but natives need not pay premium or rent for obtaining these titles. In effect this meant the abolition of customary rights and its replacement by private ownership through holding of titles. In order to 'protect the natives', they would not be allowed to sell, lease or otherwise dispose of their land except with the Resident's consent. All Unregistered Land would be State Land or Customary Land not as yet registered.

The recommendations were tabled in Bills presented to the *Council Negri* in May 1965 but faced opposition so fierce that they had to be deferred. There is no doubt that the indigenes felt threatened by the government Bills. It is obvious that replacement of customary rights by titled ownership would put the burden of proof of claim to Customary Land on the natives. As of now, the poor survey capacity of the administration has meant that the actual boundaries of 'customary lands' are very vague and hence the natives are to a large extent still free to clear and cultivate new land. If 'customary lands' are required to be registered, the natives would eventually lose claim to vast virgin forests, whereas the claim to this is still in dispute now. Hence the tremendous indignation and political heat generated against the new land proposals were only to be expected.

Although this radical proposal to change the land system never saw fruition, nevertheless customary rights to land continued to be eroded in the years that followed with changes to the Land Code.

Extinguishment of Native Customary Rights

Although there are various aspects of the Sarawak Land Code which give recognition to native customary rights over land, there are also different parts of the Code that empower land authorities to extinguish those rights. In the earlier section dealing with different land categories, we have seen how native customary rights are recognised in Mixed Zone Land, Native Area Land, Native Customary Land, and Interior Area Land. In some of these land categories, there are provisions for the removal or extinguishment of these native customary rights, as discussed earlier:

i)   Land classified as Native Communal Reserve (under native customary land) can be degazetted by the Minister (section 6 (4)).

ii) Native customary rights can be extinguished by the Settlement Officer (section 94 (2)).

iii) Customary rights can be extinguished or surrendered on State Land to facilitate alienation of the land (section (15)).

However, the most powerful clauses regarding extinguishment of native customary rights are contained in Part II section 5(3), (4), (5) of the Land Code. These clauses were introduced under the 1974 Land Code (Amendment) Ordinance. Prior to 1974, similar clauses on extinguishment already existed under Part IV, section 82(2) of the Land Code. In the 1974 amendments, this section 82(2) clause was cancelled, and instead similar extinguishment powers were instituted under Part II, section 5.

Under this section 5, the Minister is given power to extinguish native customary rights which exist on any State land. Part II section 5(3) which was created for this purpose states that the order for the extinguishment of customary rights will be published or notified in the *Gazette*, or the order will be brought to the notice of the persons affected in such a manner as the Minister thinks necessary. Upon 'expiry of six weeks from the publication or notification in the *Gazette*, or such notice having been affected as aforesaid, *native customary rights shall cease and be extinguished and the land held under such rights shall revert to the Government*'. The Minister can extinguish native customary rights on the land for any 'public purpose, . . . or . . . for the purpose of facilitating alienation . . .' Thus the powers given to the Minister to extinguish customary rights under section 5 are very wide. The definition of 'public purpose' is open to very wide interpretation. This in fact means that the Minister is given sweeping powers to extinguish native customary rights on land and 'there is hardly any scope for challenging the Minister's act . . .' (Bahrin Adeng 1975:35). Thus with a stroke of the pen the Minister can extinguish native customary rights.

Although section 5(4) provides that any person aggrieved by such a direction may within three months of the publication or notification in the *Gazette* or notice of direction may refer the matter to arbitration in accordance with the provisions of section 212 of the Land Code, in reality natives can hardly reverse or challenge the decision of the Minister. As the law stands, native customary rights will cease and the land reverted to the Government after six weeks from the day of notification or publication of the Minister's direction in the *Gazette*. It will be too late to rescind the Minister's order as customary rights would have already ceased to exist. It is also unlikely that the arbitrators will order the Minister to withdraw his decision (*Idem* 1975:37). Publication of the Minister's decision in the *Gazette* means little to natives who cannot read or write and live in remote areas. In most cases, natives whose lands have lost their status under native customary rights, are not even aware of this loss.

Another area of contention is the question of compensation to natives for the extinguishment of their native customary rights. Section 5(3) does state that where such rights are extinguished, compensation shall be paid, or other land (with native customary rights status) may be made available. However, this clause remains vague as to how the compensation can be claimed, and how much. This is in contrast to the provisions in sections 60-72 under Part IV dealing with the resumption of alienated land (or compulsory acquisition of land by the State). In these sections 60-72, several details are given on the method of calculating compensation to be paid for such acquisition. The calculations include estimation of such factors as market value and

damages suffered by the owner due to change of residence, severing
the land from other land belonging to the owner, etc. Details are also
given on payment for costs of court proceedings and the procedure for
appeals against the award. Such details on compensation procedures
and methods of estimation are conspicuously absent when it comes to
the extinguishment of native customary rights. Prior to 1974, the clauses
on extinguishment were placed under Part IV as well, in section 82.
However, even then, section 82(1) made clear that: 'The provisions
of this Part shall not apply for the purpose of extinguishing any native
customary rights'. To make this point even clearer, the previous section
82(2) dealing with the Minister's powers to extinguish customary rights
was cancelled altogether in 1974 and similar clauses were placed instead
in Part II section 5. It is obvious that the legislators wanted to ensure
that compensation paid to natives for the extinguishment of their
customary rights would be treated differently from that paid to land
owners for State acquisition of their land. In a written directive in 1975,
the Sarawak Attorney General had said that:

> 'It is obvious from Section 60 that the matters covered therein
> for the purpose of determining the amount of compensation
> apply only to cases where land is acquired in accordance with
> Sections 47 or 48 of the Land Code which come under Part IV
> of the Code. In other words, those factors that should be taken
> into consideration for the purpose of determining the
> compensation would not be legally applicable to compensation
> for the extinguishment of customary rights under Sections 5 and
> 15 of the Land Code. . . . It would appear, therefore, that
> Section 60 may be used as guidelines and no more and that the
> Department (Land and Survey) is at liberty to determine the
> amount of compensation in a realistic manner'. (Memo
> AG/10/10/5 dated 15.9.75 in folio 7 of the Compulsory
> Acquisition File 11-2/8 of the Land and Survey Department c.f.
> Abdul Razak Tready 1977:74).

It can be seen that native customary land has no 'market value' under
the Land Code. As such, natives can be deprived of equitable
compensation.

From the above, it is clear that native customary land was seen as
having no 'market value' under the Land Code and wide powers of
discretion were given to the Lands and Surveys Department as to the
quantum of compensation to pay natives. This also opened the
possibility for a high degree of arbitrariness in payment of compensation
for the loss of customary rights, and has also often led to very low rates
of compensation paid to natives.

Even before the 1974 amendment, where section 82 was invoked,
(whereby the Minister ordered the extinguishment of native
customary rights by the payment of compensation), there were
instances of arbitrary rates of compensation. In 1965, native customary
rights were extinguished to make way for the building of a bazaar at

Tiang Bekap. The payment of compensation to the affected natives were as follows:

Approximate Acreage	Amount of Compensation	Value per Acre
1.76 acres	$ 137	$ 78
1.15 acres	$ 92	$ 80
1.25 acres	$1,180	$ 944
2.31 acres	$ 326	$ 141
2.64 acres	$4,732	$1,792
0.48 acres	$ 24	$ 50

Source: Abdul Razak Tready 1977:114

From the above table, it can be seen that the value of the compensation for the pieces of land which had been extinguished of native customary rights are differently valued for each piece. In each individual case, the compensation given is far from 'realistic'. It would be interesting to find out what the 'market value' of the land would be today.

The 1979 Land Code (Amendment) Ordinance

In 1979, Part VIII section 209 of the Land Code which referred to unlawful occupation of State lands was amended. Under the amendment, the scope of offences was widened to include other activities as well. It was illegal not only to occupy State land; now, any person who 'erects any building, or clears, ploughs, digs, encloses or cultivates any State land shall be guilty of an offence'. The amendment also gave wide powers of arrest to officers of the Lands and Surveys Department. It empowered senior officers to evict any person, seize any agricultural implements, demolish or remove buildings, crops and other immovable property on the land. Previous to this, only police officers could carry out this function. Now they were duty bound to assist Lands and Surveys officers when such assistance was required by the latter. Clearly, this was to serve as a deterent to natives who want to carry out traditional farming activities. Natives who were caught farming, clearing or living on lands belonging to the State were liable to receive painful retribution from the authorities. This was to further restrict and discourage shifting cultivation among natives.

Land Development Schemes

Besides the changes in land laws and regulations, the system of land rights and use in Sarawak is also being influenced by the increasing significance of 'land development schemes' initiated and managed by government agencies. Increasing amounts of land, especially land belonging to natives, have been taken over by land development agencies, which convert the land into estates or smallholdings growing cash crops. Natives whose lands are affected by such schemes are among those 'resettled' in the estates. This of course has great significance in terms of changing the nature of the affected natives' rights, use and relationship to the land. One of the major land agencies is the Sarawak Land Consolidation and Rehabilitation Authority (SALCRA), created in 1976 under an Ordinance, whose main objective is to 'develop' native customary land by converting land under customary tenure into estates or farms of fixed size, into which natives are 'resettled'. The impact of such land development schemes on the natives is discussed in Chapter Five.

Above: Crossing the bridge across the Linau river which connects the seven longhouses of Long Geng in Ulu Belaga.

Below: Pushing the long-boat up the rapids in Ulu Baram.

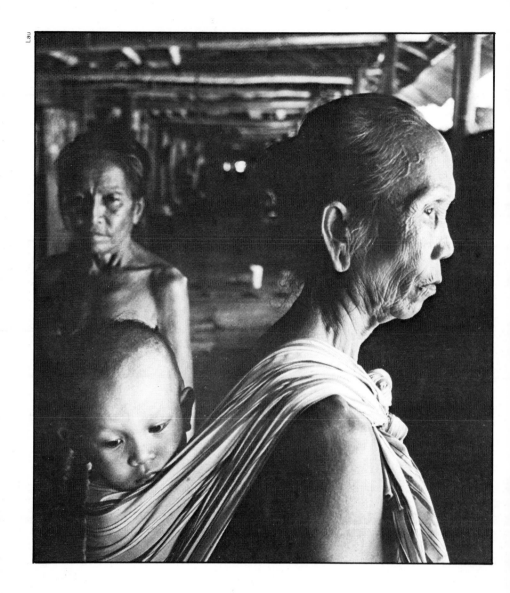

CHAPTER FIVE

Impact of Land Development Schemes

Although the classification of the various categories of land in the Land Code namely Native Area Land and Interior Area Land recognises the right of natives to land through shifting cultivation, this right as we have seen has been weakened and whittled away by various amendments in the land laws. The fact remains however, that native customary rights to land and their application are a fundamental principle recognised in the Land Code. We have also seen how this principle has been disregarded through government administration and policy.

Under customary law, any act against an individual's land can be seen as an act against the individual (Ter Haar 1962:114). Similarly any transgression against a community's land can be seen as an act of aggression against the community. Thus when the State effects the surrender of native lands and their customary rights to it, the State is making a unilateral decision to alienate native customary land (which as we have seen is inalienable under *adat* law). This decision which violates the principles of native law or *adat*, is seen as unjust and arbitrary by natives.

Thus the encroachment on native lands and the continuous infringement of native customary rights has been taking place through various changes in the land laws, forest policies and in recent years, land development policies and development agencies.

Factors Causing Loss of Native Land

We have seen in Chapter Four how the State has armed itself, through several changes in the land laws, with powers to extinguish native land rights. This has enabled the forces of the State and modern commercial enterprises to take over and make use of native lands. There are three main factors accounting for the loss of native land rights in recent years: i) commercialised agricultural policies resulting in land development schemes and private agricultural activities; ii) the tremendous expansion of the timber industry, eating into the forests of the natives; and iii) the construction of hydroelectric dams, which threaten to flood millions of hectares of forest land in which many thousands of natives reside.

In this Chapter we will examine the State's land development policies, the agencies formed to implement them, and the impact on the natives. In the following Chapters, we will examine the changes in Sarawak's forest laws, the impact of logging on native communities, and the consequences of the existing and proposed dams.

Land Development Policy

Land development appears to have top priority with the present State leadership[1]. One of the major aims of land development is the opening up of land which is presently under customary tenure. In this regard the State is going for large scale agricultural development on the plantation or estate model. This entails opening up of thousands of acres of land in joint ventures with the private sector. Under this concept, natives lands will be developed by urban private companies, both local and foreign. According to the Chief Minister, Datuk Patinggi Haji Abdul Taib Mahmud, there are about 500,000 hectares of land available for agriculture and waiting to be developed. In November 1984, the Chief Minister had announced that one million acres of land will be opened up. This would involve the development of estates, integrated area development and resettlement schemes where people will be regrouped (*Sarawak Tribune*, November 12, 1984). According to him, the government had to invite foreign firms to invest and undertake estate development 'because we are lacking technology and know-how and experience in this field'. Some M$100 million will be allocated for land development in the State under the Fifth Malaysia Plan (*Borneo Post*, February 12, 1986).

The State government has also engaged the more experienced services of the Federal agencies from Peninsular Malaysia like FELCRA and FELDA to undertake agricultural land development. In February 1985 the Director General of the Federal Land Consolidation and Rehabilitation Authority (FELCRA) Mustapha Jiman announced that the Agency's land rehabilitation programme will include the Third Division in Sarawak (*Sarawak Tribune*, February 11, 1985). The Sarawak State government had given the green light to FELCRA to develop four schemes in the Rejang Area Security Command (RASCOM). These four schemes will cover some 300 hectares of land (*Ibid*, May 3, 1985). The State government has also offered the Federal Land

---

1.   During the Confrontation between Malaysia and Indonesia in the 1960s, Iban living in the Batang Ai near the border areas were resettled in the Skrang Rubber Scheme where the Simanggang-Sibu road crosses the Skrang river (tributary of the Batang Lupar). Some 256 families were relocated in 2,500 acres of land. Each family was given eight acres for rubber and two acres for other crops. Other schemes were started in Triboh (Serian District), Melugu (Simanggang District), Meradong (Binatang District), Sibintek (Sibu District), Lambir (Miri District), Lubai Tengah (Limbang District) and Bukit Peninjau Oil Palm Scheme (near Miri). In these schemes both native Iban and non-natives participated.

Development Authority (FELDA) from Peninsular Malaysia to open up land in the State. Under this offer, 200,000 hectares of land will be opened up for oil palm cultivation. Under Phase one of the project, FELDA will develop 6,000 hectares in which 50,000 settlers will be involved (*Ibid*, December 16, 1985).

To expedite land development, a new land policy was implemented for this purpose. This involved speeding up land alienation procedures where land surveys were carried out with the view to open up land (*Ibid*, October 1, 1985). Under this Settlement programme, whereby lands will be surveyed and land titles issued to the rightful claimants (as stipulated in Part V of the Land Code), native customary lands will be further restricted. This will enable the State to open up more State land for alienation. Up to 1985, a total of 199 'settlement areas' covering a total area of 288,629 hectares (or 713,220 acres) have been gazetted as 'settlement areas' from the period 1968-84 throughout the entire of Sarawak. A total of 186,314 hectares (or 460,396 acres) have been surveyed and issued with titles. These areas will be further expanded to allow land development and estate plantations to be established (Zaidi Khaldin Zainie 1985:17). Prior to this move, the Chief Minister directed the Lands and Surveys Department to survey all lands (in lots of 10,000 acres) along all roads throughout the State. Most of these lands, especially those located along the Miri-Bintulu Road, Tahau-Bintulu Road and the Niah and Subis areas, are Native Customary Land and Interior Area Land, presently held under customary tenure. The survey was also in preparation for some of these lands to be developed into estates. The Chief Minister added that it was time to take advantage of the idle lands which had been made accessible by these roads (*Sarawak Tribune*, May 28, 1983). Many of these roads traversed 'idle lands' which were under shifting cultivation. Development committees in each Division were also upgraded. The Chief Minister announced that these Divisional Development Committees will be given greater powers to facilitate and implement development projects in their respective Divisions in the State (*Borneo Post*, April 16, 1986).

Clearly, the development of land, particularly native land, is a major thrust in Sarawak's development programme. This has been given top priority under the Fifth Malaysia Plan. 'Idle' native land will be put to agricultural development. In line with this is the policy of regrouping of natives and their longhouses into model villages. Five thousand or more people will be grouped together in such areas where infrastructural facilities will be provided. These villages will be built in strategically located areas — near roads for instance — where settlers will work together, not unlike the 'Felda schemes' in Peninsular Malaysia (*Business Times*, November 30, 1985).

In recent years, the State has also undertaken land development schemes through various bodies like the Sarawak Land Development Board (SLDB), SALCRA and the Land Custody and Development Authority (LCDA).

The Sarawak Land Development Board

The SLDB was established in 1972 to open up new land for cash crop cultivation and the breeding of livestock. It was modelled after the large scale land development schemes in Peninsular Malaysia, particularly FELDA. By 1977, 16 schemes covering a total area of 102,209 acres had been established for this purpose. Of these seven are for rubber, one each for pepper and cocoa, and the rest for oil palm (Francis Jana Wan Lian 1980:1). In the rubber schemes, each settler is given an eight-acre lot for rubber and two acres for *dusun* (orchard). In the oil palm schemes, ten acres are given to each settler. In both rubber and oil palm schemes, the settlers are also given a quarter-acre house lot. Most of the Iban settlers in the SLDB schemes have had to surrender their traditional lands for development projects. As a form of compensation, the government had made them recipients of the land scheme. Others were resettled for security reasons and given this land scheme in return. Thus they were in effect forced to enter the schemes and therefore had no choice in the matter (*Idem* 1980:7).

In 1977 the settlers in the five rubber schemes earned an average monthly income of $174. The incomes ranged from the lowest of $63 to the highest of $375. Over 95 per cent of the settlers earned an average of less than $250 a month. The poor prices from rubber did not make tapping worthwhile. Many of the settlers resorted to hill padi planting on the lands fringing the land schemes instead. In fact it has been found that the SLDB schemes have not been very popular. This was reflected in the poor response to SLDB recruitment of settlers. In 1978 the SLDB could enlist only over half of the total workers it required in the schemes. Out of this, some one-third were Indonesian contract workers. Almost all the local workers were part-time labourers (F. Jana Wan Lian 1980:4). Farmers are reluctant to participate in the land schemes because it would mean resettlement and loss of their traditional farming practices and land. The State's attempt at large scale plantation agriculture through SLDB has thus not proved successful. It has incurred huge debts which in 1982-83 were between $180 and $200 million and there have been calls to close it down (*Daily Express*, November 11, 1985).

The Sarawak Land Consolidation and Rehabilitation Authority

The Sarawak Land Consolidation and Rehabilitation Authority (SALCRA) was created in 1976 to deal specifically with native land. The purpose of SALCRA is to facilitate the 'agricultural development' of native customary land. In other words, SALCRA's role is to discourage shifting cultivation and encourage the natives to cultivate cash crops like rubber, oil palm and cocoa instead (like the FELDA scheme in Peninsular Malaysia). The prevailing official attitude is that the present customary land tenure and shifting agriculture leads to uneconomic use of land and low productivity. The permanent cultivation of cash crops and a sedentary form of agriculture is seen as a means of raising the incomes of the natives. This essentially means the consolidation of land holdings under customary tenure into economic farm units. It involves the resettlement of natives from different communities into an artificial community and the redistribution of land use (M Perpetua Kana 1975:65; Gumis 1981:100).

Before SALCRA moves in to develop native customary lands, they are first declared 'Development Areas' by the Minister through notification in the *Gazette* under the provisions in the SALCRA Ordinance. Following this, it is declared a 'settlement area' by the Director, Lands and Surveys Department (Under Part V of the Land Code) who will delineate the limits of the area within which the settlement of rights to land and registration shall be effected. This exercise is done through the Settlement Notification. On the publication of the Settlement Notification in the *Gazette*, the Settlement Officer will undertake a survey of the land, presentation of claims to the land, settlement and registration of rights and issue titles. However natives forfeit all rights to the land during this period when it is being developed. SALCRA assumes authority over the land and retains the exclusive right to develop it, according to its policies. The land titles will be issued to the 'owners' when all costs incurred during the scheme's development is recovered by SALCRA. Thus, an important consequence of land development by SALCRA is the annihilation of customary land tenure and shifting agriculture. Private land ownership will be established among natives and the issue of land titles can lead to disparities in land ownership among natives. They will be drawn completely into the cash economy. With the death of shifting agriculture and the resettlement of natives, longhouse social organisation will come to an end and with it native *adat*.

Since its inception in 1976, SALCRA has been involved in several projects. Its first scheme was implemented in the Second Division at Merindun (Lemanak) in 1978. Also known as the Lubok Antu Palm Oil Complex, this scheme had three phases namely Lemanak which began in 1978, Batu Kaya in 1979 and Pakit-Undup in 1980. It involved 757 families from 22 longhouses and covers some 5,600 hectares of land. The resettled natives were the Iban who were displaced from their land to make way for the Batang Ai hydroelectric dam. In 1981 SALCRA started the Tebakang Tea Estate at Mayan-Tembayang in the Serian District, First Division. It comprises 300 hectares and started producing tea in 1985. Another 260 hectares will be included under the Fifth Malaysian Plan (*Borneo Post*, May 31, 1986). Three Bidayuh kampungs are involved in the scheme. Under the Fourth Malaysia Plan, SALCRA developed four cocoa schemes. They are Kampung Bajo in Lundu and Kampong Taee in Serian (First Division), Batang Ai Resettlement in Lubok Antu, and Paku-Layar in Betong (Second Divison). The total area under cocoa cultivation is 2,900 hectares (*Sunday Tribune*, August

26, 1984). Another scheme has been earmarked in Bau District, First Divison. This scheme will cover 800 hectares involving 600 families (*Sarawak Tribune*, May 24, 1986). Once natives are granted titles to these lands, they lose all rights to customary tenure and native land.

In the period 1976-1980, SALCRA 'rehabilitated' a total of 4,500 hectares of land which had been held under native customary rights. (*Fourth Malaysia Plan Report*: para 652). In 1981-1985, SALCRA 'rehabilitated' another 7,610 hectares of land: 3,220 with oil palm, 2,730 hectares with cocoa, 1,460 hectares with rubber and 200 hectares with tea (*Fifth Malaysia Plan*: page 308). Although this figure is rather small presently, more lands will be opened up in the future as agricultural land development accelerates. The further expansion of SALCRA will lead to increasing disparities in the ownership of land among natives who have to surrender their customary rights to land.

The Land Custody and Development Authority

Another agency involved with the development of native customary land is the Land Custody and Development Authority (LCDA), which was formed in 1981. The LCDA has a very wide mandate and can undertake the development of *all* categories of land for agriculture, commercial, industrial and residential purposes irrespective of their location once it is declared a Development Area. It has the power to undertake the compulsory acquisition of land with the Minister's approval to further its activities. It is also expected to function as a land bank, identifying rural land and making it available for development. In this connection, it will act as a matchmaker between the owners of the land and investors who are interested in developing it. It will then coordinate and supervise the joint-venture. Once the land has been developed, LCDA has the authority to dispose the land in *any* manner it so desires. It can sell the land for a profit, it can sell it on behalf of the owners or it can transfer the land back to the owners after all costs incurred have been paid up by the latter.

Through the LCDA, the State 'will be able to undertake the development, redevelopment, settlement or resettlement of any land in the State, alienated or unalienated, both in the urban, suburban or rural areas which the Government considers proper and appropriate to develop' (*Sarawak Tribune*, June 25, 1981). This means that LCDA is empowered to undertake activities on all types of lands irrespective of their classification. Thus the activities of LCDA, given its all encompassing powers, will have far reaching implications on native land and customary tenure both in the rural and urban areas [2].

2.   Sarawak is embarking on urbanisation and there would be parcels of land belonging to natives which would be affected by urban expansion. Once these lands are declared Development Areas or acquired by the State, natives would lose all rights to it.

Through the LCDA, the State will hasten its primary objective of curtailing shifting agriculture among the natives and drawing them completely into the market economy. This will be achieved under LCDA's programme of 'estate or plantation development' where thousands of acres of lands under customary tenure (with no titles) will be opened up with outside investors who will provide the necessary capital. During this period, natives surrender all rights to their lands and become paid employees on the estate. This 'in situ' development strategy will also involve the regrouping of longhouses in resettlement schemes and the creation of model villages. With this development, native customary lands will no longer exist, and the longhouse as a social, cultural and economic entity will be destroyed. As the final authority over these lands is the LCDA , there is every possibility that natives may not even get their lands back. In the event that LCDA sells the estate, natives will stand to lose their lands ending up as landless 'plantation workers'.

Since its inception, the LCDA has earmarked areas where native customary lands will be opened up for development. In 1981 the Chief Minister, who is also Chairman of the Authority, announced that 20,000 acres of Bidayuh land in Bau will be LCDA's first project in estate development (*Ibid*, December 4, 1981). In the Baram, some 20,000 acres of land near Long Lama had been proposed for a resettlement scheme under the LCDA (*Ibid*, March 25, 1982). Another 40,000 hectares of land is planned for development by the LCDA in the Fourth Division. These lands are in the Bakong, Ulu Sibuti and Ulu Niah areas. Under the plan, the people will be relocated in a model village with basic amenities like water and electricity supply and a health clinic being supplied (*Borneo Post*, February 24, 1985). Recently the State government also announced that it will develop 10,000 acre blocks of rural land in the Fourth Division for estate plantations (*New Straits Times*, May 17, 1985). It can be seen that LCDA schemes involve very large areas of land, most of which are land under native customary tenure.

The Integrated Agricultural Development Projects

The other form of land development is the Integrated Agricultural Development Projects (IADP). In Sarawak two areas have been identified namely the Samarahan and the Kalaka Saribas basin (*Mid-Term Review, Fourth Malaysia Plan* 1984:234). According to a newspaper report the Samarahan River Basin scheme in the First Division, is an integrated package involving cash cropping, wet padi cultivation, cattle and fish farming. Presently, the area is also occupied by shifting cultivators who farm about 24,500 hectares (*Borneo Bulletin*, December 17, 1983). This scheme involves ten projects and covers 100,000 hectares of land in which 48,000 people are engaged in shifting cultivation, padi and rubber planting (*Sarawak Tribune*, March 26, 1985; February 19, 1986). The Kalaka-Saribas scheme in the Seventh

Division, is expected to cover 70,000 hectares of land (*Ibid*, February 19, 1986). Four projects have been proposed involving oil palm and cocoa cultivation, a padi irrigation scheme and 'insitu' development. Presently farmers here are engaged in shifting cultivation, rubber, cocoa, coconut and pepper growing (*Ibid*, March 26, 1985). In August 1984, the Assistant Minister for Regional and Community Development, Abang Johari Tun Abang Haji Openg, disclosed that 6,800 hectares of land near Sungei Tunoh in the Seventh Division will be developed into an integrated development area. More than 20 longhouses in and around the area would be affected by the scheme (*Sunday Tribune*, August 5, 1984). Under the IADP more natives will lose their lands and their way of life.

Other remote hill padi cultivating communities have also been encouraged to resettle, abandon shifting cultivation and engage in cash cultivation, and animal husbandry, like the Tringgos (Seringuas) people living near the border in the Bau District (*Ibid*, March 18, 1984). The nomadic Penan in other areas of Sarawak have also been encouraged to settle. Found mainly in the Fourth, Fifth and the Seventh Divisions, there are plans afoot to settle them permanently and make them farmers. On a visit to Penan areas recently, the Chief Minister Datuk Patinggi Haji Abdul Taib Mahmud announced that the State government has earmarked an area between Ulu Belaga and Ulu Mukah as a major resettlement area for the Penan (*Ibid*, May 5, 1985). Many of the Penan especially those in the Gunung Mulu area are not happy with the State's plans to convert the forest here into a National Park. This area has been their traditional home since time immemorial and they have moved in this area undisturbed for generations. Designation of the area as a Park would mean that they would not be able to find food or gather forest products from the area. It would mean they cannot carry on their way of life (Peter M. Kedit 1982:244-48). The Government is planning to resettle these groups in view of the future development of the area.

The Natives' Response to Land Development

Not surprisingly the form of 'land development' taking place in Sarawak is viewed with great distrust by the natives. Speaking of the problem the Chief Minister had said:'Most people especially the natives, regard their land as the most valuable asset and the only wealth they have for the future and they cling to the idea . . .' (*Sarawak Tribune*, February 12, 1986). These schemes involve the alienation of their lands, which in turn will be 'opened up' by outsiders whom they are not familiar with, be they private entrepreneurs or government agencies. Natives have no say in the kinds of crops grown. Very often the choice of crops is made by government agencies without prior consultation with the communties affected, at times much against the wishes of the people concerned. They see themselves as labourers, growing crops which require a lot of inputs, time and care on lands which have been taken away from them — becoming strangers on their own lands. It will take

some years before the crops bear fruit and many more years before
they will earn enough to repay the interests on the loans and the capital
which have been invested on their behalf. This is assuming that world
commodity prices remain attractive. In some years, the prices of the
cash crops grown have fallen to disastrously low levels. Natives will
be forced to eke out a living elsewhere, some abandon the schemes
and in all likelihood drift to the urban centres. In the process they would
lose whatever opportunity they would have had of owning the land in
the schemes.

Others have seen their lands being taken away from them when the
Lands and Surveys officers come to survey their lands for 'development'.
Following these surveys, some of the land is acquired by government
for land schemes of its own agencies, or else alienated to private
individuals or companies for their commercial use. Thus agricultural
development — either by government agencies or by the private sector
— threatens the natives' land. In one highly publicised case reported
in the press recently, the State government had alienated land at Balai
Ringin in 1983-4 and issued land titles to non-natives. In the process
Iban found their *Jeramie-temuda* lands (secondary forest which is fallow
land for swidden agriculture) which had pepper, cocoa, fruit trees and
dwelling houses being given away to non-natives. In a letter to the press
readers were informed that the Iban had applied for land titles but their
applications were either rejected, delayed or not acknowledged at all.
'. . . One of the saddest things happening to the Iban there because
they are now chased out of their land and the government is calling
them squatters. The Ibans are effectively becoming landless in their
own land' (*Ibid*, October 24, 1985). In response to this matter which
was brought up by the Minister for Land Development, Adenan Haji
Satem in the State Assembly, the Iban spokesman noted thus:

'Being ordinary farmers, it is unfortunate that we do not know
anything about the Land Code or Land Law or whatever name
they call it. We Ibans are poor these days and our livelihood
lies much on farming. All we know is that we have plenty of
land cleared (*di-perimba*) for us by our grandfather and great
grandfather. We have been doing shifting cultivation and some
of the land are planted with fruit trees, pepper, rubber and
some are occupied with dwelling houses . . . There are a few
hundred acres of land along the roads which were just 'robbed'
like that from the Iban and given to non-Ibans. The '*Jeramie*'
nature of the land proves that the land must have an owner.
Only 'virgin jungle' or 'untouched jungle' with huge trees that
had never been cultivated by any men should be fairly called
'State Land' or whatever technical name you can call them. The
Land Code or Land Laws are man-made and they appear to be
designed in such a way as to rob the Iban of their land. As you
know, Ibans are the most backward people in Sarawak even
though they are the largest group in terms of population and

land is our last resort to live on. Why cannot we Ibans
express our own sentiments when we are being deprived of our
land? Where is justice? Where is humanity? Above all, what's
wrong with us? Why should we be called "agitators, trouble-
makers and pseudo-champions"? . . . What we want is our land
and that is our very purpose . . . Balai Ringin case is not the
only one. Many Ibans complain about their '*Temuda* Rights' at
Siol Kandis, Tabuan Dayak, Stampin and even as far as
Matang' (*Sarawak Tribune*, November 16, 1985).

It is no wonder that natives have opposed any such survey of lands
in their vicinity. In one reported instance, along the Miri-Bintulu road,
Lands and Surveys officers were stopped at *parang* point by villagers
when the latter discovered that the area had been planned for a large-
scale development project (*Business Times*, November 30, 1985). This
fear was not unfounded. The Assistant Minister of Land Development
in February 1986 disclosed that plans are afoot to develop plantation
agriculture on native customary rights land in the Miri-Bintulu and
Bekenu-Subis area (*Borneo Post*, February 25, 1986).

In a letter to the press in 1983, a native had expressed concern about
the activities of Seatex Plantation Sdn Bhd, a company engaged in
agriculture development in the Fourth Division. According to him, the
agricultural project is displacing natives from Rumah Chang, Sallau,
Gindie and Undie. 'Almost 75 per cent of the native lands in these areas
have been taken away from the villagers against their will' he wrote.
The headman of Rumah Chang had repeatedly asked the company
to stop encroaching on the village's farmland but this had been ignored.
'The government knows that these people have no land titles and should
make an attempt to separate state and native lands so natives will not
become victims of economic oppression' (*Borneo Bulletin*, November 19,
1983).

Agricultural land development is not the only threat perceived by
the natives. In Bau, a group of 12 Bidayuh families claim that land
which had been leased to a mining company belongs to them. According
to a Member of Parliament, the Bidayuh had been farming the land
Bikajang long before the first mining lease was issued in 1952. The
Bidayuh claim that the piece of land has been farmed for generations.
The land has been gazetted as mining land. However the Bidayuh had
planted padi on it unaware that the government had issued a mining
lease to the Bukit Young Goldmine totalling 300 acres. The 12 families
want to be allowed to stay until the 36 acres of padi they have planted
are ready for harvesting. However the company has demanded their
immediate departure. A similar dispute has also taken place in two
other areas, Pijiru and Kroking Puak (*Ibid*, October 5, 1985).

It comes as no surprise that natives find it difficult to identify with
'land development'. This development has increasingly led to the loss
of their customary lands, their impoverishment, deprivation and robbed
them of their identity and dignity.

They find it impossible to grow enough food to feed themselves and their children when their farms are destroyed and when they are restricted from felling new forest. Their integration into the market economy and resettlement into 'schemes' and 'estates' have traumatised them further. Hunger, malnutrition and destitution have stalked their existence in this alien environment. In these artificially created communities, their cultural and spiritual needs find no anchor and natives lose their cultural moorings and experience alienation.

A party of Penan trekking in the forest in Ulu Baram.

CHAPTER SIX

Forest Policy and the Natives

In Chapter Four we had examined how the Sarawak land laws had been designed to restrict the rights of the natives with regard to land use. To complement the land policy and laws, the State also instituted policies and laws regulating the use of the forests in Sarawak. As changes in the land laws took place, complementary changes in the forest laws also occurred to further strengthen government policies towards land and their dealings with natives. In fact both the land laws and forest laws had the effect of progressively restricting native customary practices on land and their access to the rich forests.

Forest Policy and the Forests Ordinance 1953

The main instrument regulating forest policy is the Forests Ordinance 1953. Although this legislation dealt mainly with forest management and exploitation, it had very wide ranging implications for land administration and policy *vis-a-vis* the natives. Under this Ordinance, the forests of Sarawak were divided into two main categories: Permanent Forests (over which the Forest Department have full control) and Stateland Forests. Permanent Forests are those parts of the forests which have been selected to be 'protected' to serve the forest needs of the State in perpetuity; whilst the rest of the forest (Stateland Forest) is available for agriculture or other purposes. Areas of Stateland may be constituted as Permanent Forests, thus increasing the Permanent Forest estate.

As at 31 December 1984, the forests of Sarawak covered 95,232 sq. km. of which 32,821 sq. km. (or 34 per cent) had been constituted as Permanent Forests whilst Stateland Forests and the 6 national parks constituted 62,411 sq. km. (or 66 per cent of total forests) (Forest Department Sarawak 1984:90).

Under the broad category of Permanent Forests, there are three types of forests: (i) Forest Reserves; (ii) Protected Forests and (iii) Communal Forests. Forest Reserves are the most protected category, being set aside as a permanent source of timber and other produce. Entry into a Forest Reserve is forbidden, except when a licence is issued for a specific purpose. Natives are not allowed to exercise customary rights over this forest, to farm or to hunt, fish or collect any forest produce in it. On

Table 2
Sarawak: Forest and Other Land as at 31.12.84
(square kilometres)

Division/Section	Total Land Area	Permanent Forest				Other¹ Forest Area	Total Forest Area	Other Land	% of Land Area			
		Forest Reserves	Protected Forest	Communal Forest	Total				Perm. Forest	Other Forest	Other Land	Land
1st Div.	8,630	1,238	281	16	1,535	3,014	4,549	4,081	1.2	2.5	3.3	7.0
2nd Div.	9,977	300	984	10	1,294	2,707	4,001	5,976	1.1	2.2	4.8	8.1
3rd Div.	12,784	935	3,111	7	4,053	4,097	8,150	4,634	3.3	3.3	3.8	10.4
4th Div.	38,490	4,392	7,089	3	11,484	22,533	34,017	4,473	9.3	18.3	3.6	31.2
5th Div.	7,734	791	164	4	959	5,747	6,706	1,028	0.8	4.7	0.8	6.3
6th Div.	5,949	290	1,194	9	1,493	1,208	2,701	3,248	1.2	1.0	2.6	4.8
7th Div.	39,689	533	11,463	7	12,003	23,105	35,108	4,581	9.7	18.8	3.7	32.2
Kuching	18,607	1,539	1,265	26	2,830	5,721	8,551	10,056	2.3	4.7	8.1	15.1
Sibu	55,729	922	15,710	23	16,655	26,799	43,454	12,275	13.5	21.8	9.9	45.2
Bintulu	14,509	2,691	3,544	3	6,238	6,105	12,343	2,166	5.1	5.0	1.7	11.8
Miri	34,408	3,327	3,767	4	7,098	23,786	30,884	3,524	5.7	19.3	2.9	27.9
All Sections	123,253	8,479	24,286	56	32,821	62,411	95,232	28,021	26.6	50.8	22.6	100.0

Total Land Area = 123,253 sq. kilometres
Total Water Area = 1,197 sq. kilometres
Total Area of Sarawak = 124,450 sq. kilometres

¹ Other Forests include 6 National Parks

Source: *Annual Report of the Forest Department Sarawak, 1984*, Appendix F (Form 1)

Protected Forests, customary tenure is also forbidden. However, the law allows natives to collect, produce, hunt, fish and pasture cattle in these forests for their own needs, provided they apply for and are granted permission by the Forest Conservator. Communal Forests, on the other hand, are meant to be constituted for the benefit of a settled community 'to set aside a convenient area of woodland to provide its domestic needs of forest produce . . . Communal Forests will normally be large enough only to supply permanently the domestic needs of the community specified, allowing for a reasonable increase in population' (*Ibid* 1982:3).

As at 31 December 1984, out of the total 32,821 sq. km. of Permanent Forest, Forest Reserves comprised 8,479 sq. km., Protected Forests 24,286 sq. km. and Communal Forests only 56 sq. km. (*Ibid* 1984:90).

The Forests Ordinance 1953 in effect prohibits the natives from practising shifting agriculture and from exercising customary rights over the designated areas. Indeed, the Ordinance preceeds the Land Code in its prohibition of the creation of customary land by natives. It is also clear that the real objective of the Forests Ordinance was to curb the rights of the natives. The Forest Department's 1968 Annual Report states:

'The constitution of protected forests is directed against shifting agriculture. The Land Code affords protection in theory because it makes felling of virgin jungle on Interior Land an offence without prior permission in writing from the District Officer. In practice, without the protection of demarcated and patrolled boundaries to define the locality, or a nearby timber licensee interested enough to report them, offences are rarely detected. The constitution of Forest Reserves is directed towards complete control of the forest. Removal of forest produce for domestic purposes, and pasture of cattle, is allowed in Protected Forests but not in Forest Reserves; otherwise protection is very similar in each, and control is entirely vested in the Forest Department' (p5).

It is thus obvious that the aim of the Forest Ordinance was to complement and strengthen the land laws in curtailing natives from practising shifting cultivation and exercising customary land rights.

Although native activity is highly restricted in Protected Forests and Forest Reserves, the Ordinance allows logging activities to be carried out under permit. In these areas, logging is controlled by the Forest Department through 'Working Plans' in which restrictions are placed on the maximum yields permissable. The intention is that logging will be done on a 'sustained yield' basis. On Stateland Forests, logging is also allowed only under licence, but there is no management over this activity by the Forest Department. Logging companies only submit 'Felling Plans' to the Department, and unlike 'Working Plans' there are no restrictions placed on permissible yields.

It would appear from the above that the creation of Permanent Forests is really to 'protect' large parts of the forests from being claimed by the natives, so that these areas can be made available to logging companies to exploit timber, although in a manner more controlled and regulated than in the 'free-for-all' situation prevailing on Stateland Forests.

Indeed, the conversion of the status of areas from Stateland Forest to Permanent Forest has taken away large parts of the forest from the jurisdiction of native customary rights. This has caused substantial unhappiness among native communities.

Under the Forests Ordinance, the Minister of Forestry has the power to 'constitute' areas as Permanent Forests; including areas in which natives had already established customary rights. The law provides for people who are unhappy with the proposal of the Minister to designate selected areas as Permanent Forests to lodge their objection, but it is very difficult for a native to so lodge an objection and near to impossible in practice to reverse the decision. Section 4 of Part II of the Ordinance (which deals with Forest Reserves) states that before any piece of land becomes a Forest Reserve the notification shall be published in the *Gazette*. The notification which will be announced by the Resident will specify the extent of the forests. It also provides that 'any person who has any objection to the reservation of such forest, or who wishes to make any claim' can do so either 'verbally or in writing to the District Officer' within three months from the date of the publication of the notification (sections 3-5). Should there be objections, the District Officer will hear the claims of the persons objecting as well as the case of the Forest Conservator, and decide whether to allow or reject the objections. The District Officer's decision can be appealed against within 14 days to the Resident, whose decision will be final (section 8). After the three-month period is up, and all objections and appeals have been disposed of, the Minister will publish a notification in the *Gazette* declaring the area a Forest Reserve. Similar clauses exist regulating the procedure for the hearing of objections to the creation of Protected Forests.

Although the procedures are laid out in the Ordinance, in practice it is almost impossible for the unlettered native living in the far interior to gain access to information in a *Gazette* announcing the designation of his land as a Forest Reserve or Protected Forest. It is thus even more unlikely that he can place an objection against such a declaration within the three-month period. According to the Forest Department's 1982 Annual Report, 'Permanent Forests are constituted . . . after an inquiry in which the local people are consulted and the existence of rights investigated'. In practice, such a personal approach to affected communities is not taken. The natives are very often unaware that their customary lands have been declared a Forest Reserve or Protected Forest and that their customary rights have been 'extinguished'.

In many instances, forest areas over which native communities practise customary rights are converted through *Gazette* notification to

Permanent Forests, and concessions are given to timber companies to log these forests. The natives, who may not even be aware that they have lost their customary rights, become resentful of both the loggers and the government's disregard for their rights. The devastation caused by logging activities threatens the forest environment and the natives' way of life, as we shall later discuss.

What about Communal Forests? Although the creation of Communal Forests recognises the rights of the community to the use of the forests for their domestic needs, this right is very limited in scope and in practice. The government is not bound to create these forests; Part IV states that the Minister *may* (using his discretion) at the request of the community constitute any State land a Communal Forest. Members of the community may remove free of charge any forest produce for his own use only. The community is allowed to remove timber from Communal Forests subject to the direction of the District Officer, who 'may regulate the method and extent of any fellings or other operations' (Part IV section 46). Apart from these provisions, section 48 states that *the Minister has the sole power to revoke Communal Forests by mere notification in the Gazette*. This again means that the community which is living in the remote interior may not realise that their rights to the Communal Forests may have been revoked.

Of the three classes of Permanent Forests, only the creation of Communal Forests can be said to be in the natives' interest. It is thus interesting to note that Communal Forests constitute a very minute proportion of Permanent Forests. On 31 December 1984, Communal Forests constituted only 56 sq. km., a mere 0.17 per cent of the total 32,821 sq. km. of Permanent Forest. Moreover, we find that the areas under Forest Reserves and Protected Forests have increased, whilst the already meagre area under Communal Forest has shrunk very substantially through the years. Between 1968 and 1984, the total area gazetted as Permanent Forests rose from 30,875 sq. km. to 32,821 sq. km. The area under Forest Reserves rose (from 6,472 to 8,479 sq. km.) as did Protected Forests (from 24,100 to 24,286 sq. km.). But the area under Communal Forests shrunk from 303 sq. km. to only 56 sq. km. (Forest Dept. Sarawak 1968: Appendix F, Form I; 1984:90). In the space of a few years the Communal Forests have been drastically reduced by 82 per cent, thus depriving the natives from having access to forest produce in the vicinity of their communities.

Moreover this discrepancy is bound to increase in future years. The *1984 Report of the Forest Department* notes the State's target of making 35 per cent of the total land area of Sarawak come under Permanent Forest by 1985. In 1984 the proportion was only 26.6 per cent so another 10,318 sq. km. of land is targeted for conversion to Permanent Forest. In 1984 itself, much effort was put in by the Department to prepare land for such conversion. Altogether, 2.42 million hectares were under preparation, and within a few years these will be brought under Forest Reserves or Protected Forest status (*Ibid* 1984:6-8). It can be

Table 3
Sarawak: Classes of Forests, 1968-84 (sq. km.)

| As at Year End | Total Forest | Permanent Forest | | | Other Forest |
		Forest Reserves	Protected Forest	Communal Forest	
1968	94,325	6,472	24,100	303	63,450
1974	94,325	7,001	24,100	303	62,921
1979	94,305	7,480	23,955	306	62,564
1980	94,315	7,555	24,224	54	62,482
1981	94,411	7,651	24,224	55	62,481
1982	94,316	7,557	24,224	54	62,481
1983	94,296	7,491	24,214	56	62,535
1984	95,232	8,479	24,286	56	62,411

Sources: *Annual Report of the Forest Department Sarawak, 1968 & 1984; Annual Statistical Bulletin Sarawak, 1983.*

expected that quite a lot of these lands would have been under customary rights, which will now be extinguished.

Meanwhile, it is clear that the forest and State authorities will not favourably consider the natives' requests for land to be given Communal Forest status. According to a report by the Sarawak Study Group, top government officials in Sarawak's Seventh Division agreed at meetings in 1981, 1982 and 1983 that native applications for Communal Forests were not genuine but were filed only to disrupt timber operations. Thus, all applications should not be investigated but instead automatically turned down (Sarawak Study Group 1986:p14-15). As will be discussed later, even the existing Communal Forests of the natives are not secure: they are increasingly being trespassed upon and invaded by logging companies.

1979 Amendments to the Forests Ordinance

As pointed out in earlier sections, the land and forest laws in Sarawak have progressively restricted the geographical scope under which customary rights of the natives can continue to be exercised. Many areas of forest and land are now legally shut off from shifting cultivation and even from native collection of jungle produce, hunting and fishing. In order to tighten these restrictions further, and to enable enforcement, amendments were made in 1979 to the Forests Ordinance. Changes were made in section 90, to include two new clauses, which were henceforth cited as sections 90 and 90A. Under these amendments, wide powers were given to forestry officers to evict and prosecute natives who were found trespassing, felling timber or collecting forest produce in a Forest Reserve, Protected Forest or State land. Under the new section 90, any person found guilty can be evicted from these forests so long as the Director of Forests applies to the court for such an order. 'The court shall issue a warrant addressed to all police officers or forest officers requiring them to evict such person from the forest reserve, protected forest or state land in which the offence was committed, and to take possession . . . of all buildings, animals, crops and other property . . .'. Prior to this amendment, the eviction and the removal of property was left to the discretion of the court. Under the amendment, where the Director applies for an order, the court shall issue the order. Section 90A empowers any forest officer not below the rank of Assistant Director of Forests to take punitive action if the following offences have been committed in Forest Reserves: namely, trespassing, pasture cattle or permit cattle to trespass, erect any building or clear or break up any land for cultivation or for any other purpose; and in Protected Forest namely clearing any land for farming or any other purpose, or erect any building, or fell, cut, burn or remove any timber, firewood or charcoal (Part II section 21; Part III section 36).

These wide ranging powers given under the amendments enables senior forest officers to:

i) remove ... any person whom he has reason to believe to be committing the offence;

ii) seize any vehicle, tractor, chainsaw or other implement or thing which he has reason to believe was used or is being used in the commission of the offence;

iii) demolish or remove any building, or take possession in the name of the Government of all buildings, cattle, crops and other property.

It also provides that 'no forest officer or police officer shall be liable for any loss, injury or damage caused to any person or property' in carrying out his functions. Further, every officer in the exercise of the powers conferred upon him 'may call upon any police officer or forest officer for assistance and it shall be the duty of every such officer to comply with such request' (section 90A(2)(3)).

The overriding powers vested in forest officers under the changes in the Forests Ordinance discussed above reflects the State's policy towards customary tenure and shifting cultivation. Natives can now be severely dealt with for trying to make a living on Protected Forest or State land by practising shifting agriculture. The 1979 amendments to the Forests Ordinance 1953 serves to complement and reinforce the 1979 amendments to the Land Code 1958. These amendments have been shown to be very similar in nature and reflect the primary objective of the State towards native customary tenure and shifting agriculture, which is to restrict its practice and eventually to seek its demise.

Consequences of Land and Forest Laws
on the Natives

It can be seen from the above analysis that Colonial domination of Sarawak which began first under the Brookes and subsequently the British government has drastically altered and undermined the traditional concept of property and ownership of land and resources in native society. Laws which were taken from the various British colonies were plucked and grafted on to the Sarawak Land Code. These laws and legal concepts of property and ownership which were embedded in a market economy were diametrically opposed to native concepts of rights and justice. In the post Colonial era, further amendments to the laws resulted. This was bound to happen as the independent State embarked on a programme of 'development' which in essence meant the increased exploitation of the State's natural resources and modernisation of every sector of the economy, including agriculture. In such a 'climate' of thinking, natives who were tied to a subsistence 'primitive' economy (which was seen as a stumbling block) had to change. And to expedite these changes, laws which impeded this progress had to change as well.

From the discussion in Chapter Four and this Chapter, it can be seen that changes in land and forest laws and policies, especially the Land Code and the subsequent amendments made to it, have drastically affected native rights to their lands. It has been officially projected that the peculiar classification of lands in the Land Code was for the purpose of protecting native rights. In reality this has not been true. The law treats natives as mere licensees to the land on which they have lived and toiled for generations. Although the law recognises the existence of native customary rights to land, it also contains numerous provisions making it all too easy to have these lands taken away from the natives and for their rights to native customary tenure extinguished. This is found in various provisions in the Land Code and Forests Ordinance. The irony is that the land laws also allow for non-natives to acquire rights to land at the natives' expense as well. Given this situation, it would appear that native rights to their lands are not really protected, let alone being enshrined in the Land Code. In the words of a native law student: 'It will not be surprising in the not-too-distant future, native customary rights will not exist anymore' (Bahrin Adeng 1975:40).

Given the unsatisfactory treatment of native rights, the native has never been able to come to terms with government policy towards land and the forests. To them, the land, its resources and their right to it had always existed even before the 'arrival' of the State. That the State should arrogate to itself ownership to the land was both immoral and unjust. In the words of a native elder: 'The land belongs to the countless numbers who are dead, the few who are living, and the multitudes of those yet to be born. How then, can the Government say that all untitled land belongs to itself when there had been people using the land even before Government itself existed?' (Gumis 1981:44 footnotes).

'How' they (natives) ask 'can the Government consider them as mere licensees when they have "sweated and bled" for the land they now occupy? How can the Government give them a licence to what it does not itself own? The land they say is theirs, their rights thereto are permanent; how can a piece of paper (the land title) given by the Government make their rights "more permanent"?' (*Idem* 1981:47).

Natives cannot comprehend why they should be accused of wrong doing, when they fell new forests. 'We have committed no wrong. How can it be wrong? The jungles have always been ours — our forefathers have been using these forests from time immemorial, and we are just continuing a long tradition' (Das Murthy 1980:77). 'We are the natives, the people of the land. Our ancestors farmed and lived on this land and so did their descendants. We are only following their "path". The Government is meant to protect us. If this is so, why should it drive us out of our land?' (Gumis 1981:56).

It is not surprising that natives view government policy as unjust and the laws used against them as oppressive. This is made worse when they see outsiders being granted licences to log with gay abandon forests which rightfully belongs to them. Not only have they been deprived of their rights, the wanton destruction caused by the large scale logging activities have caused them extreme and dire hardship when their farms are destroyed before their very eyes, their rivers and water sources polluted, their sacred ancestral lands desecrated and their very existence threatened. This is seen as rubbing salt into their wounds.

Above: Iban farmers set out for their farms with their faithful hunting dogs.

Below: A Penan settlement in Ulu Baram. The Penan are the only nomadic people in Sarawak and especially dependent on forest resources for their needs.

Above: Kayan native longhouse settlement of Uma Bawang at Long Murum. Land surrounding longhouses in Sarawak can be classified as "communal forest" on request, but many requests have not been approved and the size of such forests has declined through the years.

Below: Traditional fishing is an important activity in the interior.

CHAPTER SEVEN

Natives versus Timber: Fight for the Forest

We have seen in Chapters Four and Six how the laws on land and forest were designed to restrict the activities and rights of the Sarawak natives with regards to agriculture and land. It is tempting to conclude that this restriction is motivated not so much to protect the forest ecology, but to protect the interests of the timber industry. Despite the laws, and the system of Permanent Forests, Sarawak's forests are being devastated — and not so much by shifting agriculture, but by massive logging activities. The issue as to who causes forest destruction — swidden or logging — we will leave to Chapters Eight and Nine. In this Chapter, we will examine the impact of the timber industry on the land and livelihood of the natives.

The Clash between Traditional and Commercial Systems

Timber is big business in Sarawak, and increasingly so. In 1985, the industry produced 12.2 million cubic metres (cu. m.) of logs (39 per cent of Malaysia's total output) and earned $1,315 million in exports (49 per cent of the country's total saw log earnings) (Bank Negara Annual Report 1985:142-3). This was much higher than the 4.4 million cu. m. of logs and $242 million in exports produced in Sarawak in 1976 (Annual Statistics Bulletin Sarawak 1977:132; 1981:57). With the expansion of such an important industry, the timber lobby is very influential. Logging is carried out through concessions and licences on both Permanent Forests and Stateland Forests, and the amount of land involved is tremendous. Official data on Working and Felling plans indicate that as at 31 December 1984, timber concessions in operation involved 5,752,996 hectares of forests, of which 1,342,826 hectares had already been exploited and the balance of 4,410,170 hectares are scheduled to be logged (Forest Department Sarawak 1984:80-89).

According to the environmental group, *Sahabat Alam Malaysia*: 'It is not always easy to identify the real owner of these timber concessions. Normally, individuals are given grants/licences, who then commission the licences to major timber contractors to work the commissioned area. Sometimes the major contractor will sub-contract it out to different contractors. This practice of sub-contracts, forming a kind of hierarchical structure, makes the original licensees virtually "invisible", they may never actually visit the logging camp yet profit enormously from it. Whoever they may be, it is common knowledge that timber licences are usually owned by politicians or those related by blood or money to them. The main reason for the development of the timber industry is economic. Yet, only a minority of the population benefits from the development' (SAM 1983:60).

Another study by the Sarawak Study Group investigated the ownership of the 12 timber concession areas in operation in January 1985 in the Belaga District, Seventh Division. The study found that among the prominent shareholders of companies holding the timber licences were politicians belonging to the ruling party, senior civil servants or close aides to political leaders, or their relatives. Most of the licensee companies did not extract timber themselves, but went into production-sharing arrangements with other companies responsible for the actual ground operations. Taking one company holding licence as an example, the study found that out of the total timber sales of $15.5 million in 1983/84, the contractor was paid $12.2 million (79 per cent of revenue) as fees; royalty and premium payments were $3.6 million; and the net profits of the licensee company itself was $1.4 million (9.3 per cent of revenue) (Sarawak Study Group 1986:5-8).

Given the lucrative timber trade, it is not surprising that the land and forest laws have increasingly controlled the movement and activities of the natives, since it is essential that they be geographically restricted to facilitate the logging companies' easy access to the forest and smooth operations in logging it. Moreover, as we have seen, the laws provide for the extinguishment of the rights of natives over various types of land and forest areas where they had previously established customary tenure. In many instances, the extinguishment of native rights was carried out to enable the granting of licences to logging companies to exploit the lands which until the 'extinguishment' had come under the jurisdiction of the natives. Often, the natives do not even know that their lands had been handed over to the loggers, who turn up with their bulldozers and their timber licences in hand. Sometimes, the loggers make a private deal with influential individuals in the community, who 'sell' the land rights over without the agreement of other members of the community. At other times, the companies illegally trespass on the natives' lands, or damage their crops, pollute their waterways and cause landslips or soil erosion which affect the natives' lands. These are sources of several conflicts between natives and logging companies which have broken out in different parts of Sarawak in recent years. The natives have responded to the loggers' intrusion with demonstrations, removal of parts of the tractors or bull-dozers, and physical fights. The State has replied with arrests, fines and even jail sentences. The immediate clashes over land rights manifest a deep-seated conflict of systems: of economic systems (between profit-motivated companies and

the natives' customary tenurial system), of ecological and techno-
logical systems (between the modern destructive technology and
careless technique of the loggers and the ages-old conservationist style
of swidden agriculture), and of cultural systems (the get-rich-quick
vulgarity of the modern enterprise versus the natives' ancient *adat* tied
to the land).

The contest between these systems is not between equals. Though
it may well be argued that morally and ethically, right is on the side
of the natives (who, after all, have lived on the land for generations),
the crux of the matter is that the might of money and modern
technology, backed by the power of the State, is on the side of
the timber industry. Thus the rapid expansion of logging has also meant
the progressive retreat of the natives and their swidden way of life.

Encroachment of Logging Into Native Lands

Obviously in an industry such as timber extraction which requires
modern engineering facilities, the individual native farmers are in no
position to compete with timber companies. Only the companies have
the capacity and resources to obtain timber permits from the
Government, but since the industry involves large scale deforestation,
it obviously has an adverse effect on native interests. Natives find the
extensive lands of their old domains whittled away. Since all primary
forest is State land, forest can only be felled on issue of permit by the
Government. Since the Government has the ultimate right to issue these
permits to individuals to take timber or for development schemes, the
Government's policy is often seen by the natives as arbitrary and
damaging to the community's right to land. Even worse, the already
restricted territory which is given to native customary rights is rapidly
being taken over by logging companies without natives even realising
it. In a letter to the press in June 1985, SAM revealed that many of
the timber licences issued to timber companies in fact stood on lands
where natives exercised native customary rights. SAM's study also
showed that natives did not receive any notice from the authorities
informing them that their rights to the land had been extinguished.
Neither has any compensation been paid to them (*Sarawak Tribune*, June
8, 1985).

In the previous Chapter, it was pointed out how ungenerous the
State has been in reducing the area of Communal Forests which had
already been granted to the natives. To make matters worse, even the
existing Communal Forests are now being exploited by outsiders for
timber. In some cases, the Government has made claim to marketable
timber within the territory of a community or longhouse (Richards 1961:
Part V para 31). A recent report by SAM states that most forest areas
within the territory of longhouses in the interior have been licensed
to timber companies (*Sarawak Tribune*, June 8, 1985). In other cases,
chiefs 'show a tendency to appropriate community rights for their own
personal or family disposal. They will personally sponsor outsiders to

come and trade or work timber in one or more of the *menoa*[1] of their area, and they will increase the "gifts" required of such strangers in the process, both for their own profit and because they are strangers. Complaint of such deals is now more often made than in the past and this, again, is a sign that the chiefs, by past behaviour, have to some extent alienated themselves' (Richards 1961: Part V para 30).

Among Iban communities, Sutlive has noted that village chiefs were paid by timber companies for the rights to fell Communal Forests. When an agreement is reached between the company and the village elders, the *tuai rumah* will apply for a logging permit on behalf of the company. In return, the timber companies will lavish gifts in the form of drinks and money to the *Penghulu* (area chiefs) and *tuai rumah*. In one instance, two *tuai rumah* were given fifty dollars each and plane tickets to Kuching to negotiate with the State authorities. When the deal was finalised, the company made a cash gift to the community. Sixty per cent of the money went to the *Penghulu*, 20 per cent to the *tuai rumah* and the rest was shared between other members of the community (Sutlive 1978:132). Iban chiefs have been using their political titles to cash in on the timber industry. Native Forest Reserves belonging to the community have been given over to logging companies for timber extraction. These '*Penghulu* and headmen who have been able to acquire rights to forests sought by timber operators have been able to convert political advantages into personal economic benefits' (Sutlive 1978:151).

This shows that even communal lands have not been spared from encroachment by timber activities. In recent years such 'joint venture' agreements involving influential natives of considerable social standing have been made. These natives apply for timber concessions as licensees and have agreements with businessmen who have the capital and resources to finance and operate the logging. The premiums paid out to licensees usually run into six figures.

Because native customary tenure is not protected under the Land Code, it has led to the occupation of non natives (as well as influential natives) on native lands. This can be seen in the large scale invasion of native lands by timber licensees who now enjoy the freedom to exploit the forests. 'Ironically, in the timber-rich state of Sarawak there are some longhouse communities *without* rights to any forests, and others that by sale of their lands are totally impoverished of natural resources' (Sutlive 1978:151).

The intense hardship of the people is poignantly revealed by this Kayan headman in the Baram when he appealed to a senior government official (during a visit upriver) to give them aid:

> What you have said is right. When are we going to build the house? (He pauses). These few years, we have been here for

---

1.   *Menoa* refers to all lands surrounding the longhouse whose members have exclusive rights to the use of the territory, forests and all waters running through this territory (Richards 1961: Part IV para 10).

four to five years, there has not been enough to eat, that's why
we haven't built the house. That's why I ask you to ask *plentah*
(*perintah* or government) to help us . . . That is why I ask help
because the boundary has been made already, but now with
larger families we don't have enough land. What are we going
to do? That's why I ask for some land. We have built our
house in *temuda* forest land for many times. That's why we need
land because now there're more people. That's why I ask you to
ask *plentah* not to give any more land to *kompeni* (timber
company), to *orang luar* (outsiders), to think of us instead. I've
heard they've brought outsiders to the ulu. Kebing Wan (a
pseudonym) has brought them. . . . . I've heard that . . . there's
going to be *kompeni* opening up land and people can buy shares.
But we are not educated people so I ask you to help get *sare
kosong* (shares) for us' (Hong 1977:288).

Cases of Native Communities Affected
by Logging Activities

There are numerous cases of native communities having grievances
against timber companies for disturbing and damaging their land and
river system. Many such cases have been documented by public interest
groups (particularly *Sahabat Alam Malaysia*) and also highlighted in
newspapers, especially Sarawak papers. Some of these cases are
summarised below.

Many of the reported cases of native grievances have occurred in
the Baram District of Sarawak's Fourth Division. The Baram river is
the second largest river in Sarawak. It is fed by three major tributaries,
the Tinjar, the Apoh and the Tutoh rivers. There are dozens of
longhouses along the Baram and all its tributaries, and logging has
affected almost all the longhouses.

In the Baram river alone, there were over 40 logging camps operating
in 1979. On the Tutoh and the Apoh rivers, Hanbury-Tenison who
led the Royal Geographical Society Mulu Expedition, reported in
1977-78 that: 'Longhouses and lumber camps already alternate. Almost
all the land is allocated in concessions for logging and its character is
changing fast' (Hanbury-Tenison 1980:144). Amidst all the timber
concession areas are the longhouses of the Kayan and Kenyah and
wandering in these forests are the nomadic Penan. There are some
180 longhouse and forest communities in the Baram (Leigh 1975:256-8)
which depend on the forest for their livelihood. These communities
now find that the primary forests surrounding their *temuda* (secondary
forests) have been taken over by the timber concessions to which they
have no access. Land could not be expanded to meet their need to
establish new swiddens.

Logging activities on communal lands also frightened away animals
making it very difficult for natives to hunt them. According to a SAM
report in 1981, in the Tutoh, Penan who are hunters and gatherers

leading a nomadic existence in the forest have been forced out of their areas by logging operations. Wild sago (their staple diet) is being destroyed by the felling and the wild boar and other animals are being frightened away by the noise of tractors and chainsaws. Timbermen also shoot these animals and use *tuba* to poison fish depriving the Penan of their food. This has also been reported by Hanbury-Tenison. According to his observations: 'Deforestation of surrounding areas is forcing more Punan (Penan) to move into the park in search of the remaining relatively undisturbed forests . . . under pressure from logging operations, the future for both the people and the wildlife looked grim' (Hanbury-Tenison 1980:136-7).

On 19 June 1982, 1,400 residents in the Upper Baram sent an appeal letter to the Prime Minister, Chief Minister of Sarawak, Minister of Forestry and various officials including the Member of Parliament for the Baram to stop the logging activities of a timber company in the area. According to the residents, logging began about four years ago when the forest area behind the longhouse was given to a timber company. Since then their activities have been destroying the illipe nut trees and *rotan* vines. These forest products were collected by the people for sale to supplement their subsistence. 'We are full-time subsistence padi farmers who mainly live on the forest resources. If the felling continues and destruction to the canes (*rotan*) goes on, our very survival is greatly threatened' they wrote in their letter (*Borneo Bulletin*, June 19, 1982).

A week later in the Apoh river, natives of Long Layun who had lived there for over 50 years were told by the manager of a logging camp that they were not allowed to farm the land 'just above our longhouse because the land belongs to the company'. The manager had told them that 'the government owns the land and gave it to us'. These villagers only discovered that the communal forest reserve was occupied when they saw bulldozers coming. Not only was the land taken away, the village cemetery was also desecrated in the process. According to one native: 'They didn't bother to show us any respect. They thought we were just wild animals'. Another native said: 'How come we are simply told to get out from the place where we've been settled for ages?'. Occupation of native lands meant a threat to their very survival. 'Taking the land away from us is just like taking our pot of rice' added a spokesman. They felt that the government is responsible for their welfare (*Ibid* June 26, 1982).

In the Patah river, (a tributary of the Baram) a group of Penan who had been resettled at Long Itam were shocked to find their farmland included in a concession given to a logging company. These nomadic people had been given the land by the authorities six years ago when they agreed to settle down permanently. They also claimed that some prominent people in the State are connected with the logging company and they are appealing to the authorities (*Star*, September 12, 1982). One logging company had damaged the farm land belonging to the Long Bunau community in the Patah river. When the residents demanded compensation they were ignored by the company and their appeals to the authorities have gone unheeded as well (*Ibid* September 12, 1982).

In recent years, the onslaught of loggers and machines in the forest has accelerated in the Baram District. A SAM survey has estimated that some 40 longhouses comprising 16,000 people residing in the Baram, Apoh, Tutoh and Tinjar rivers are directly affected by logging activities (SAM 1983:62). In fact in many longhouse communities, the stillness of the surrounding forest is now continually broken by the jarring sounds of the chainsaw. In the Pelutan river, the licensing of 800,000 acres of forest for logging has affected the lives of various groups of Kenyah, Kayan and Penan. The area between the Tinjar and the main river Baram contains rich *Kerangas* forest which has been licensed out. This will affect the Kayan and Kenyah longhouse communities of Long Kesseh, Long Loyang and Long Atun. One native community which tried to apply for a licence to lease out *Kerangas* forest was told that 'the feature of the forest is very mountainous and it does not possess the economic potential to be exploited'. Not long after, however, the same forest was leased out to a logging company (*The Sunday Star*, June 17, 1984).

This has happened in the Ulu Tutoh as well. In a letter to a newspaper, the people of the Upper Tutoh wrote that they had in the past applied for a licence to extract timber along the upper reaches of the Tutoh river. This request was refused. Then in 1986, in the same area that they had applied for, 'a logging company is now making its way through the hills and dense forest with their mighty tractors, leaving behind its way only the uprooted trees and areas that look as if a massive landslide has occurred' (*Sarawak Tribune*, April 23, 1986).

Loggers have also destroyed *engkabang* (illipe nut trees) belonging to the local people. These forest trees (which bear illipe nuts[2]) are an important source of income for the natives. The tree is protected under the Forest Rules and felling them constitutes an offence. In 1985 SAM sent a memorandum to the State government concerning the Kayan longhouses of Long Pilah, Long Kesseh, and Long Naah in the Upper Baram: these communities have complained and made numerous appeals to the Forestry authorities to take action against the logging companies which continue to fell and extract the nuts from their *engkabang* trees. However nothing was done by the authorities. According to the natives, when they protested to the loggers concerned, the latter boasted that even if the natives were to report the matter to the local Forestry authorities, they (loggers) 'could use their money to buy over the authorities concerned to close the case' (SAM Memorandum 1985). Very often, damage or loss of property has never been adequately compensated by the timber companies. In the Middle Baram, the Kenyah of Rumah Akeh had agreed to give up their forest lands

---

2. Illipe nuts are valued for their fat which are extracted for use in chocolate manufacturing. They are exported for this purpose.

Above: Timber camp invading swidden farm areas in Ulu Belaga.

Left: Women who depend on the forest for important products such as the rattan they have just collected.

Below: Natives examining recent damage to the forest caused by movement of heavy vehicles dragging logs.

when they were promised compensation. During the State elections in 1979 the timber company gave each family M$48. However since then, the timber company which was given the forest concession has not lived up to its promises (*The Sunday Star,* June 17, 1984).

As the timber companies increasingly encroach upon their surrounding forests, natives find their resources dwindling rapidly. The forest is the storehouse for their daily and domestic needs; wood and *rotan* for their homes, boats and agricultural implements, medicinal herbs for their ailments, and plants and animals for their food. Today, these forest products are scarce and difficult to find. Increasingly their quality of life has suffered. Houses are built with poor materials, and one has to go further and deeper in the forests (if they have not been already logged) to look for game and forest products. As a result of these negative developments, natives have applied for Communal Forests but their requests have not been granted.

Between August 1984 to May 1985, the seven longhouse communities of Long Miri, Long Kesseh, Long Naah in the Baram; and Long Lutin, Long Lilim, Long Kawi, Long Han in the Patah tributary, wrote numerous letters to the District Officer, Resident, and various Ministers, requesting for communal forest status to be given to land near their longhouses. 'The receipt of their letters and applications was not even acknowledged', according to a SAM memorandum addressed to the Chief Minister, the Ministers of Forestry, and Resource Planning on the matter. The memorandum pointed to the fact that natives were prevented from collecting wood and forest products within the concession areas although this was sometimes allowed, depending on the goodwill of the timber companies concerned. 'Local people cannot afford to buy woods needed to repair or rebuild their houses or for making boats and other essential purposes from the sawmills'. From its investigations SAM said that there is a legitimate and an urgent need for a Communal Forest to be reserved for the longhouse communities as in most cases, 'the forest areas around their longhouses have been licensed out to timber companies'. There was thus 'no reason why the authorities and the law restricts to accommodate (sic) a request for a Communal Reserve ... which would be for the exclusive use and welfare needs of a community when the Government could freely license such a reserve to timber companies'. SAM in its appeal said that 'the longhouse communities would be seriously deprived of vital resources in the future' (SAM Memorandum 1985).

It has become increasingly clear that natives have little control over the decisions that affect their lands and their livelihood. According to SAM: 'No matter what the profits from logging, it is only the small elite that benefit; the majority of the tribal communities have to bear the brunt of destroyed forests and barren lands ... Sarawak tribes ... have no say in their future, or are misled by timber companies or government authorities. Their future is being decided by businessmen and politicians

— whose only concern is profits, not their welfare' (*The Sunday Star,* June 17, 1984). Time and again natives have been told that they must not reject development, that they have to accept change and progress. It is a bitter irony that natives living in the remote interior often equate development with logging companies. Not unexpectedly, natives want 'a share of this development' as well. In April 1985 a Member of Parliament told the House: 'It would appear that after years of accelerated timber exploitation very few rural dwellers have benefited directly except as labourers . . . This disappointment has been made all the more glaring because in many instances timber have been cut in places very close to kampungs and, indeed, in areas usually regarded by natives as traditional property and hunting grounds' (*Sarawak Tribune,* April 11, 1985).

Native Resistance in the Fourth Division

In recent years, there has been growing resistance by Sarawak natives against the encroachment of timber activities on their land, their trees, their ancestral graves, water systems and other resources and properties. They have become painfully aware that 'development' takes the side of the timber companies and does not benefit them. They have come to realise that it is only a privileged few who have been able to enrich themselves. Instead this 'development' had left barren lands, mutilated forests and farmlands. The shock, the fury and bitterness is often impossible to bear. There is a deep sense of injustice, treachery, painful loss and uncertainty for the future. This is often articulated through the only means available to them — resistance and confrontation with the loggers. The bitter experience of other natives who have suffered at the hands of the logging companies, and fears of further exploitation and encroachment of their forest lands have forced many communities to take matters in their own hands. Some of the cases of this confrontation between native communities and timber companies are recounted here. This section describes land conflicts in the Fourth Division (mainly the Baram District), whilst the next section examines cases in the Seventh Division (mainly the Belaga District).

In 1981, 400-500 Kenyah from Long Apoh, Baram went to the Sam Ling Timber Company at Long Bedian in the Apoh river, armed with parangs, spears and blowpipes. The Kenyah had demanded compensation from the company for damage done to their land. They threatened to burn the camp if the money was not paid. They had asked for a 'commission' of $40 for every ton of timber extracted. Their action was prompted after earlier petitions asking for negotiations had been ignored, said one of the spokesmen who was arrested (*Borneo Bulletin,* March 19, 1983).

In November 1981, some 70 to 80 natives from 22 longhouses in the Baram arrived at the Lamat logging camp and demanded compensation. A spokesman from the group, told the court that ever since the logging companies started operating, their animals vanished, the river became dirty and their *engkabang, damar, rotan* and *jelutong* (latex from this tree is used in chewing gum manufacture) were destroyed. The company had refused their demand of $2 a ton for the timber extracted as compensation, which they thought was justified. The people had applied for their own timber licence but had been refused. The company had been given a licence to log 168,272 acres of the Baram River area under the Forest Department's Tinjar-Paong Management Plan. This lease expires on June 30, 2002. During the incident, the camp manager was given a letter containing 55 thumb-prints and asked to stop logging (*Ibid* December 26, 1981).

In another dispute in 1982, five Iban from Rumah Berandah, Niah, armed with a shotgun and parang set up a road block and stopped the manager as he drove to work. He was made to pay them $7,000 compensation for damages on their land when the company cleared the jungle to build the camp. They had originally been promised compensation but since nothing had been paid, they felt cheated and decided to 'waylay' the manager. They were arrested when the manager reported the incident to the police (*Ibid* November 6, 1982).

In February 1983, ten villagers threatened to burn down a logging camp in Ulu Nyalan, Niah if their demands for compensation were not met. The natives had demanded $100,000 in compensation and $10 for every ton of timber extracted. The villagers were upset because the stream near their village which they used for cooking, drinking and bathing became polluted after logging started near the village three months ago. The village headman told the court that as a result, all the 15 families in the longhouse had to walk very far to fetch water from another stream. Two days after the incident, the police arrived by boat and arrested the ten men (*The Sunday Star*, March 6, 1983).

In October 1983 a group of angry Iban set fire to several blocks of living quarters at a timber camp in the Batu Niah area. Forty-seven were arrested and taken to the Miri Sessions Court which placed them on $1000 good behaviour bonds for a year.

In the same month, a group of 12 Iban from Sungai Ridan, just outside Marudi, went to a timber camp and took control of a large caterpillar machine. One of the men used the machine to push a large log across the road leading to the camp, thus blocking the way of log-carrying lorries and other heavy vehicles. They also painted a warning in Malay on the log informing lorry drivers they would have to pay $3,000 if they moved the log in order to use the road. The conflict arose because the Iban said that the timber company was logging their native customary land. The company pointed out that they were extracting timber from a concession area that belongs to the State — not to the Iban.

In January 1984, 200 Iban barricaded a timber road with logs at Lubok Lalang in Sungai Medamit. They demanded $2 million compensation from the company which is owned by prominent

Sarawak businessman — politician Datuk James Wong[3]. The Iban say that the logging had damaged their water supplies (*Borneo Bulletin*, January 28, 1984).

At Long Pilah in the Baram District, the longhouse community banned loggers from removing timber and trespassing on their land. The logging contractor bulldozed a 1.6 km road through their farmland without permission. This land was their *temuda* which had been left fallow. It was last farmed in 1976. It was very fertile 'but now all that is left is barren rock' said a spokesman. When the farmers approached the manager, he told them he had no power to negotiate compensation as this could only be done by the company manager. According to the spokesman, neighbouring longhouses had been involved in long and tedious negotiations with the timber company and were only compensated $5 for every 20 metres of land damaged, which they considered unfair. 'We don't want any repetition of this injustice' added one of the farmers whose land the company had built workers' quarters. The farmers will not take their protest to court because their land will be classed as Native Customary Right Land and they will only be compensated at the $5 per metre rate. They claimed the company went ahead with its road because it knew that it would not face a large compensation claim (*Ibid*).

In 1985, Laeng Wan, a Kayan from Long Miri, built a fence across a logging road leading to his land. He was arrested for unlawfully restricting a trespasser from encroaching on his own land. In 1977 he had signed an agreement leasing his land for ten years to a timber company when he found his land licensed out. In 1983 the timber contractor moved out. It was replaced by another timber company. This company without his permission or additional compensation, continued logging activities. The new company insisted they were the agents of the earlier company, therefore compensation was not necessary. Since Laeng Wan disagreed, he had built the fence to protect his land from further damage (*Suara Sam*, October 1985).

The plight and suffering of the *orang ulu* in the Baram was related to me by a Baram native in December 1981:

'We *ulu* people have complained that the pollution caused by
the timber companies is killing the fishes and muddying the
rivers. The logging has caused erosion, silting of our rivers,
chasing away the animals and leaving no timber for our people.
In some areas like the Upper Tutoh, Penan have been forced
out of the area by the timber company which had destroyed
their wild sago. This area which was traditionally their home, is
below the Mount Mulu National Park. It is now being
extensively logged. The area which comprises 60,000 acres has
been given out as timber concession to Kayan politicians. Now

3.   Datuk James Wong is the President of SNAP (Sarawak National Party) one of the political parties in the ruling State coalition.

the wild boar and other animals are either being shot by the
timberman or else the noise of the tractors and chainsaws have
frightened them away. They have also been using *tuba* to poison
the fish in the rivers. And the *rotan* vines and sago trees have
all been destroyed by the logging. The source of food for the
Penan have all been destroyed as a result. Because of this, they
have now migrated to the Patah and the Apoh to look for food.

In the Baram alone, there are more than 30 logging
companies working on about one million acres of forests. And
amidst all these timber concessions are the longhouses of the
Kayan, Kenyah and the people wandering in the forests — the
Penan. All these forests are next to our *temuda*. In fact timber
companies have moved into our *keharah aya* (old secondary
forests, 20-40 years old). When our people tell the timber
companies that these lands belong to us and you have to pay
compensation for destroying it, they say: "Where's your land
title?". Now the whole of Apoh, Tinjar and Tutoh and about
two thirds of the Batang Baram are affected by logging
activities. In these areas are found not less than 40 longhouses
with a population of ten to fifteen thousand people.

In 1975 in the Apoh, about 50,000 acres of forest in the area
were leased out to Mohamad Tahir (pseudonym), the son of a
prominent former State dignitary. Our people had felled the
forest here 40 to 50 years ago before the land became a timber
concession. At first the people of Apoh did not realise this as
everything was decided in Kuching, and so nothing was done.
It was only when the contractor came with his machines and
men to open up the area, did the people realise and they
immediately petitioned the authorities to intervene. They also
appealed to their State Assemblyman but nothing was done.
When 500 *ulu* people approached the camp manager, they were
told to meet the management (contractors) in Miri. Then they
sent their representatives to meet the contractor in Miri, and
they were told to go to Kuching to meet the licensee. Then they
made a trip all the way to Kuching, but when they got there,
they were told that the licensee had gone overseas. This has
been going on for sometime. Petitions after petitions had been
sent to the authorities including the Prime Minister. In their
letter to the Prime Minister, the *ulu* people appealed for the
recognition of historical rights to their lands, requested for
communal forests, for timber licences and an equal share of the
timber wealth, and called for an investigation of the licensing of
timber concessions (This letter is reproduced in Appendix *4*).
Many meetings had been held too, but nothing was
forthcoming.

The people dare not stop the company because they were
warned not to take the law into their own hands by the
authorities. Yet these authorities remain cold and indifferent

to the plight of the people. The people could no longer farm on new land because all the land around their longhouses — altogether there are five longhouses involved — had already been leased out to the company. They even took the land next to our rubber gardens. And if the people tried to farm on new land, they would be charged for felling the trees illegally and would be prosecuted. But they need to farm and extend the farm when the family grows and becomes larger. How can they farm on the same piece of land year after year? In fact 20 families from these five longhouses have left the Apoh because they couldn't farm anymore. They have left to join the SLDB Miri-Bintulu Scheme to plant oilpalm. They were told that after six years, they will be given three to four acres of the land.

Since they could not get any help from the authorities, the people realised that they have been left to themselves to handle their problems. Now they have decided and are determined to defend their land and fight for their rights. Many meetings were called among the longhouse people who have been affected by the logging operations. Many others not affected were called upon to lend their support. The people decided that they have to do something themselves to stop the timber company from polluting the river and robbing away their lands.

One morning about four to five hundred people from the five longhouses went to the camp site. The Penan also came with their blow pipes. They had gone with the purpose of meeting the timber company officials for negotiations. The camp manager told the *ulu* people that the contractor and licensee would arrive at the camp in the afternoon. The people waited until the following afternoon but there was still no sign of the contractor and the licensee. This agitated the people and they removed some parts from the tractors. It was only when this happened that the authorities responded with a show of force. They sent the military to the area and arrested people. They even threatened to beat up the people. A platoon (30 members) of police field force were brought to the logging camp. They fired their rifles to frighten the people. The people were told to go to Marudi for negotiations with the timber company officials. During the negotiations at Marudi, the timber company officials told the people that they (natives) will not get a single cent from the timber company. After the meeting, four orang *ulu* were arrested. Over two thousand orang *ulu* from all over the Baram came to Marudi to lend their support during the trial which began on 23 March 1980. (Details of the camp incident and the above events are noted in Appendix 5). The *ulu* people also invited Members of Parliament based in Peninsular Malaysia to witness the proceedings. [A letter to a Member of Parliament is reproduced in Appendix 6].

In the Batang Baram and the Tinjar, many other longhouses which had been affected by the timber companies took courage and followed suit. Many were also arrested and brought to court. Yet till today, there is no help forthcoming from the authorities. Instead the people are warned time and again not to take the law into their own hands.

The people have been called barbarians, thieves and other insulting terms. The police called the people *kurang ajar*[4]. Even the local newspapers have their share of bias portraying the people as uncivilised and bad.

The chiefs are of no help. They are the 'frontmen' of the politicians and it is they who have betrayed our people. Most of the longhouse chiefs or headmen (*ketua kampong*) have been paid monthly salaries ($400-$500 every month) by the companies and are as happy as ever. The contractors have also brought many of the chiefs to Miri and Kuching nightclubs for entertainment. Some of the Baram chiefs are licensees themselves. Many longhouses want to elect new leaders but the authorities will always interfere and make the people accept the former's choice for the longhouse communities. Even the companies are involved: they offer bribes and jobs to the community leaders and their families.

For example in one longhouse in the Apoh, the longhouse people decided to elect a new *tua kampong* because the *tua kampong* which was the government's choice was not heeding the wishes of the people. So an election was held. The SAO (Sarawak Administrative Officer) from Marudi came to witness the election. Even the *Temenggong* (the government appointed Paramount Chief of the *orang ulu* in the Baram) was there. The peoples' choice won. But the government didn't want to recognise the elected leader. So the people met the District Officer and the Resident. The Resident told the people: "Changing the *tua kampong* is not like changing your clothes. The government is not in favour of election. In fact we have a directive from the State Secretary that the *tua kampong* should be appointed by the Government. So long as there is a majority of four people in the village committee (or council) who support the nominee, he gets elected". But the rest of the committee members were government supporters and they were the *tua kampong's* men. The people even met the State Assemblyman to help them solve this problem, but he said he could not do anything.

The land and pollution are not the only problems. Erosion and silting cause floods. At the end of last year (1980) until early this year (1981) there were four big floods affecting some

---

4.   Literally in Malay it means 'not properly taught'. It is a poor reflection of one's parents or upbringing if one is ill mannered or not properly taught.

ten longhouses and towns like Marudi and Long Lama. Many padi farms and other crops were washed away. This has led to a big rice shortage in the area. In 1980 there was famine in the Middle Baram. About 200 families from three longhouses, Long Banio, Long Laput and Long Lian did not have food to eat. In the last two years, four to six floods have occurred just before the harvest and after weeding time. In 1978 and 1980 the Government provided seeds to the people to plant because of the floods. Each family was given six *gantang*. Some had to eat tapioca and sago to survive.

In 1979, about three to four longhouses were short of food. In 1980, more longhouses suffered food shortage because of the increase in logging activities. This time eight to nine longhouses involving some 200 families were affected. Those who could afford bought rice from the bazaar. Others were forced to look for work in the logging camps and the construction sites. Many families did not even have seeds to grow rice for the next planting season. In the last three years, most communities of the Lower Baram had to depend on the. Agriculture Department to provide them with seeds to plant. In the last ten years or so, the rotation of the fields had been shortened. Nowadays, all the longhouses have to grow our *parei tu'an* (hillrice) in the *sepiteng*[5] because there is no more land.

Nowadays, timber work has brought many people from all over to the Baram. These are the Iban, Land Dayak (Bidayuh) and Chinese men who work in the camps. This has also caused a lot of problems for the local people. As many of the logging camps are near the longhouses, the timber workers often go to the longhouses and bring along all kinds of influences. These men marry local girls. In many longhouses in the Baram today, you can hear of young girls who have been abandoned by their husbands who work in the timber camps. When the company has logged the area, it moves out and these men leave as well deserting their wives and children.

In our suffering, we now realise that the authorities have forgotten us and have neglected us. They are the ones who hold the breath (life) of these companies and they are the ones who are in the most powerful position who can set right the wrongs and the injustices committed against us. But they are again the owners of the timber companies. In fact there are at least four very senior State politicians who own timber concessions in the Baram. It is they who have made these things happen, who have created unjust laws. And they are the protectors of these laws'.

---

5. *Sepiteng* in Kayan refers to land which have been in fallow two years after the last harvest and three years after the last planting season. The trees here are still very small about 10-20 feet high and with girths about the size of a man's wrist.

Native Resistance in the Seventh Division

Similar examples of land conflicts between native communities and logging companies can be found in the Belaga District in Sarawak's Seventh Division, where logging operations first began in the early 1980s. In 1984 a newspaper report highlighted the plight of the longhouse people in Belaga. Loggers who have started clearing forests along the Betun, Penuan and Lebuwai rivers (tributaries of the Balui[6]) have frightened animals and fish life (on which they depend for food), and ruined the rivers as a source of drinking water. In fact logging activity here was seen as a prelude to the Bakun dam project. The natives had marked the forest areas where they get their supplies of *rotan*, *damar* (a resin used as fuel), bamboo and illipenuts and appealed to the loggers to spare them. However, these markers had been ignored. Residents had been promised both compensation and jobs, but so far nothing has been paid and people from Kuching have been hired instead. An official from the Sarawak Electricity Supply Corporation (SESCO), which is involved in the Bakun dam project was quoted as saying that all logging areas was on State land and no compensation was therefore required (*New Sunday Times*, November 27, 1983).

In many instances, the position taken by the authorities and elected representatives (State Assemblymen and Parliamentarians) reveal a callous indifference to the problems of the natives. This can be seen in the case of Long Bulan, a Kenyah longhouse in the Ulu Balui, which had desperately sought help and advice from the authorities when they found logging operations on their forests lands. Below is the story of what happened as it was told to me (during my visit in October 1985) by the former headman who retired in 1984 after 20 years of service:

'This happened in 1983. From the beginning I didn't know. When the Kenyah wanted to celebrate the New Year, I was surprised to see the Penuan (tributary of the Balui) silted. I asked the young men to go hunting there — when the river is silted, there may be lots of wild boar there. Two boats went and met the Iban there. Our people were scared because they thought they were communists. Then the Iban told our people they are not. Our people went near and the Iban asked, "Why do you come here?" We told them: "We want to hunt wild boar — usually when the river is silted, there's wild boar". "It is not wild boar, but it is bulldozers and the company that is silting the river", the Iban told us. After hearing this, our people came back and told me everything. They said we cannot go up to hunt because the river is silted by '*kompeni*' (logging company).

---

6.   The Rejang (called the Balui in the upper reaches) is fed by three major tributaries, the Linau, Murum and the Belaga rivers. It is 350 miles and the longest river in Sarawak, navigable for coastal vessels as far as Kapit 150 miles upriver.

I told them, "Let us go and see the *kompeni*". I went to see the '*kompeni*' with a few men, about ten persons. We met the '*kompeni*'. I asked the manager, "Why are you working here, this is our area". The manager asked, "Did *perintah* (government) tell you?" I said, '*ta'on*' (no in Kenyah). He said, "We come to work because we have licence from *kerajaan* (government)". (The headman paused). "Since you have the licence, you should come to tell us as Penuan is our area". "We didn't know, we expected the D.O. (District Officer) to tell you" he said. We came back to Long Bulan. I went to Belaga to see the D.O. I told the D.O. "Why don't you tell me about '*kompeni*' in my area?" The D.O. said he didn't know anything. Then the D.O. asked the Forest Department whether they knew about it. Forest Department said, "no". I told them all, "You should know about it because you are in office. If that is the case, I will go to Kuching". I went to Kuching with Bai (pseudonym) and a few of the kampong people in August 1983. I told Lejau (pseudonym) and the others from our longhouse who were in Kuching. Then I brought them to see Dato Nawan[7] (pseudonym). Dato Nawan said, "I don't know anything about this". He said "be patient". Then I told him, "If we are patient, in time to come our land will be destroyed, *habis kayu, habis tanah — semua rosak*" (The wood will be finished, the land will be finished — everything will be useless). Then I got very worried because if he didn't know anything, who did? Then I asked my kampong people in Kuching for the office of the authority who issues the licence. They said it is Y.B. Entinggi's[8] (pseudonym) office. Then I went to ask Entinggi about this, and he said, "I don't know anything". He said, "I am too busy" and he gave me $50 and told me to go and have a drink. I was lucky because he had a clerk who told me that the place they issue licences is the office Masyarakat, (this building is behind the new museum) Kuching. I went there immediately and met a Malay officer. I asked him whether they have issued the licence to a company in the Penuan. "*Kami tidak tahu*" (We don't know), he told me. "*Mana boleh kamu tidak tahu?*" (How can it be that you don't know?), I told him. "If you don't know, where's the map?" Then he brought the map and both of us looked at the map. Then I pointed to the area on the map. Then they confessed, "Yes, we have issued the licence already". So I asked them what is the name of the '*kompeni*' and they said they don't know, "*boleh tanya orang lain*" (you should ask somebody else) — then I came out.

7. Dato Nawan is a State Assemblyman.

8. Y.B. Entinggi is a Member of Parliament and a senior party member of the PBB Party (*Parti Pesaka Bumiputra Bersatu*).

Then I came back to Long Bulan and told our people what happened and told them we have no more hope. We went to see the *'kompeni'* again. Then I told the manager, "you should leave a piece of land for us to search for wood for our house". Then I asked for help from them — "give us *sago hati* — *pengelesau*[9]" (give us something as consolation). Then the manager said, "I don't know anything, wait for my boss". Until today the *sago hati* has not come. Then I came back and went to Kapit to see the forest officer there. I asked him "why didn't you even tell us that the company is coming here", and he told me, *"mana boleh, kerajaan yang berkuasa semua tanah"* (How can I, the Government has the authority over all land). *"Apa macam saya?* (What about us?) *Kami orang ulu, hidup di tanah kerajaan* (We are orang ulu, we live on the government's land). *Kalau kami tidak ada kuasa, memang tiap-tiap kampong ada batas, ada kuasa"* (If we don't have authority, for sure every kampong has a boundary, therefore we have authority). He said the Government will get the land next to your *temuda*, it won't take your *temuda*. *"Mana boleh, sebab kerajaan telah kasi lesen sampai temuda* (How can that be because the Government has given the licence up to our *temuda*). *Apa macham kami hidup kalau itu macham?* (How can we live if the situation is such?) *Memang susah rakyat kalau itu macham* — *ta'ada tempat bikin perahu, rumah, ramuan rumah, tidak dapat dalam temuda* (For sure the people will suffer if the situation is such — no place to make boats, and house as *temuda* does not have wood big enough). *Sedang besi, batu pun buruk* (Even iron, stone can rot). The same with our *temuda*". "I cannot clarify everything to you" — the officer said to me. "I can ask *kerajaan* (the Government) — *Kalau boleh dapat. Kalau tidak, tidak lah"* (If it's possible, you will get land, if not then you won't get). (This was with reference to the headman's request for communal land).

I came back to Long Bulan and asked the kampong people to make boundary, to ask *'kompeni'* not to enter the border of our lands any more, but still they cut the timber within the boundary. So we made another one and yet it was not successful — the *'kompeni'* couldn't care less and kept logging. After that we went to the *'kompeni'* roads leading to our land, showing them a warning — a blow pipe pointing at the bulldozer. Then the news went to the Government that the Long Bulan people are threatening to kill the loggers. Then the D.O., the forest officer, General Manager of the company, and the police came to the longhouse and had a discussion. This took place in April 1984. They asked us, "Why do you want to

9.   *Pengelesau* in Kenyah means to show your mercy or sympathy. To have pity on someone.

kill the people working in the company?" I answered, "*Berapa orang Long Bulan sudah bunuh kompeni, siapa nama dia orang?*" (How many people have the Long Bulan residents killed?). They said, "Our purpose here is because we heard about the threat to 'blowpipe' the workers in the logging company".

Then I told them, "What do you understand if one were to say there is no entry? Everywhere, at sea, in the other countries, there's always warning which says 'no entry'. Whoever goes against the order will be punished. Another thing I want to say, soldiers give warning that those who trespass will be shot because they will be regarded as criminals. That is the reason I have drawn the limits of our land to inform others not to trespass but '*kompeni*' doesn't care. Where have I killed people? We have asked for wood, we cannot get because the Government has.given a licence. If we do not follow what is said in the licence, we will be punished by the Government, so they tell us. That's it, there's no more to be said". Then I asked help from the Government to fulfill *sago hati,* — until now there is nothing. I even spoke to D.O. to give money *sebagai kopi-o tiap-tiap bulan* (as a monthly payment to us), but the D.O. said he has to discuss with the *orang besar* (the important people), *sampai sekarang tidak ada* (until now there is nothing). The kampong people went twice to see the manager for *sago hati* — '*mintak belas kasihan dari kompeni*' (to ask for compassion from the company) — but the manager refused. Until now nothing has happened. I am very disgusted and angry with them, because they think we are fools, they never want to *ngigo* (consider) our complaints.'

In August 1985, four Kenyah communities involving more than 3000 people were shocked and angered that their ancestral burial ground along the Penyuan river in Ulu Belaga had been desecrated. A Bintulu-based timber company, 'Lau's Timber'[10], had bulldozed the ten acre site when building a road in the area. According to a spokesman, several verbal requests for compensation had been rejected by the timber

10. Also known as Richwood Sdn Bhd. the logging contractors for Delapan licensee company. The shareholders include Datuk Tajang Laing, PBB State Assemblyman for Belaga; Haji Idris Abdullah, Political Secretary to the Chief Minister; Norlia Abdul Rahman, daughter of the previous Chief Minister; and *Pemanca* Kupa Kayan a community leader of Belaga (Sarawak Study Group 1986:6-7). The PBB (*Parti Pesaka Bumiputra Bersatu*) is the senior party (Melanau based) in the State's four party National Front coalition. The others are SNAP (Sarawak National Party — multiethnic), SUPP (Sarawak United Peoples' Party — Chinese based), PBDS (*Parti Bangsa Dayak* Sarawak — Iban based). PBDS was formed when some members of SNAP broke away in June 1983. *Pemanca* is a government appointed position for a native Chief of a District which is higher in status than a *Penghulu* (native Chief of an area), but below that of a *Temenggong* (Paramount native Chief).

company. A group of Kenyah journeyed to Bintulu to meet the General Manager of the company. The latter told the delegation that he could not make any decisions and had to refer it to his office in Singapore. He was given a letter signed by three headmen and a representative of the Baram Kenyah declaring that the burial ground belonged to them (*Borneo Bulletin*, August 10, 1985).

The gravesite (which is one day's journey by boat and foot from Belaga bazaar) is the ancestral burial ground of the Kenyah Lepo' Tau, Kenyah Badang and Kenyah Sambop. According to Kenyah oral history, this graveyard is said to be over 400 years old. Today the descendents of the deceased Kenyah Lepo' Tau are found in Long Moh in the Baram and Long Nawang in the Apo Kayan in Indonesia. The Kenyah Badang and the Kenyah Sambop are found in Long Geng in the Linau river and Belaga river (tributaries of the Rejang) respectively. Below is an account of the graveyard problem related to me by some of the Kenyah Badang village[11] elders during my visit in October 1985:

> 'This happened in 1982. The Sambop people had seen the bulldozers while on the way to their farms and told our relatives in Belaga about it. So we went to see and we found some of the *belian kelireng biok* (big ironwood burial posts) still standing, some others damaged. So we went to see the manager of the company. Six Kenyah representatives went to see him. The manager said, "I cannot make a decision now because all of you own graveyards. The graveyard is owned by Kenyah in the Belaga and Baram". He also said, "where's the proof? Where's the letter from D.O. (District Officer) that you own the graveyard?" The manager said to us "*memang saya bayar,*

---

11.   The lands surrounding this village has been converted to the Danum Permanent Forest which has been gazetted by the Ministry of Forestry. The Danum Permanent Forest covers 180, 820 hectares of land (Forest Department 1984:7). According to the *tua kampung* sometime in early 1985, a man came to the longhouse and delivered him a letter and a map. The map showed the location of the Danum Protected Forest. Eighteen longhouse communities will be affected by this conversion. This means that natives are now forbidden to exercise customary land tenure in this area. They may collect forest produce, hunt and fish in this area for their own needs *provided* they are granted permission by the Forest Conservator (see Chapter Six). The designation of the Danum Protected Forest is in preparation for the area to be logged. When I asked him whether he understood the contents of the letter and the map, he said he did not know. He showed them to me as he had wanted me to explain the contents to him. The 18 longhouses affected are Uma Penan Geng, Long Luar; Uma Penan Geng, Long Tanggau; Uma Penan Apo, Long Malim; Uma Penan Tanyit; Uma Penan, Long Kajang; Uma Penan Lerong, Lusong Laku; Uma Penan Busang, Long Lidam; Uma Badang, Long Busang; Uma Kulit, Long Jawe; Long Geng; Long Wat; Penan Geng; Uma Nyaving, Long Linau; Uma Bawang, Long Murum; Uma Belor, Long Sah 'A'; Uma Lahanan, Long Panggai; Uma Kelap, Long Sah 'B'; and Uma Penan Talun, Long Belangan.

tapi saya mahu bukti itu benar benar pulong" (of course I will pay, but I want proof that it is really your graveyard). The D.O. also promised to look into the matter. Five times we went to see the manager. We also went to see the State Assemblyman. He said, "you can approach the manager". Then Kehing (a pseudonym) approached the manager. The manager said, "I want proof and a letter from the D.O.". We said to him, "we have approached you many times and you have not properly settled our demand for compensation, so I will not deal with you, I will write to the newspapers". We want compensation because of our (*adet*) *adat*. Our traditional belief is that if our graveyards are disturbed, all *parib* (disharmony or harm or bad luck) will befall all of us and our future generations. We are demanding $125,000 but the company tells us it is willing to pay $30,000. We also asked for one pig (100 *kati*), one *tawak* (an embossed gong), one *baeng sek* (a ritual *parang* — *parang ilang*), two *lukat kesala*[12], one *lampang pagang*[13] and one chicken. We asked for all these because four communities are involved. We are not selling our graveyard. We want to settle the problem by appropriate means — the *tawak* is required so that nothing ill will befall us according to Kenyah *adat*. Until this day, we have not received compensation'.

Other communities have also complained of the loss and destruction of illipe nut trees by loggers. Again requests for compensation have been ignored. One community in the Balui told me that they had lost over 20 *engkabang* trees when loggers bulldozed a road through the forest. They were collecting illipe nuts once every two years before the *kompeni* came. According to them they were able to get M$130 for every *pikul* of illipe nuts. One family said they could harvest four to five *pikul* everytime it fruits. In the Ulu Belaga, longhouse communities have complained that ever since the loggers came, life has not been the same. Graveyards have been destroyed. Likewise *temuda*, fruit trees and farm lands and hunting dogs have been killed by landrovers running over them. Hunting dogs are very important to the longhouse people in their search for wildgame.

Recounting their experiences a Kenyah told me: "We were never informed that the timber companies were operating on our land. We only knew when we saw the big tractor coming. Since the timber companies came, animals and fish are becoming very rare. Fish are also dying by the river bank. People find it harder to fish and hunt. *Rotan* is now difficult to find. Some of our new forest lands were

---

12. *Lukat kesala* is a very ancient bead, in the old feudal days, the value of one was equivalent to a slave.

13. *Lampang pagang* is another type of ancient beads.

also destroyed. We have asked for communal forest since 1971. We
have also applied for *belian* licence. They told us they cannot give it
to us".

In many of the cases of destroyed farmlands, fruit trees and hunting
dogs, compensation paid was arbitrary and grossly inadequate. Below
are some instances which were related to me by the natives of Ulu Balui
and Ulu Belaga:

> *Long Bulan longhouse*: 'They didn't come to tell us, but when our
> people went to search for fish and wild boar in the Penuan then
> they met the surveyors. This happened in 1982 I think. They
> thought it was *penyamun* (people who kill and kidnap) so they
> returned to the longhouse and informed the people and we sent
> two boats to investigate. They were surprised to find that they
> were surveyors. But nobody told them what they were doing or
> why they were there. One month later the people notice the
> Penuan was silted. So they went up the Penuan again in four
> boats to see what was happening. They saw a timber camp.
> They saw them bulldozing and cutting timber. They asked the
> manager for compensation because all the fish and wild boar in
> the river had disappeared and they fell our *engkabang* trees. But
> the manager refused. He told us to go and see his *towkay* (boss)
> first.
>
> We just came back. We went to see the manager of the camp
> many times but he refused to entertain us. Now the river has
> very little fish. Wild boars have run away, our *rotan* killed and
> our illipe nut trees destroyed. We wanted to report the felling
> of the illipe nut trees to the Forest Department but the manager
> said, "if so, I won't pay you but I will pay the Forest
> Department". Our longhouse people consulted the Forest
> Department in Kapit — and the Forest Department said they
> were not aware of the problem. This took place in 1984. We
> brought this up with Dato Tajang Laing[14] and asked him
> whether it was his '*kompeni*' which was responsible. He said "no"
> and told us to write an official letter of complaint addressed to
> him. Two of our longhouse representatives even went to see
> Dato Tajang Laing and the Forestry Department in Kuching.
> But no action has been taken so far. Even the District Officer
> came to our longhouse to tell us that we cannot stop the
> '*kompeni*' from coming because the land now belongs to the
> '*kompeni*'. They also came to survey another area further up the
> Bulan river. They are restricting us from shifting
> cultivation. In 1984, the Forest Department told us we
> cannot chop down new forest anymore, they showed us on

---

14. Dato Tajang Laing is the State Assemblyman for Ulu Belaga. He is a Kayan
from *Long Linau*, a longhouse some two hours by longboat from Bakun. He resigned
from PBB in May 1986 to return to his former party SNAP.

the map which area we are not suppose to fell. They just brought a map to show us but there was no letter or map given to us'.

Uma Sambop longhouse: 'In 1983, they bulldozed our graveyard to build a road. They did not even ask permission. Some of our *kampong* people went hunting and found it destroyed. Our people went to see the manager of Lau Timber and told him "your workers have destroyed our graveyard". The manager said there is no evidence that it is your graveyard. But the *belian* (ironwood) posts were still there. The manager did not compensate us'.

'In 1980 my farm was bulldozed for a road. This happened just before *nugan* (sowing). Seven peoples' farm were involved. Ten chains of my land were destroyed. The rest had 16, nine and seven chains destroyed. We asked the company — Belaga Sawmill Company for compensation. They paid us a total of $200 to be shared among the seven families involved. Even during *nugan*, padi was destroyed in one farm because they drove the tractor across the farm to get the logs. When the owner asked for *ganti rugi* (compensation) for the padi destroyed (i.e. one *parang*, one pig weighing 50 *kati* and some money)[15], the manager laughed at him. They never paid him any money until now'.

'This company Lau Timber Contractor first arrived at Sambop in September 1982. They set up camp in Kapelutan. They did not contact our people. Maybe they asked *tuai rumah* himself, but he did not call for a meeting of the longhouse. We only knew that the bulldozer bulldozed my father-in-law's *temuda* at the end of 1982. Approximately ten acres of *temuda* which had fruit trees — rambutans, *buah pulasan*[16], sago and *mata kuching*[17] were destroyed. He was paid $3,000 as compensation'.

'After this they destroyed my *temuda*. About 100 chains[18] of our *temuda* land were affected when they started to build the road just above the timber camp. They said that this was

---

15. According to Kenyah *adat* you have to pay a ritual 'fine' for breaking the ritual prohibition (*pemali*) in the farm during planting time. This is required so that harmony and balance can be restored between people and their environment.

16. *Buah pulasan* (Nephelium mutabile) is a fruit that resembles the rambutan though not as hairy.

17. *Mata kuching* (Erioglossum edule), literally 'cat's eyes', are the fruits of the *mertajam* tree. The fruit has a semi-transparent pulp which encloses small round seeds which resembles 'cat's eyes'. These small fruits are produced in big bunches.

18. 1 chain = 66 feet.

not *temuda* land as the trees were old. They have not paid me anything to this day'.

'Lau Timber also destroyed my *temuda*. The bulldozer paved a road through my land. They destroyed (18 chains) of my *temuda*. Three *mata kuching* trees, five *pohon rotan* and ten durian saplings were killed. They paid me $900'.

'Opposite the river about ten acres of my neighbour's *temuda* was also affected. He was given $4,000. He had coffee, rubber and fruit trees growing. Then next to this was my cousin Gau's (pseudonym) land. He had six acres of *temuda* which was destroyed by the bulldozer because they had put up camps on the land. They paid him $3,000'.

Long Bungan longhouse: 'Kastima Timber Sdn Bhd[19] built a bridge below our kampung Rumah Long Bungan. The bridge is still there. It is very dangerous. The site of the bridge is near the rapids so when it was built across the river, it became like a waterfall. Our people cannot pass through the bridge with their boats. Lakek Lugan who was 40 years old capsized in his boat and drowned. His family was paid $1,500 as compensation. The company has also destroyed the *temuda* of our kampung people'.

Ulu Belaga: The 1983 Timber Dispute

In 1983, a timber company started operations in the Ulu Belaga area. The natives were soon complaining about silting of their river. Then the company erected a long bridge across the river, half a mile upstream from the longhouse. The bridge hindered the passage of the natives' boats on the river. The natives' requests for compensation (of $6,000 per month) were rejected by the company. This led to a dispute between the timber company and the natives. The police intervened and arrested eleven natives, including three *tuai rumah* (headmen) and four teachers. According to a newspaper report, the Sarawak Commissioner of Police said the natives destroyed the bridge when their demands were not met, and that the eleven were arrested on charges of 'mischief, illegal assembly and extortion' (*Sarawak Tribune*, November 22, 1953). Actually the bridge was not destroyed and was still standing in October 1985. Three of the four teachers arrested subsequently lost their jobs. Below is an

19. Kastima Lumber is the logging contractor for Baltim Timber the licensee company. Some of the shareholders are Wan Habib Syed Mohamed, PBB State Assemblyman for Balingian; Wan Madzihi Mohdzar, PBB Central Committee member and Mohd. Yahya Lampong, vice President of USNO in Sabah (Sarawak Study Group 1986:6). USNO is a member of the *Barisan Nasional* the ruling coalition government. Because of intra-party squabbling, Wan Habib Syed Mohamed left PBB in May 1986 to form a new party, United Sarawak Natives Association (USNA), which was still awaiting registration in July 1986.

account of the events concerning the bridge dispute as narrated to me by some of the natives[20]:

'The water became muddy in the river two or three months after Lau Timber started operating in our area. It was during the dry season (June, July and August) of 1983, and the tractor could move across the river. As a result the river became oily and muddy. We asked for compensation, the company refused. Many people in the longhouse got diarrhoea after using the water from the river. They had to go to Bintulu to get medical treatment. When the dry season was over, they stopped pulling logs across the river with the tractor. They put up the bridge across the river (which was about 100-150 yards wide) about half a mile upstream from our longhouse. Then we asked for compensation because the bridge was not built in a proper manner. Because of this, our boats could not go up and down the river. The camp manager did not care. He just ignored our pleas. When the bridge was completed, we kept on asking for compensation. We had asked for $6,000 every month, which would be divided among all the longhouses in Belaga namely, Kenyah Long Bungan, Kajang Uma Seping, Penan Uma Pawa', Penan Long Urun (who are semi nomadic) and Penan Long Kupang, we informed the manager[21]. This was in October 1983. All the longhouses grouped together and about 100 people went to Lau Timber camp to ask for compensation regarding the bridge. We went peacefully, led by the *tua kampong* (village headman) but there were two policemen who came and stopped us when the camp manager heard about it. We went back home.

On 17 November 1983 evening, some policemen came to our longhouse and told the six headmen to go to the timber camp for a meeting the next morning. On 18 November morning, all the people of the longhouse went by boat to the camp one mile from the longhouse. We arrived at 8 a.m. The police Superintendent Mr Heathcliff (pseudonym) arrived at 11 a.m. by chopper. Then he showed us the anonymous letter with the names of the six *tuai rumah* typed on the letter but with

20. This narration was given by a number of natives who were either present or heard accounts of the various incidents from others who participated in them.

21. Earlier in the year the six headmen from Long Bungan, Uma Sambop, Uma Seping, Uma Pawa', Long Urun and Long Kupang in Ulu Belaga held a meeting in Uma Pawa' to discuss the formation of a company 'Syarikat Batu Belalang'. Their aim was to approach all the logging companies operating in their area for a monthly contribution based on the volume of timber extracted. The money given would be used by the company for the welfare of the people in the six longhouses, for example, subsidizing their children's education, medical care in the towns, buying boat engines and generators (Sarawak Study Group 1986:11).

no signatures or thumbprints of the headmen and no name of
the sender of the letter. He said: "You people are wrong
because with this letter you are threatening the company and
you have no right to claim any compensation for the bridge".
But the longhouse people said: "*Tolong lah*, (please) *Tuan*[22] police
help us to settle the matter of compensation with the company".
He sounded threatening and was very *kasar* (crude), he was
looking very fierce too, he said: "You people are so mercenary
— You keep asking for money all the time. You think it is easy
to get money, money falls from the sky, does it?" Only the *tua
kampong* were allowed to sit in the camp office where the
meeting was held. Every time a *tua kampong* tried to explain the
matter to him, he brushed it aside, interrupting them when
they tried to speak and told them to keep quiet. He held his
hand out and said: "Don't speak".

About 3 p.m., the *anak biak* (longhouse people) waiting
downstairs asked for food. "Now we are hungry, go and get
food". The manager then said, "I cannot, there are hundreds of
you here". But they said: "We are hungry already". The
manager said: "I did not call all of you to come here". Then the
longhouse people said: "It is because you have been responsible
for this matter that we are hungry now while waiting for the
discussion to be settled". Then the police inspector said, "You
people cannot ask for food but you still insist". Then they
stopped asking.

Those upstairs (the *tua kampong* and also some *anak biak*) were
still listening to the manager and the *Tuan* police Heathcliff and
insisting on their right to compensation. Then Heathcliff said,
"Cannot" — so the people got very angry and said: "The police
are biased for the company" and they walked towards the
bridge. Some took the axe and chainsaw from the camp and
started cutting a few planks off the bridge. Heathcliff went
away to the chopper. A man with the camera wanted to take
photos and one *anak biak* grabbed his camera. He stopped. He
went into the chopper and took photos from the chopper. The
police watched from the camp. They did not try to stop the
people at all. Some of us told the people not to cut the bridge,
so they stopped. About 20 minutes later, they wanted to burn
the bridge. They took all the discarded tyres — carried it to the
bridge intending to burn it. Then the police went down and
told them: "*Jangan*" (don't). They did not listen to the police.
Some of the policemen said: "If you don't stop, we will shoot".
Then some *anak biak* said: "*Tuan polis boleh tembak kami, biar kami
mati habis*" (*Tuan* police can shoot us, never mind if we are all
killed). They stood in front of the police, stuck out their chests,
some took off their shirts. Some of us pleaded with the

22. *Tuan* is a respectful term of address meaning 'Sir'.

people: "*Ayen ti lan*" (please don't do it anymore, in Kenyah). Then they stopped. We went back to the camp and back to the longhouse. Before we went back to the longhouse, a police constable told the headmen to go to the camp the next day.

So, next morning, 19 November, all the people from the various longhouses followed the *tua kampong* to the camp. About 9 a.m., a big Nuri landed in the timber camp with 80 fieldforce parapolice. Heathcliff came by landrover on the same day at night. The police asked a few of the people to go to the camp to discuss the problem again. When they arrived, they were taken into a room to be questioned by Heathcliff and another fieldforce officer. Heathcliff threatened to detain them. They asked him: "What have we done? We are not against the Government, we are not killing people. We are not using any weapon, what we do is we are fighting for our right, we are claiming compensation for our people". Then Heathcliff said: "You have no right to compensation for this bridge". Then suddenly the manager spoke out, he said: "There are so many rapids below your house and above your house. Why don't you people claim compensation for that? Why claim for this bridge?" Then the natives replied to him: "You are mad, General Manager, how can you expect us to claim from nature? The natural rapids belong to God. If you can claim, please claim it for us from God". Then he kept quiet. Heathcliff motioned to him to keep quiet. Later, the people were interviewed more by other police officers, and then they were allowed to go home.

The next day, 20 November, some of the natives were asked by the police to the camp again. They met Heathcliff again, the General Manager, and asked for compensation again, but still they were refused. About noon, they put all 13 natives in a room. At about two p.m. they were brought to Belaga by landrover. They asked the police constables why they were going to Belaga. The police told the natives they were already under arrest. The natives said: "How can we go to Belaga, when we have nothing with us, not even a shirt". While they were detained in the room, they told our longhouse people through the window that they were now under arrest by the police and were going to Belaga at two o'clock: "Please go and tell our families and get our *baju* (clothes) and some money". Before they left the camp, many people arrived from the longhouse. Some brought all their belongings, and wanted to follow them, some of them were crying already because they thought the police would harm those arrested. The police then asked those arrested to go to the landrover. Then all the people held onto them tightly. They said: "Don't go, let us fight the police here". Some of them said: "Police, what are you going to do with our people?". All the fieldforce were on alert, they surrounded us, pointing their weapons at us. Some of the

Above: The bridge at Ulu Belaga which was the subject of dispute between natives and the timber company. The company built the bridge to transport logs (seen at left of photo) to the other side of the river. The logging operations also caused extensive silting, evident in this photo.

Below: A longer view of the bridge. Natives complained the bridge hindered the passage of their boats on the river to their farms.

police fieldforce told the longhouse people not to worry and to
calm down. Some mothers who were crying bitterly, climbed on
the landrover and got hold of their sons. All the people were
shouting in anger: "*Apa kamu polis ini, datang bunuh kami kah atau
datang jaga rakyat?*" (What are you police, are you come to kill us
or are you come to protect the people?). Then the landrover
left.

Some of those arrested later told us what happened after
that. They arrived in Belaga around 6 p.m. There were already
about 20-30 fieldforce personnel from Kapit there. They were
closely guarded throughout the night. There was a public
community hall which was poorly maintained and had rubbish
littered all over the place. Heathcliff said: "You people stay
here". Then the people said: "*Tuan* polis, please don't put us
here, please look for a better place for us, the room is full of
rubbish and it smells". Then he said: "You just stay here, I can
put you anywhere". They ate their food in the dirty room.
After that, they were taken to the government rest-house
ground floor and were locked up for one day and one night.
They were asked to go to the police station to give a statement
at 2 a.m. in the morning. They were very rudely treated and
asked to give confessions.

The next day, 21 November, around 8 a.m., the Belaga
Councillor, Bilong Bit (pseudonym) came and bailed the people
out for $2,000 each for all 13 of them. They were released at
about 10 a.m. They were asked to gather at the Belaga
conference room in the District office, where the Magistrate and
some police were present. They were told to come back to the
conference room on a certain date for a court case against
them.

Subsequently, the natives who had been arrested had to go
before the Magistrate for a 'summons'. Then in January 1984,
they went back to the Belaga court again for the trial. But the
case was postponed. Then they went again another two times.
At the last hearing, they were told the case against them had
been dropped. When the bridge incident was reported in the
newspapers, three teachers received letters from the Education
Department which said that they had been dismissed from the
teaching service'.

From the above account, it would appear that there had been little
understanding or sympathy for the problems of the natives caused by
logging activities and the erection of the bridge. The official attitude
was apparently to 'control' the feelings and actions of the natives, rather
than to assess the damage caused by the logging company in
constructing the bridge in a manner which prevented the natives from
having access to their river. The bridge is still standing across the river
and natives find it very dangerous to bring their boats under the bridge

because of the swift currents. They have not been paid any compensation either for the hardship and risks imposed on them as a result of the bridge being built across the river.

Ulu Belaga: Unsuccessful Requests for Communal Forests

Sympathy has also been lacking towards natives in their applications for Communal Forests. The longhouse communities in the Belaga District have submitted more than 30 applications to give 'communal forest' status to land in the vicinity of their longhouses. The majority of the longhouses concerned have applied more than twice. Except for Rumah Lassah, a Kejaman longhouse, none of the others have had their applications approved. At a meeting in August 1982, the Chief Police Officer of the Seventh Division DSP Clive Howell was reported to have 'stressed that all applications for Communal Forests *should not* be investigated. Instead, these applications should be *automatically* turned down and the local population informed of this promptly so that they would not hold up logging operations in those areas'. This position was again reaffirmed by the Resident in a meeting in 1983 'in which he was reported to have said that *no application for Communal Forests in the Seventh Division should be considered or entertained'* (Sarawak Study Group 1986:13, 15).

This clearly reflects a negative stance towards the natives in their application for Communal Forests (a right upheld in the Sarawak Forest Ordinance). Yet the same forests are often given over to timber companies, as shown in the following example cited from the study by the Sarawak Study Group.

Rumah Sing (Uma Seping) first applied for Communal Forests land in the mid 1970s. This was turned down on the grounds that their longhouse population was too small to be granted a Communal Forest. They applied again, this time jointly with Uma Pawa', Long Urum and Long Kupang. These applications were turned down. Another attempt was made for a smaller area in a different region. This was also rejected. In 1984 Uma Seping again applied for a much smaller area just behind their longhouse. Forestry officials came and surveyed the area. Months passed but there was no reply from the Forest Department. Then the logging company 'Lagi Sdn Bhd' moved into the area. The longhouse residents appealed to the loggers to delay their logging operations. They agreed at first, but after several days, the company returned and started chopping the forests. The angry longhouse residents confronted the loggers, took away some chainsaws and told the latter to leave. The next day, the Bintulu police arrived and picked six natives for questioning concerning the theft of the chainsaws. They were released after one night and had to pay their own way back all the way from Bintulu (on the coast) in the Fourth Division to their longhouse. The area has since been logged (Sarawak Study Group 1986:14).

Ecological Damage Caused by Logging:
Impact on Native Communities

Apart from the impingement of native lands by non-natives and native entreprenuers alike, the ecological effects of timber activities have also inflicted great damage on native communities. Logging companies have been known to build roads on swidden farms, destroying the crops grown. The havoc wreaked by timber operators on native lands was highlighted in a letter to the news weekly the *Borneo Bulletin* on April 4, 1981: 'In recent years as many new camps have appeared in their jungle, they have begun to realise the devastating impact of timber operations on their territory .... They (timber operators) have come with their bulldozers, destroying the forest. In so doing, they have chased the animals away and have contributed to the spoiling of farmland. Those once beautiful rivers and streams with clear water have been blocked by broken logs and other debris. The waters have turned muddy and polluted, the fish have become scarce. The longhouse people find they are no longer free to cut trees if they do they will be prosecuted for illegal felling. As long as these *ulu* people still rely on the forest, and its rivers and streams, for their source of food, they will continue to regard the timber operators as interfering with their livelihood'.

In another case, logging operations in the sungai Silas in Bintulu had broken and blocked the water-pipe systems supplying water to longhouses in the area. In their letter to the press, the affected natives reported that the timber company refused to repair or rebuild the damaged water supply which is government property. This has inflicted great hardship on the people, whose only source of drinking water had been cut off when logging damaged the water catchment area. The affected villagers had written: 'How can we respect the law if the law does not seem to respect and protect us?' (*Ibid* October 17, 1981).

The 1981 Baram District Officer in his Annual Report had this to say:

'The logging operators bring along tons of their plants and equipment for land and riverine usage such as giant bulldozers, trucks, locomotive engines, electric generators, small vehicles,· fuel tanks, tugboats, barge and so on. With these equipment they can work out their concession areas by building crisscross roads and railways bulldozing hills, mountains and plains with great ease but devastating effect. Sometimes it has to cross over the local peoples, customary land, padi farms, gardens, cemeteries, pipelines and catchment area and other private properties.

Extraction of timbers in fact has caused extensive and irreparable damage to the natural land surface and vegetation. It has frightened and threatened the life and habitation of wild,

rare and precious birds and animals depriving the local people
of their hunting grounds. In fact, reports have been received
from local cave owners that the production of birdnests has
been declining since the start of intensive timber extraction in
the Baram. Complaints of water pollution by timber camps and
damage to the jetties by tugboats, barges and floating logs have
often been received from the longhouse people. Genuine claims
for land compensation were sometimes not promptly entertained
simply on the grounds that the lands were not held under title.
In the past two years the Baram District has experienced
successive severe flooding causing extensive damage to crops
and livestock, cutting communications for weeks and causing
hardship to people from all walks of life. To this, there is a
theory that the dwindling vegetation caused by logging
operators in the course of extracting timber has resulted in the
deprivation of elements which could have readily absorbed and
retained large quantities of rain water. One huge tree is able to
retain one hundred gallons of water let alone the thousand acres
of forested land. The existence of several miles of timber roads
in the interior also facilitate the flow of rain water into the
main rivers. Soil erosion is not ruled out' (Baram District
1981:19-20).

There is abundant evidence that disturbances to the tropical forest
ecosystem has profound epidemiological and health consequences.
According to a UNESCO Report, clearance of forests encourages
malaria carrying mosquitoes which normally live in the forest canopy
to come down and feed upon human beings and deforestation along
streams gives ideal conditions for breeding (UNESCO/UNEP/FAO
1978:381, 387-8). Knudsen has shown that logging or deforestation
increases the incidence of jungle-transmitted haemorrhagic dengue fever
among the human population. According to him, this is due to the
fact that the natural vectors of the disease are forest canopy dwellers
like the macaques, leaf monkeys and mosquitoes. Complete
deforestation or forest exploitation disturbs the habitat, resulting in
either the vector moving towards populated areas or increasing the
possibility of human (loggers, settlers) contact with the disease-vectors
or both (A.B. Knudsen 1977:41-7). Ruts made by heavy machinery
and tractors in the forest also allow water to collect there. These
make ideal breeding sites for many anopheline vectors of malaria
(UNESCO/UNEP/FAO 1978:397). In a local newspaper report the
Director of the Antimalarial Programme Dr Mehar Singh Gill was
quoted as saying that: 'The anopheles mosquito is normally reproduced
at a high rate in the presence of sunlight and the clearing of these thick
jungles is believed to be one of the factors leading to the increase of
(Malaria) cases' (*Sunday Mail*, October 17, 1982). Ten days following
this news report, the Health Minister stated that the number of malaria
cases in Sarawak has increased over the past year. Most of these

victims were loggers (*New Straits Times*, October 27, 1982). In May 1985, the Medical Officer of the Third Division, reported 20 cases of malaria, nine of which were attributed to loggers in the Sibu District (*Sarawak Tribune*, May 9, 1985).

Logging operations can thus bring about an increase in malaria and pose a health threat to the rural communities. Damage by logging operations has been increasingly felt by natives in the Baram as timber companies continue to expand their activities. In September 1982, six longhouses in the Upper Baram sent letters to the Government to investigate the problems caused by timber companies. In the letter, they stated that: 'Our method of shifting cultivation has often been blamed for the water pollution, soil erosion and flooding problems of the Baram area — but the loggers seem to us farmers to be responsible for most of the damage', and added that 'logging is causing the quality of the land to deteriorate'. They also reminded the authorities that they had suffered a great deal from the effects of floods and droughts (*The Borneo Bulletin*, September 11, 1982). In April 1985 representatives of the Sarawak Orang Ulu Association made a call to the Government to check river pollution caused by logging operations which has reached serious levels in the Belaga, Baram, Apoh, Tutoh and Trusan areas (*Ibid* April 19, 1985). Villagers living in the Trusan, Tutoh and Apoh rivers have frequently found dead fish floating in the water (*Ibid* March 30, 1985).

The increase in sawmilling activities, one of the by-products of the timber industry is also causing widespread pollution to the rivers. The Department of Environment and Technology has reported that great quantities of sawdust and other wastes were being dumped into the Rejang river (*Ibid* March 30, 1985). According to two researchers, floating logs downstream gives rise to the leaching (dissolving) of water soluble chemical compounds from them. Other preservatives, wastes and sawdust disposed into the streams and rivers also contaminate the river. Many of these wastes contain toxic chemicals which are harmful to human beings and aquatic organisms. As logging exploitation accelerates and sawmills sprout up, sawmill toilets along the river banks discharge an added pollutant into the rivers (Hii and Tay 1980:239). This has a significant impact on health since the communities in these areas are largely dependent on the river for their drinking and domestic needs. One such case occurred in Long Pilah in the Baram. The timber camp built a hanging toilet at the edge of the steep river bank. This toilet is situated some 200 yards on the river *above* the longhouse which relies on the river for its drinking and washing needs. Appeals by the natives to the timber company to remove the toilet several times on the grounds of health have been ignored (*Borneo Bulletin*, April 16, 1983). In recent years natives have complained that the Baram river has become too dirty for drinking and bathing (*Ibid* August 13, 1983). Besides polluting the water system, the timber industry also pollutes the air, since rural sawmills practise open air burning of other wood wastes as well. This creates further air pollution and poses a danger to populated areas (Hii and Tay 1980:241).

As deforestation accelerates and spreads to the higher hills, the threat of severe floods, water pollution, drought[23], and timber shortage worsens. In the Baram, logging has ascended the hills and reached the headwaters of the river itself. This area of Sarawak is the home of swidden farmers, where hills are extremely steep and soils poor. The people here have seen how disastrous logging has been to the natives in the downriver areas and wish to avoid becoming victims suffering the same fate. In another appeal to the authorities eight longhouses comprising a total of 4,000 residents sent appeal letters to the authorities to 'keep the forests in our upper Baram from being taken and destroyed by timber companies'. In their letter these natives pleaded that: 'They were subsistence farmers whose lives depend entirely on the forested land and waterways. If these are allowed to be destroyed, our very lives will be threatened. It would also show that the authorities have no interest in us, and we would consider them responsible for any harm to our surroundings . . . We hope our leaders will, in good conscience, consider our situation and decide in the interests of the majority rather than an already privileged few' (*Ibid* August 28, 1982).

In recent years, floods have become an increasing occurrence in the Baram. In the two years between 1979 and 1980 a SAM report stated that four to six floods had occurred. These floods had all occurred before the harvest and deprived many communities of their food supply. In January 1981, floods hit the Fourth Division including the Baram inundating areas as far as Long Lama in the Middle Baram. Damage in terms of rice fields, crops and livestock amounted to over $12 million. In his report, the Chief Co-ordinator for evacuation said that 'the wounds to farms would take years to heal'. Speaking of long term measures he mentioned that: 'Vast areas within the State, particularly at the respective river water-head regions, should be preserved and kept untampered in its natural state. Denudation of natural vegetations either through forest harvesting process or for crop cultivations, particularly in the interior hilly regions and along

---

23. Droughts have appeared to be a frequent occurence in Borneo. In April 1983, outbreaks of cholera appeared in several areas in Sabah. In Sarawak's Fourth Division thousands of fish and prawns had died when the 2,000 acre and 15 feet deep lake, Logan Bunut in the Upper Tinjar 'dried up' (*Borneo Bulletin*, April 2, 1983).

· Two weeks later a press report stated that the three month long drought had reduced the Baram river to a jungle stream. As a result villages in the Upper Baram were cut off from food supplies from Marudi. In Long Akah, about a day's boat ride from Long Lama in the Middle Baram, the people were living on tapioca. A mile upriver in Long San, children were eating two meals a day because rice supplies were running low. Even the timber industry was hit as the logs could not be towed downstream (*Borneo Bulletin*, April 16, 1983).

the riverine belts, needs to be discreetly regulated' (Wong Leong Do 1981:12-6).

Flooding has led to increasing and frequent food shortages in the Baram. Not only are farms destroyed, seeds for the next planting season are not available. Natives are forced to look for employment elsewhere at construction sites or in logging camps as paid labourers. Thus what was not taken from them by the law, development policies destroyed by their execution.

CHAPTER EIGHT

Logging and Forest Depletion in Sarawak

There is increasing international realisation and concern that the world's tropical forests are being destroyed at an unprecedentedly rapid rate. This is bringing about tremendous adverse ecological effects, such as loss of topsoil, reduced trapping of water through the soil, silting and pollution of rivers and long-term climatic changes.

There are varying estimates of the rate of current tropical forest destruction. In her comprehensive study of the world's rainforest, Catherine Caufield summarises these estimates: i) A United Nations study in 1976 found that of the 2.4 billion acres of rainforest left in the world, 14 million are completely and permanently destroyed each year. ii) In 1980 the U.S. National Academy of Sciences announced a worse figure — 50 million acres destroyed or seriously degraded each year. iii) An FAO study in 1980 says at present rates almost one fifth of the world's remaining tropical forests will be completely destroyed or seriously degraded by the end of the century. The study says at current rates, Indonesia would lose ten per cent of its remaining forest in 1981 by the year 2000; Philippines will lose 20 per cent; Malaysia 24 per cent and Thailand 60 per cent. In Africa, Nigeria and Ivory Coast will be completely deforested by 2000, Guinea will lose a third, Madagascar 30 per cent and Ghana 26 per cent of their remaining forests. In Latin America, Costa Rica will lost 80 per cent; Honduras, Nicaragua and Ecuador more than half; and Guatemala, Colombia and Mexico one third their remaining forests (Caufield 1984:37-38).

Who Is To Blame for Forest Destruction?

For many years, the blame for such forest destruction has been placed squarely on swidden agriculturalists. This slash-and-burn practice has been said to be wasteful, causing the loss of forest, and soil erosion. Very little was said of the large-scale logging carried out by modern commercial companies. However, in recent years, it has been increasingly realised that whilst swidden agriculture has contributed to deforestation, the role of the timber industry has also been major, and possibly much greater. Caufield quotes FAO data to show that in Indonesia peasant agriculture affects only 500,000 acres of rainforest a year, one quarter of the area annually affected by logging. In Peninsular Malaysia, where there is very little swidden agriculture, half the rainforests have been logged since 1960. In the Ivory Coast, one million acres are cut by loggers annually, and there will be no timber left by 1985. The Congo has 60 per cent of Africa's rainforests; its government has scheduled 68 per cent of its rainforest to be logged (*Idem* 1984:41). From these statistics, it is clear that the timber industry, with its modern technology, has a rapacious capacity to destroy the forest in very few years, which swidden agriculturalists could not do in generations.

Ironically, most of the logs from the rainforests are not used by the local people but are exported to the rich countries:

> 'Only 20 per cent of the world's industrial wood comes from rainforests, but more than half of that is exported to the richest nations. Thus, virtually all the hardwood logs and more than half the hardwood sawn timber in world trade comes from the rainforests. In 1979, for example, 58 per cent of the world production of hardwood logs and 75 per cent of all log exports came from Malaysia and Indonesia alone. The developed countries, which produce 80 per cent of the world's industrial wood, keep almost all of it and import much of the rest of the world's harvest as well. Japan alone takes more than half and Europe more than one quarter of all wood exports. The rainforest countries of Asia and the Pacific export 70 per cent of their industrial wood, half to Japan and most of the rest to countries (mainly Korea, Singapore, and Taiwan) that process the logs and immediately re-export them to North America, Africa, and the Middle East. West Africa exports just over half of its harvest, largely to the EEC; Latin America exports less than 10 per cent of its harvest, mostly to North America and the EEC' (*Idem* 1984:150-51).

Forest Depletion in Malaysia

Let us look more closely at Malaysia, the world's biggest exporter of tropical hardwood. As stated earlier, half of Peninsular Malaysia's rainforests have been logged since 1960. In 1977, the then Deputy Prime Minister (and presently Prime Minister), Dato Seri Dr. Mahathir Mohamed, warned that uncontrolled forest exploitation would deplete the nation's timber resources in 12 years, with serious implications on the economy: 'By 1990, the rate of timber production would not be sufficient to meet local demand, the timber export industry would collapse and most timber factories will have to be closed. Then we will be forced to import timber'. He said only 540,000 acres of forest reserves had been reafforested in the past 20 years (1957-76) compared with the *average of 680,000 acres logged annually* (*New Straits Times*, August 30, 1977) In other words, 13.6 million acres of forests ·had been logged in the 20 years to 1976. Most of it had been logged in the later years of the two decades, as Dr. Mahathir revealed that 5.5 million acres of forest were cleared in the last six years (1971-1976) and 1.015 million acres were logged in 1976 itself. Dr. Mahathir called for a national forestry policy, mentioning that if forest clearing was reduced from the average rate of *680,000 acres a year* to *140,000 acres a year*, the life of the forests could be extended by 35 years.

At the time of Dr. Mahathir's warning, the forest situation in Peninsular Malaysia had already reached critical proportions. Although he spoke of 'the nation's timber resources' it is believed that the data he gave referred to Peninsular Malaysia. The speech he gave was before a meeting of the National Forestry Council, attended by all Chief Ministers and five Cabinet Ministers. In 1978, the Council approved a National Forestry Policy, whose objectives were: 'to conserve forest resources to meet ecological requirements for the protection of the environment, to sustain the yield of the productive forest known as the Permanent Forest Reserve, to reduce resource wastage through an efficient utilisation of timber in forest as well as processing mills; and to introduce into the market the under-utilised species' (Ministry of Primary Industries Malaysia 1986:68). However, this Policy covers only Peninsular Malaysia and *excludes the East Malaysian states of Sabah and Sarawak*. Under the Policy, the National Forestry Council agreed to gradually reduce the annual cutting rate in Peninsular Malaysia from about 400,000 hectares (990,000 acres) in 1979 to 220,000 hectares (554,000 acres) in 1983 and 149,000 hectares (360,000 acres) by 1986 and hereafter (Ministry of Primary Industries 1986:68). This reduction plan has been put into effect and in 1985 the area logged was estimated to be 177,000 hectares (440,000 acres) (Bank Negara 1986:142).

However, whilst logging has been cut down in Peninsular Malaysia, the reverse seems to have happened in Sabah and Sarawak, which does not come under the National Forestry Policy. Indeed, it would appear that logging has increased tremendously in the past decade in East Malaysia to compensate for the slowing down of logging in Peninsular Malaysia. Table 4 shows that log production for Malaysia as a whole rose from 17.8 million cu. metres in 1970 to 20.6 million cu. metres in 1972, 27.9 million cu. metres in 1980 to a peak of 32.8 million cu. metres in 1983 and 31.3 million cu. metres in 1985. Thus, the timber output for the country as a whole has been increasing in the past 15 years. However, timber output in Peninsular Malaysia dropped from 10.5 million cu. metres in 1980 (37 per cent of overall output) to 8.3 million cu. metres in 1980 (27 per cent of the total). The share of the East Malaysian states therefore rose from 63 per cent to 73 per cent of overall output. Looking at Sarawak, we find that log output increased tremendously from 4.4 million cu. metres in 1976 to 8.4 million cu. metres in 1980 and a record 12.2 million cu. metres in 1985. The Sarawak share of total log production jumped from 13 per cent in 1975 to 26 per cent in 1979 to 39 per cent in 1985. In Sabah, where data is available to the writer for only 1980-85, we also find output rising from 9.1 million cu. metres in 1980 to 10.8 million cu. metres in 1985. These figures indicate that whilst logging has indeed slowed down in Peninsular Malaysia (output fell by 20 per cent between 1980 to 1985), it has increased in Sabah (19 per cent rise in the same period) and especially in Sarawak (which experienced a tremendous 45 per cent jump in log output). For the country as a whole, log output also rose from 27.9 million cu. metres in 1980 to 31.3 million cu. metres in 1985, a 12 per cent increase. Thus, despite the 'National' Forestry Policy, the log output and thus the acreage of forest logged has been increasing in the past decade, and even in the past five years, especially in Sarawak.

Most of the log output in Malaysia is exported, either as sawlogs or sawn timber. Most of the timber in Sarawak and Sabah are exported as sawlogs, whilst most of Peninsular Malaysia's timber is processed first as sawn timber, and exported. In 1985, Malaysia produced 31.3 million cu. metres of logs and 5.5 million cu. metres of sawn timber.

Table 4: Production of Logs in Malaysia
('000 cu. metres)

Year	Total	Peninsular Malaysia	%	Sabah	%	Sarawak	%
1970	17,792					4,685	26
1971	18,230					3,911	21
1972	20,618					3,172	15
1973	24,064					3,251	14
1974	21,372					2,827	13
1975	19,164					2,511	13
1976	26,595					4,414	17
1977	27,573					4,880	18
1978	28,685					5,977	21
1979	28,762					7,571	26
1980	27,916	10,453	37	9,064	33	8,399	30
1981	30,655	10,226	33	11,732	38	8,697	28
1982	32,724	9,842	30	11,639	36	11,243	34
1983	32,794	10,238	31	11,991	37	10,565	32
1984	31,088	9,183	30	10,504	34	11,401	37
1985	31,300	8,300	27	10,800	34	12,200	39

Sources: (a) Ministry of Primary Industries, *Statistics on Commodities*, April 1986 (for all 1980-84 data).
(b) *Bank Negara Malaysia Annual Report 1985* (for 1985 data).
(c) *Annual Statistical Bulletin Sarawak, 1981, 1983* (for 1970-79 data on Sarawak).

Note: There is a slight discrepancy in Sarawak data published in Source (a) and Source (c). Thus, the Sarawak data in this Table and Table 5 differ for years 1980-83.

In the same year, 18.8 million cu. metres of sawlogs and 2.7 million cu. metres of sawn timber were exported (*Ibid* 1986:169).

The export of sawlogs thus comprised 60 per cent of log output. The volume of sawn timber exported was also equal to nine per cent of the weight of total log output. However since a lot of wood volume is lost when logs are processed into sawn timber, the sawn timber exported would have been processed from significantly more than nine per cent of the total logs produced. We can conclude that about three quarters of the logs produced in Malaysia are exported. Most of the wood ends up in the industrial countries. In 1985, of the total sawlog exports of 18.8 million cu. metres, 61 per cent went to Japan, 15 per cent to Taiwan, 15 per cent to South Korea and five per cent to China (*Ibid*). A lot of the logs exported to Taiwan and Korea is processed and re-exported. Of the 2.7 million cu. metres of sawn timber exported in 1985, 32 per cent went to the EEC, 23 per cent to Singapore (where it is re-exported), nine per cent to Japan and seven per cent to Australia (*Ibid* 1986:1970).

Rapid Forest Depletion in Sarawak

Turning now to Sarawak, we have already shown how log production has increased at a tremendously rapid pace in the last ten years. The year of lowest output was 1975, where 2.5 million cu. metres of logs were produced. By 1979 output had shot up to 7.6 million cu. metres and it reached a peak of 12.2 million cu. metres in 1985, by which year it had become the nation's most important producer, accounting for 39 per cent of the total output.

How many hectares of forests have been logged in Sarawak? Although estimates of area logged exist for Peninsular Malaysia, there are no easily available estimates (at least to the public) for Sarawak. We therefore have to make our own estimates, based on assumptions regarding the yield of timber per unit of area logged. There are a number of estimates of timber yields. In a paper for the FAO, Chandrasekharan (n.d.:3) gives an average log yield for hill forest of 15-20 Hoppus tons per acre, or 67-89 cu. metres per hectare. This estimate appears to be too high compared to other estimates. Hj. Sulaiman bin Sebli (n.d.:4.2.3.) a senior forester in Miri, gives an estimate of 44.5 cu. metres of timber per hectare in Sarawak. Tan Yaw Kang (1980:146) gives a similar estimate of ten tons per acre (44 cu. metres per hectare) as average yield for Sarawak. He also estimates that in 1979, about 250,000 acres (around 100,000 hectares) of hill forests were logged in Sarawak. Finally, we can also estimate the average yield for Peninsular Malaysia. According to Bank Negara's Annual Report for 1985, around 177,000 hectares of forests were logged. The output of sawlogs was 8,300,000 cu. metres (1986:142-3). Thus the average yield for Peninsular Malaysia was around 47 cu. metres per hectare. This comes closer to the estimates of Sulaiman (44.5 cu. metres per hectare) and Tan Yaw Kang (44 cu. metres per hectare) for Sarawak.

It is also interesting to note that Peninsular Malaysia, producing 8.3 million cu. metres of logs, (or 26.5 per cent of total log production in Malaysia), cleared 177,000 hectares of forest in 1985 (see Table 4 and *Bank Negara Annual Report 1985*). This gives an average rate of 21,325 hectares of forest cleared for every 1 million cu. metres of logs produced. If the log yield is similar for Malaysia as a whole, this would mean that for the country's total log production of 31.3 million cu. metres, 667,000 hectares of forest were logged in 1985. This rate is equivalent to 1,827 hectares logged a day, or 76 hectares an hour, or 1.27 hectares a minute. Or a rate of logging of 1.65 million acres a year, 4,514 acres a day, 188 acres an hour, or 3.1 acres a minute.

If we take the Sarawak log yield as 45 cu. metres per hectare (somewhat between the Sulaiman, Tan and Peninsular Malaysia estimates), then we can give an estimate of the area of forests logged in Sarawak over the past two decades. Since we know the output of logs, we can divide this by the estimated yield of 45 cu. metres per hectare to provide estimates of area logged for each year. This is undeniably a rather crude method of estimating area logged, but it is the best we can do given the lack of other information.

Using this method, we are able to construct Table 5 giving estimates of forest area logged for each year between 1963 and 1985. We find that in the past 23 years between 1963 to 1985, a total of 2.8 million hectares (seven million acres) of forest were logged. The average annual logging rate increased from around 45,000 hectares (1963-65) to 90,000 hectares (1966-70), fell to 70,000 hectares (1971-75), and rose rapidly thereafter to 140,000 hectares (1976-80) and 240,000 hectares (1981-85). In the latest year, 1985, around 270,000 hectares (or 670,000 acres) were logged.

How do our estimates compare with Tan Yaw Kang's? Tan estimated (1980:146) that in 1979 about 100,000 hectares of *hill forests* were logged. Our estimate is that in 1979, about 170,000 hectares of *all forests* (hill, peat swamp and mangrove swamp) were logged. In 1978, according to FAO and UNEP (1981:321), the production of logs in hill forests in Sarawak was 3.1 million cu. metres compared to 2.9 million cu. metres for logs from peat swamp forests. Using this ratio (and assuming similar log yields in both types of forests), Tan's estimate of 100,000 hectares of hill forests logged would translate into 194,000 hectares logged for hill and peat swamp forests in 1979. This is not far off from our estimate of 170,000 hectares in 1979.

Using our estimates, we find that logging has been responsible for clearing a tremendous amount of forests in Sarawak. In the period 1963-1985, 2.82 million hectares were logged, or 28,217 sq. km. This is equivalent to 30 per cent of the total estimated forest area in Sarawak, which is 95,232 sq. km. In 1985, 270,000 hectares (or 2,700 sq. km.) of forests were logged. This was equivalent to 2.8 per cent of Sarawak's forest area. Should logging continue at this rate, another 28 per cent of Sarawak's forest will be logged in the next ten years. We can see from these estimates what a devastating effect logging has had on the Sarawak forest.

Forest Concessions in Sarawak

In Sarawak, logging is carried out under licences and concessions. For logging permits within the Permanent Forest Area, companies have to follow certain regulations concerning the maximum permissable amount of logging per area and per year. This is regulated through a 'Working Plan'. In Stateland Forest, companies are supposed to adhere to a 'Felling Plan' but the Forest Department has little capacity to monitor actual

Table 5: Sarawak: Estimates of
Forest Area Logged 1963-1985

Year	Production of Logs ('000 cu. metres)	Estimate of area logged (hectares)	
1963	1,704	37,867	
1964	1,841	40,911	
1965	2,311	51,356	
1966	2,983	66,289	
1967	3,622	80,489	
1968	4,228	93,956	— 440,934
1969	4,324	96,089	
1970	4,685	104,111	
1971	3,911	86,911	
1972	3,172	70,489	
1973	3,251	72,244	— 348,266
1974	2,827	62,822	
1975	2,511	55,800	
1976	4,414	98,089	
1977	4,880	108,444	
1978	5,977	132,822	— 695,266
1979	7,571	168,244	
1980	8,445	187,667	
1981	8,802	195,600	
1982	11,319	251,533	
1983	10,598	235,511	— 1,207,111
1984	11,401	253,356	
1985	12,200	271,111	
TOTAL		2,821,711	

Sources: (a) For log production: *Annual Statistics Bulletin Sarawak, 1981* (for years 1972-78) and 1983 (for years 1979-83); Ministry of Primary Industries, *Statistics on Commodities*, 1986 (for 1984); and Bank Negara Annual Report 1985 (for 1985).

(b) For estimate of area logged: calculated on the assumption that the average log yield is 45 cu. metres per hectare (see text for reason behind assumption).

implementation. Data on the geographical areas and the size of forest coming under the 'Working' and 'Felling Plans', as well as the size of forest worked during a particular year, are available in the Annual Reports of the Forest Department, Sarawak. These figures reveal the number of licences currently under operation, the amount of forests given out under concession, how much of that have already been logged up to that year, and how much remain to be logged. The figures change from year to year, as logging may be completed in some areas (which are therefore removed from the Plans the subsequent year) whilst new areas coming under the Plans for the first time in that year are added on.

Table 6 shows that as at 31 December 1984, 5,752,996 hectares of forested area were currently under concession under both Working and Felling Plans. During the year 1984, 225,033 hectares were exploited. (This comes close to our estimate in Table 5 of 253,356 hectares of forest logged in 1984). By the end of 1984, a total of 1,342,826 hectares out of the total concession area had already been logged, leaving a balance of 4,410,170 hectares still to be exploited in future years.

In Table 5, we had estimated that in the period 1963-85, 2.82 million hectares (or 28,217 sq. km.) of forests had been logged, equivalent to 30 per cent of Sarawak's forest area. From the end of 1984, another 4.41 million hectares (44,101 sq. km.) of forests are scheduled to be logged. This is equivalent to another 46 per cent of Sarawak's total forest area. Every year, new concessions are given out, so even more forest will be logged. By the time the forest under current concessions are exhausted, there will hardly be any forest left in Sarawak.

Table 6: Sarawak: Forest Area Under Logging Licence in Working and Felling Plans, as at 31.12.84 (hectares)

Section	Forested Area under Plan	Exploited Area (during 1984)	Total Exploited	Balance of Area
Register of Working Plans				
Kuching/Simanggang	243,233	7,766	106,962	136,271
Sibu Section	1,961,217	68,818	254,751	1,706,466
Bintulu Section	795,581	42,366	186,316	609,265
Miri Section	867,292	17,413	197,263	670,029
Register of Felling Plans				
Kuching	106,777	6,328	46,026	60,751
Sibu Section	449,439	32,860	105,595	343,844
Bintulu Section	376,481	27,411	139,188	237,293
Miri Section	952,976	22,071	306,725	646,251
TOTAL	5,752,996	225,033	1,342,826	4,410,170

Source: *Annual Report of the Forest Department Sarawak, 1984*, Appendix E.

Table 7 shows how much forest has been given out for logging concession in each of the seven Divisions of Sarawak, and what percentage of total forest area it constitutes. The year referred to is 1984, which means these are the areas given under concession (already logged plus the balance still to be logged). The table shows that the total area currently under concession was a very high 60 per cent of Sarawak's total forest area. In other words, three-fifths of Sarawak's forest was then currently licensed out for logging. The situation is most serious in the Fourth Division, which is rich in forest land. Out of 34,017 sq. km. of forest, 24,579 sq. km., or 72 per cent, had been given out under concession for logging in 1984.

Table 7: Sarawak: Forest Area Under Logging Licence (Management Plan Areas) as % of Total Forest Area, Sarawak, 1984

Division	Area under Management Plan (sq km)	Total Forest Area (sq km)	%
1st Division	1,575	4,549	35
2nd Division	1,589	4,001	40
3rd Division	5,550	8,150	68
4th Division	24,579	34,017	72
5th Division	2,749	6,706	41
6th Division	1,464	2,701	54
7th Division	19,261	35,108	55
TOTAL	56,768	95,232	60

Source: *Annual Report of the Forest Department Sarawak, 1984,* Appendix F, Forms 1 & 6.

The data in this Chapter shows that logging carried out by the timber companies is the most devastating factor responsible for the rapid pace of deforestation that has been taking place in Sarawak.

Above: Loading recently-felled timber onto rail tracks for transporting to the timber camp.

Below: Logs being debarked at timber camp.

Above: Logs being transported through the forest.

Below: The logs are fastened together and floated down the river towards the port for export.

CHAPTER NINE

A New Look
at Swidden

When discussions take place on the destruction caused to tropical forests, the blame is more often than not placed firstly on swidden agriculturalists, whilst the role of logging is correspondingly played down. This is certainly not fair, at least in the case of insular Southeast Asia (Malaysia, Indonesia, Brunei, Philippines, and Papua New Guinea), where, according to an ESCAP (Economic and Social Commission for Asia and the Pacific) report: 'Logging is undoubtedly the primary cause of degradation and indirectly of deforestation too' (ESCAP 1986:44).

How destructive is shifting agriculture? Are the estimates of the extent of forest clearance by swidden farmers correct? This Chapter provides a review of the criticisms levelled against shifting agriculture in Sarawak.

Extent of New Forest Opened Up by Swiddeners

The efforts to curb swidden farming which is practised by natives is supported by the current official thinking that views this practice as an 'evil' which must be stamped out at all cost. Many of the arguments against swidden are based more on prejudices than on an understanding or proper analysis of swidden and the native economy. One outstanding example of the anti-swidden position is given in the much quoted paper 'The Effects of Shifting Cultivation On Sustained Yield Management for Sarawak National Forests' written by Lau Buong Tiing, a senior executive forester in 1979. From aerial photographs taken in 1966 and 1976, Lau (1979:418-9) estimates that about 150,000 acres (60,000 hectares) of virgin forests are 'destroyed by shifting cultivators every year'. Lau also estimates that the 36,000 swidden households in Sarawak use 250,000 acres (150,000 acres primary forest; 100,000 acres secondary forest) annually. This estimate is based on the assumption that each family uses an average of seven acres per year. This estimate appears to be an exaggeration.

According to several studies on swidden farming, an average family is able to farm only three to five acres per year. In 1949 Freeman estimated that for an Iban *bilek* family of 5.7 members, the average farm was about 4½ acres (1970:249). According to him the crucial factor limiting farm size is the area which the available labour force of the family can effectively weed. Under normal conditions, the maximum area which one worker can effectively weed is about two acres[1] (Freeman 1970:196). Comparative studies of swiddeners in Burma, French Indo China, East Indies, Land Dayak and Iban between 1945-51 have revealed that for a swidden family of five, the average size of the swidden was 3.2 acres (that is .6 acre per person) (Freeman 1970:250). More recently, Hatch states that a swidden household with an average size of six persons will *seldom exceed* 6.2 acres (2.5 hectares) of swidden land (Hatch 1980:487). Even if we take a (relatively high) estimate that each family uses five acres a year, the total land used for swidden by the 36,000 families is only 180,000 acres or 73,000 hectares (not 250,000 acres estimated by Lau). Our estimate in fact matches the figures provided by the *Sarawak Department of Agriculture Annual Report* which estimates the area for hill padi for the 1979-80 year at 74,208 hectares or 183,368 acres (Department of Agriculture 1980:37).

It is also well known that when primary[2] or new forest is used, swidden farmers crop the land for at least two or three successive years. This is because the soil is fertile enough and the tremendous work involved in clearing the forest inhibits the farmers from annual forest clearing. Assuming that the Sarawak swidden farmers use primary forests for two years running, and even assuming they do not return at all to clear secondary forests to farm, then only 90,000 acres (36,000 hectares) of primary forests are chopped every year. That is, in any one year, out of the 180,000 acres farmed, 90,000 acres are on primary forests newly cleared and 90,000 acres are on virgin forests cleared the previous year. Since the swidden farmers in fact also cultivate on secondary forests (i.e. they return to land which they had already farmed seven or ten or 20 years earlier), it is likely that significantly less than 90,000 acres of primary forest are cleared by them annually. In fact it is widely recognised by anthropologists that swidden farmers use more secondary forest than primary forest at any time because of the labour involved in clearing virgin forest. Even assuming half the land used is secondary forest, then only 45,000 acres (18,000 hectares) of new primary forests are cleared by swidden farmers each year. In fact, less

1.   The bulk of the weeding falls on women in the family. Men had to help out when the women were sick or pregnant.

2.   It is becoming increasingly evident in the literature that much of the tropical rainforest regarded as 'primary' has in fact been re-established on sites affected in one way or another by humans. According to Spencer: 'In fact virgin forest in the sense that it has never been cleared by human or natural agency, may actually exist in numerous small areas. It is likely that most of the mature forests of the Orient today are not virgin forests in the proper sense, but merely old forests that have reached a fairly stable equilibrium of ecological succession after some earlier clearing by human or natural means' (Spencer 1966:39).

than half of their land is on primary forest so it is likely that much
less than 18,000 hectares of new primary forests are cleared by swidden
farmers each year. This conflicts with Lau's estimate that 150,000 acres
(60,000 hectares) of primary forests are 'destroyed' by swidden farmers
every year. The primary forest opened for swidden agriculture each
year (less than 18,000 hectares) is also only a small fraction of the
270,000 hectares logged by the timber industry in 1985 (see Table 4).
So it is clear that the timber industry and not the swidden farmers are
mainly responsible for deforestation in Sarawak.

Use of Forest Resources By Swiddeners

Lau also estimates that because of swidden agriculture, the State
economy loses M$377 million a year. This has been described as the
export value of logs which 'goes up in smoke' when the estimated 150,000
acres of virgin forest is burnt for swidden farming. But this argument
is erroneous on many scores. Firstly, since Lau's estimate of 150,000
acres of virgin forest being opened up seems overblown, the sum of
$377 million purported to be 'lost' is also exaggerated. Secondly, this
'loss' to the abstract 'State economy' does not take into account the value
of the farmers' economic activity, i.e. the value of the crops produced
on the land. Surely this too is part of the economy? Thirdly, it is wrong
to assume that all the timber is burnt or 'goes up in smoke'. The farmers
leave a fair number of trees on the land. They also select a good number
of the felled trees for their own use as timber and wood resources.
Freeman records that cultivation of virgin forest by the Baleh Iban avails
them of timber for building, making boats, farm and other implements,
rotan for mats and baskets, palm fronds for thatching, *belian* for roof
shingles, *damar* for lighting and boat building and bark for padi bins
(Freeman 1970:283). Pollarding (cropping the leaves and branches off
the tree) is also practised by the Iban (Janang Ensiring 1975:240). Chin
reports of the Baram Kenyah that desired plants 'were protected from
the axes and fires of farm-making'. Desirable trees were also planted
in forest clearings that later would revert to forest[3] (Chin 1981:9).
   In other words, some of the valuable timber which would otherwise
have been exported is well used by the local people. They would
otherwise have to purchase these resources at very high cost to

3.   Similar observations have also been made of the Lua' by researchers. When Lua'
fields are cleared and burnt, a number of strumps are left from which coppices grow.
The villagers deliberately protect the forest at the ridge tops and in rills, gulleys, and
creek beds from the field fires, so there is relatively undisturbed forest in the immediate
vicinity of the fields to provide seed for regeneration (Sanga Sabhasri 1978:160). In
fact firebreaks are built around the sides and tops of fields before burning by cutting
a 5-10 metre wide corridor and sweeping it clear of underbush to protect future swidden
areas (Peter Kunstadter 1978:83). Iban also construct firebreaks to prevent the spread
of fire. This is done by burning a strip around the perimeter of the farm before burning
the farm (Sutlive 1978:74).

themselves. The use of local resources by native people is also of economic value. One can argue it is of greater economic value than having the same resources exported to developed countries for the use of foreign people. It is surely more appropriate for our own poor people to use their wood for houses, boats and farm implements, rather than for our wood to be exported to be used as exotic and expensive furniture and packaging materials in the West or Japan where tropical hard wood furniture is a prized item in houses of the rich. It is typical of the prejudices of commercially oriented writers to judge that the use of resources by poor farmers who obtain the resources through their own efforts is 'of no economic value' (or represents 'wood gone up in smoke') just because there is no monetary transaction involved. Or just because the State government obtains no revenue from traditional activities, unlike the royalties obtainable from log exports.

Pro-timber, Anti-swidden Prejudices

The above analysis shows that many of the prejudices and statements made against swidden agriculture in Sarawak are not fair. The rapid destruction of the State's forest has been wrongly blamed on swidden agriculturalists, whilst the real factor responsible, the timber industry, has hardly been focused on for its role in depleting forest resources. Our estimates are that swidden is responsible for chopping 18,000 hectares of primary forest at most, and in reality far less than this. The timber industry, on the other hand, logged 270,000 hectares in 1985 alone. It is clear from this that the timber industry has far more capacity to destroy Sarawak's forest, and has used this capacity with increasing effect in recent years. The State's land and forest policies clearly supports this timber industry because of the vast profits and revenues to be made out of logging, and thus smoothens and paves the way for the industry to flourish. The people and bodies supporting these policies have been silent on the destructive capacity of the timber industry and instead diverted public attenton to the swidden agriculturalists, blaming them for the loss of Sarawak's forest. They also treat the forest which swidden farmers use as being a 'loss' to the State since profits are lost to the timber industry and revenue is lost to the government — failing to take into account the fact that the forest used by swidden farmers are of great value to them in terms of the produce of the land and the forest itself. We can therefore conclude that State policy has championed the cause of the timber industry, whilst unfairly throwing bad light on swidden agriculture, thus attempting to create a justification for restricting the rights and activities of Sarawak's native peoples.

In the next Chapter, we continue our examination of the effects of the timber industry from the social and environmental points of view.

Kayan woman sieving recently pounded rice, perhaps for making cakes.

Above: Besides land for farming, the forest also provides many resources to meet the farmers' needs. Here, a Kenyah man is splitting a lengthy piece of rotan, which is then used for making mats, baskets and lashing material.

Below: A Kayan woman in the Baram weaving a mat made from rotan. The mat is dyed with natural dyes extracted from forest plants.

Below: Making a dug-out boat from a single log.

Above: Young Kenyah women cleaning tapioca from the swidden to make flour, snacks or wine.

Tractor track in the deep forest, causing damage to trees and extensive soil erosion.

CHAPTER TEN

Social and Environmental Impact of the Timber Industry

In recent years, timber has played a major role in the Malaysian economy. Earnings from timber has provided the revenue for the rapid pace of economic growth in the last two decades especially in the case of Sarawak. Massive fortunes were made by individuals and enormous profits entered the State's coffers. However, this wealth was achieved at great cost to the State and the natives. This Chapter will examine the timber industry in Sarawak and its impact on workers and the tropical forest ecosystem.

Sarawak's Timber Industry

Timber is big business and an important industry in Sarawak. It is the State's second export earner (only behind petroleum), accounting for 20-30 per cent of total export earnings (varying from year to year). In 1983, timber exports were $1,179 million, or 21 per cent of Sarawak's total exports of $5,707 million. In 1985, timber exports were $1,328 million. In the decade 1976-1985, timber fetched a total of $9,070 million in export earnings (see Table 8).

In terms of contribution to Sarawak's Gross Domestic Product, timber is also among the top two sectors. In 1983, the forest sector accounted for 15.5 per cent of the GDP, second only to the mining sector, and in 1979-82 it was the most important sector (*Annual Statistical Bulletin Sarawak 1983*:183).

Timber is also a major revenue earner for the State and Federal governments. In 1983, forest revenues accruing to government totalled $403 million. These comprised royalty, premium and fees ($254 million), export duties ($119 million), timber cess ($10 million) and timber development premium ($20 million) (Forest Department Sarawak 1983:i) It is interesting to note that the $403 million in government revenue was a high 34 per cent of the value of the timber exports ($1,179 million) in 1983. This shows that a large part of the income derived from timber flows to the government, which thus has a large interest in the timber industry.

The timber industry is also a major provider of jobs. In 1980, logging

Table 8
Export of Sawlogs and Sawn Timber,
Sarawak, 1976-1985
($ mil)

Year	Timber Exports
1976	359
1977	344
1978	400
1979	912
1980	920
1981	897
1982	1,363
1983	1,179
1984	1,368
1985	1,328

Sources: Department of Statistics, *Annual Statistical Bulletin Sarawak* (for 1976-83); *Bank Negara Annual Report 1985* (for 1984-85).

and forestry employed 19,839 people and the wood manufacturing industry (mainly sawmills) employed 9,748 people. Thus almost 30,000 people were involved in timber, or 3.5 per cent of the total workforce of about 850,000 (Department of Statistics 1983:773-83). If we include people involved in timber transport and trade, the numbers employed by timber would be even higher.

There is thus no denying that timber is a very important industry in Sarawak, in terms of providing income, foreign exchange, State revenue and employment. The problem is that the acceleration of the rate of logging in recent years has led to the widespread destruction of the forest, which makes the timber industry unsustainable in the long run. At current logging rates, Sarawak will have no more forests left to chop down, within a matter of years. Moreover, as we have seen, the granting of massive amounts of forest land as concessions to logging companies has disrupted the lives and livelihood of the natives who live in the forest interior.

Finally, the way in which the timber industry carries out its logging activities has caused adverse environmental and social effects, which in turn will affect the land and forest base, and the economy in the long run. These effects include the high and horrendous rates of logging accidents, massive soil erosion, damage to residual stands (the unlogged parts of the forest), and damage to the forest ecology caused by logging roads. These social and ecological effects are examined in the rest of this Chapter.

Forest Exploitation : Who Benefits?

The crucial question we should ask is who actually benefits from the felling of timber. The Sarawak timber industry is an export oriented industry. As such most of the timber felled are for the international market. The people who gain from the export of logs are the timber owners, the State in terms of revenue, the foreigners who obtain the wood, and the timber workers who earn wages from the industry. In fact it has been argued that the exporting country may not earn as much foreign exchange as is often shown in the export value figures. According to Y. Shudhakara Rao, FAO Regional Forestry Economist, since much of the exploitation of the timber is carried out through foreign based transnational corporations, the net foreign exchange earnings to the country, in effect will be the residual after deducting from the gross earnings such items as profit repatriation, imports of equipment and material, and expenditure towards employing expatriates in the operations. 'One estimate' he says, 'is that net foreign exchange earnings in timber operations may not exceed 30 per cent of gross foreign exchange earnings' (Y. Sudhakara Rao 1982:22). In a speech he delivered at a Seminar in September 1984 on the Sarawak economy, Datuk Leo Moggie, the Federal Minister, revealed that 'the marketing of Sarawak timber is still very much controlled by the Japanese trading houses, as Sarawak timber companies are largely dependent on these trading houses for their intricate line of credit' (*Sarawak Tribune* September 15, 1984).

On the other hand, the use of the forest by swidden farmers benefits this large group comprising 25 per cent of the Sarawak population. The issue at hand is that economic gains from timber revenue cannot be equated with the social cost incurred to a swiddening community when their source of subsistence is cut off. Swiddeners comprise some one quarter of the total population. When such a sizable segment of the population is deprived of their means of livelihood in the absence of a viable alternative, the socioeconomic costs incurred will be very substantial. Thus who benefits from forest exploitation? As the FAO Assistant Director-General for Asia and the Pacific, D.L. Umali noted in his keynote address at the FAO/SIDA Seminar on Forestry in Rural Community Development at Chiang Mai in 1980, forest exploitation as hitherto practised in the tropical moist forests of Southeast Asia was a manifestation of 'tunnel vision' where profit was the main criterion and where the end result has been the creation of corporate ghettoes in a sea of impoverished forest communities.

There is also the widely touted argument that forest exploitation benefits the economy in the form of dividends, infrastructure development, transfer of technology and skills, and it creates employment for the local people. However a case can be made that the timber industry benefits few local people like the timber concessionaires. There is no publicly available estimate of the extent of foreign outflow of the timber revenue of Sarawak. However, leading government leaders have lamented the fact that little of Sarawak's timber profits are reinvested in the State or used to uplift the socioeconomic conditions of the people. This was disclosed by the then Chief Minister of Sarawak in 1974. According to him timber tycoons had made huge investments in foreign countries. Some even had accounts in Swiss banks (*Ibid* August 12, 1984). This point was again lamented in September 1984 by Leo Moggie, the Federal Minister for Energy, Telecommunications and Posts when he said in a speech that timber profits continue to be invested outside the State (*Ibid* September 15, 1984).

Low Skills and High Safety Risks for Timber Workers

The argument that logging brings about technology transfer and creates job opportunities is offset by the fact that the skills involved are of a low level; many of the jobs created are taken by foreigners; and moreover once the forest is logged so too do the jobs disappear. A study on the timber industry in Indonesia shows that although it created as many as 11,000 new jobs during the period 1968-76, not all were filled by Indonesian workers. Many expatriates had been employed instead (M. Gillis 1980). Sudhakara Rao also notes that the natives who are employed in logging are given unskilled jobs. 'There is little evidence of concern for training them and enriching their skills or seeking their participation in the management and exploitation of these forests' he added (Sudhakara Rao 1980:23).

In Sarawak, logging is a labour intensive industry largely based in the remote areas. In 1970, it employed 10,906 local natives out of a total of 22,490 jobs created. In other words 48 per cent of the workers employed in logging activities were local natives. In 1977, 16,000 local peoples mostly from rural areas, were employed. They comprised some 57 per cent of the total 27,800 jobs in the industry. Labour was also imported from the Philippines for jobs requiring high skills (Chandrasekharan n.d.:5). Logging activities include felling and preparation of logs and haulage, road making, rafting, driving tractors, boats, trucks and locomotive, measuring for royalty, surveying and counting of trees, loading, measurement and grading for export, yarding and machine maintenance. Most of these jobs do not require any skills. On the other hand, the work is often dangerous to life and limb.

Indeed, the record for occupational safety in logging and the woodwork industry is atrocious. The timber sector has the highest incidence of accidents and deaths among all sectors in Sarawak. In 1979 there were 987 reported accidents in logging and 671 in the woodworking industry. Thus the timber sector recorded 1,658 accidents, which accounted for an astounding 73 per cent of all accidents in all industries in Sarawak. The 61 fatal accidents in the timber sector also accounted for 74 per cent of the total industrial accidents in the State. There were 930 injuries in logging (42 per cent of total injuries in the State) and 57 deaths (68 per cent of all industrial-related deaths) whilst in woodworking there were 667 injuries (30 per cent of the total) and four deaths (five per cent of the total). These were only the reported cases; many other accidents went unreported (STIDC 1981:2).

Taking the logging industry alone, we find that the number of fatal accidents has risen from 28 in 1977 to 87 in 1984 whilst the number of non-fatal accidents rose from 726 to 1,553 between the same two years. In the period 1973-1984, there were 603 logging deaths and 11,648 non-fatal accidents (Abang Naruddin Zainorin 1985:2). The incidence of accidents is shocking. In 1980, there were around 20,000 workers involved in logging activities. In the same year there were 52 deaths and 967 injuries related to logging. This means that 5 per cent of workers (one in twenty) were injured and 0.26 per cent of workers (one in 400) were killed. At the same incidence of accidents, if a worker were to work for ten years in logging, he would have a 50 per cent chance of getting injured and a three per cent chance of being killed.

A senior timber officer, Abang Naruddin Zainorin (1985:4) estimates that for every one million cu. metres of logs produced in Sarawak at least seven lives are lost. This is a very high incidence since in Canada there is only one death to every three million cu. metres of logs produced. The Sarawak logging death rate is over 20 times higher than Canada's.

In the period January 1984 to June 1985, there were 108 fatal logging accidents. Of these, the major causes of death were: hit by falling tree or branch (44 cases), hit by log (30 cases), lorry or truck carrying logs overturned (ten cases), and other accidents involving tractor or vehicle (18 cases) (Sen Gupta 1985:Appendix II).

The high incidence of logging accidents reflects the lax attitude of the management and the authorities in accident prevention measures. 'Even fatal accidents are soon forgotten in places where labour is cheap and abundant' (Ministry for Forestry 1982:7). This problem is most likely to increase as more and more of the timber industry in the State moves into the hill forest areas which requires more capital intensive machinery and infrastructural back-up systems.

The plight of workers is made worse by the poor compensation they get if they are injured or die at work. However, present compensation schemes give such miserable compensation that it is really a double tragedy for the worker and his family if he is injured, disabled or killed. Indeed, workers are getting a raw deal under both the Workmen's Compensation Scheme (governed by the Workmen's Compensation Act, 1977) and SOCSO (under the Social Security

Act, 1969), for instance:

- The maximum limits of compensation are very low. For example, the compensation for death of a worker is only $14,400 under the Workmen's Compensation Scheme, and 70 per cent of average monthly earnings under SOCSO. These amounts are low when compared to court awards for fatal road accident victims.

- Compensation for permanent disablement is also very low under the Workmen's Compensation Scheme and SOCSO. Take the case of chainsaw operator Lutau who lost his right leg due to a falling tree. He was given only $14,760 as compensation. If he had been covered by SOCSO, he would also get very little — $190 every month. Compare this with the case of shopowner Soon Song Lee who was knocked down by a lorry. As a result of the accident, he was permanently disabled due to a shortening of his right leg. The Court awarded him $64,000 in damages.

- The Social Security Act forbids an injured worker from suing his employer in court to recover damages for work injury. The worker has to accept the SOCSO benefits and cannot take further action even if he thinks the compensation is not fair.

- There is no provision for the rehabilitation of injured workers (*Utusan Konsumer*, November 1985).

The epidemic proportion of accidents found in logging is due to a number of factors. Firstly, there are no laws existing to protect the safety of workers engaged in the timber industry. Accident prevention is thus not mandatory or regulated. Management is therefore not compelled to institute protective measures for their workers. Moreover, management only pays small sums under the Workmen's Compensation Act or SOCSO which is then responsible for paying out compensation in the event of accidents. The employer is not liable, thus he does not have the incentive to prevent such accidents.

Secondly, logging is carried out through a multi-tiered system. The concession owner often contracts the whole work to someone else who in turn may sub-contract the work to a fourth person. These subcontractors are only interested in getting the job done as quickly as possible and moving on to the next contract. In this situation 'they will try to maximise profits to get maximum financial returns while neglecting the welfare and social aspects of the workers' (STIDC 1981:4). Hence safety is of low priority.

Thirdly, most of the workers engaged in logging activities are contract workers with minimal education. This means they are paid according to the amount of work they do. Most of these workers have no idea how hazardous the work can be neither are they in a position to articulate for better preventive measures and proper maintenance of tools and machinery.

Some of the most dangerous aspects of hill logging operations are tree felling, skidding, debarking, loading and trucking. According to the STIDC 'Notes on Forest Industrial Safety and Accident Prevention in Sarawak', most tree fellers are local inhabitants paid on contract basis who are never briefed on safety aspects and are usually not given adequate protection. No consideration is given to the proper method of felling trees and no escape routes are made prior to felling. Most of them are not trained to handle and maintain chainsaws properly. Tree fellers are not protected with safety helmets, ear protection and safety shoes. No proper warning system is used by tree fellers especially when felling beside the roads and skidding areas. Loading is another activity which can cause fatal accidents. Loading is done at the forest landings where the logs are measured and recorded before they are transported. Scalers measure the logs immediately before the logs are loaded. This involves lifting the logs a few feet from the ground by the loader. Logs can slip from the loader's fork and this is very likely to happen as the debarked logs are slippery. Accidents of this nature are very often fatal. Truck drivers also court death when they squat on top of the truck's cap (which is often the case) directing the loading process. Logs can either hit them or fall on top of them. Speeding trucks on forest roads are another major cause of accidents. Very often these trucks are over-loaded. This causes a strain and impairs the ability of the truck to brake during emergencies. Little care is taken to design roads which are safe especially those on steep gradients. Most of the surveyors in the logging camps are not qualified to execute road planning and design. These roads are a hazard to truck drivers (*Ibid*:5).

The other area of danger is the woodworking industry. According to a Forest Safety Industrial Consultant, G.W. Noris, little attention was paid to accident prevention although workers are doing their work in an acceptable manner. 'The danger of operating modern, fast moving equipment with man-power inadequately trained cannot be stressed too strongly'. Some of the areas requiring attention referred to machinery. These included poorly built ladders; lack of guards on all chains and sprockets; V-belt drives and revolving shafts to prevent accidental contact; swing trim saws many of which are not secured to prevent it from rebounding past the straight edge by a latch; circular rip saws many of which do not have a splitter to prevent material from binding, riding up on the saw and being kicked back by the top teeth; lack of adequate fire protection and poor housekeeping resulting in non clearance of waste materials.

As in logging, there is also no adequate physical protection afforded to workers in the woodworking industry. Supervision and training is not given and workers actually learn about the dangers on the job and the fatal mistakes of their fellow workers (*Ibid*:2-3,14). The woodworking industry comes under the Factories and Machinery Act 1967. This means that the registration and inspection of machinery,

Native timber workers pulling a heavy log across the forest to the timber camp.

the control of safety, health and welfare of the workers are required by the law. However, there appears to be minimal inspection and enforcement is most inadequate. This is reflected in the observations made by the Forest Industrial Safety Consultant mentioned above.

Apart from the physical dangers and injury that workers are exposed to in the workplace both in felling operations and wood-working, the environment in which workers live also leaves much to be desired. According to the STIDC Notes, 'in Sarawak, poor accommodation and living conditions prevail in most logging camps. Poor housing conditions can be the reason for the spread of certain insect-borne diseases like malaria or typhus . . . Medical supervision and care is non-existent in the logging camps' (Ibid:5). The nutrition and food consumption of the camp workers need to be improved, and contract workers are not given sufficient rest periods when they do heavy mechanised work. 'Workers start work at dawn and continue until dusk without any proper break. Accumulated fatigue, low efficiency and high accident rates are the result'.

Forest Exploitation:
The Environmental Impact

Shifting cultivation, according to official opinion, has also been responsible for widespread environmental destruction. According to Lau, 'Additional and yet incalculable damage must result from soil erosion and degradation, pollution of waterway and air (during the burning seasons), siltation of waterways, damage to fish spawning grounds, and down river flooding. The total loss of the various genetic value of fauna and flora and habitat for wildlife is irreversible' (Lau 1979:419). Such a portrayal of the effects of swidden is unwarranted and untruthful. As shown earlier in Chapter Three, swiddening is a form of agriculture which is dependent on the sustained productivity of the forest system. Swidden is an ecologically sound system with a minimum of soil erosion and regeneration of forests. The negative effects which Lau attributes to swiddening are in fact the very effects resulting instead from logging, as shown by many studies. In fact, the very people (timber industry) destroying the forest environment are blaming the ecologically sound swidden farming for the ecological damage. The real culprits are blaming the victims as culprits.

On a boat trip in the upper Baram, I happened to see a whole hill striped bare of vegetation and a 'landslide' had occurred. The natives were visibly upset by the occurrence. One of them told me that 'this is not the way to log the forest. When we farm we always make sure that the forest above the farm is not felled or else when it rains all the soil from the top of the hill will be washed down'. This shows the farmers' depth of understanding that one of the cardinal rules in hill farming is the preservation of natural vegetation above the swiddens and the prevention of soil erosion.

According to Grandstaff (1980:6) 'In regard to the likely causes of watershed deterioration, several researches feel that commercial interests and modern "bulldozer technologies" are likely to be of more danger in this regard . . .' According to Dasmann *et al* (1973:175) 'In the more humid tropics, over-population relative to carrying capacity is more likely to be evidenced by malnutrition . . . and environmental deterioration may not be so dramatic under subsistence methods of resource exploitation . . . it will very probably be modern methods of agricultural and forestry exploitation that are doing the more serious damage'.

The following sections provide details of the ways in which logging activities have destroyed and are destroying the forest ecology. First, we examine the impact of logging on the tropical forest in general, with examples from various countries, especially Peninsular Malaysia. Then, we examine the specific case of Sarawak.

Increased Soil Erosion: Soil erosion is perhaps the most serious environmental impact of logging. Commenting on the effects of large scale deforestation, Eckholm says it 'upsets the normal workings of the hydrological cycle by affecting the course of fallen rains; instead of sinking into hillsides for later seepage into streams, rains on denuded lands run down in one major flood' (Eckholm 1976:91). The erosion of topsoil can be very severe. According to Alan Grainger writing in *The Ecologist* (1980:45): 'A watershed covered with natural rain forest loses one ton of soil per hectare per annum' from soil erosion. Should this forest cover be removed and the land cultivated 'between 20 and 30 tons may be lost'. According to a UNESCO/ UNEP/FAO study in the Ivory Coast, negligible erosion (0.03 tons/ha/yr) was found on land with a seven per cent slope covered with secondary forest. When annual crops were cultivated soil erosion increased to 90 tons/ha/yr. When the ground was left bare the damage was 138 tons/ha/yr (UNESCO/UNEP/FAO 1978:264). In a preliminary study conducted by Malaysia's Federal Land Development Authority (FELDA), in Peninsular Malaysia, it was found that the soil loss after forest clearing was very substantial. Soil loss was 79 tons/ ha/yr. The most serious effect of this was the rapid depletion of soil organic matter which reduced the soil fertility (A.H. Ling *et al* 1979:21-4).

It has also been observed in Pasoh Forest Reserve, Negri Sembilan, that within two years following forest clearance for oil-palm plantation, the litter and A_o (absorption) layer of the soils are completely washed out by rain, resulting in increased run-off (E. Soepadmo 1979:54). Furthermore, other studies in Peninsular Malaysia have shown that logging operations or complete deforestation followed by cultivation of crops increases the rate of soil erosion from 39-104 kg/ha/yr to 2,800 kg/ha/yr while total sediment load of the streams draining the area increased from 6 m³/km²/yr to 1,350 m³/km²/yr (*Idem* 1979:55).

Soil erosion will disturb the structure of the soil and lead to soil infertility. Impoverished soils will be useless to agriculture and will not be able to support any regeneration of the forest either (Aiken and Moss 1975). Thus the clearing of vast jungle areas due to logging activities (in some cases followed by agriculture) has led to adverse hydrological changes and increased soil erosion and flooding. These changes also affect the local climate. It has been claimed that a large tree has a cooling effect of 20 air-conditioners (Tan Yaw Kang 1980:146). If a million of such trees were felled, the effects can be ecologically very damaging. In areas or countries (such as where the forests have disappeared), there have been frequent severe floods in periods of heavy rains and severe long drought during the dry seasons. In Malaysia, rapid deforestation has also resulted in more occurrences of flooding, long droughts threatening food production, rivers, and reservoir siltations (Radzuan A. Rahman 1979:85). All these activities have posed serious environmental deterioration in the coastal zone as well (Jamaluddin Md Jahi 1983:9).

In comparison to the ecological devastation caused by logging, the environmental damage from swidden farming is small. Referring to shifting cultivation in Africa, Chin cites from studies that on slopes of less than ten degrees, soil erosion during three years of cropping does not exceed 50 tons per acre, often much less. This loss is at most one tenth of the fertile top layer and has little effect on the nutrient content in the top soil (Chin 1981:3). A study by the Sarawak Forest Department on soil erosion in primary jungle cleared by shifting cultivators on slopes of 25-30 degrees revealed soil loss of 0.15 tonnes/hectare a year (*Sarawak Tribune* March 21, 1981). Compared to the loss of soil in logged areas, this amount is very negligible. The interesting fact is that this negligible 0.15 tonnes/hectare soil loss was used by the Forest Department to insinuate that shifting cultivation causes serious erosion. This again indicates the prejudices that exist against shifting cultivation.

Damage to Residual Stands: When a forest is logged, the timber companies only extract certain trees which are commercially useful to them. Ideally the other trees which are not wanted should remain undamaged in the forest. These remaining trees are called 'residual stands'. Some of the major criticisms against logging is the extensive damage inflicted on the young trees. An FAO study has shown that as much as 50 per cent of the residual stand may be damaged, and the surface soil may be destroyed, when up to 30 per cent of the ground surface is exposed. According to the study, it will take more than 40 years for such a disturbed forest to recover, which is longer than the desired rotation cycle[1]

1.   Rotation cycle is the system based on selective felling or 'creaming'. The remaining trees are to be left on the site to grow into merchantable trees in the next rotation. In Sarawak the Selective Felling System of hill forest adopts a rotation of 25 years.

(Sastrapradja *et al* 1978). In another study, Setyono Sastrosumarto (1978) concludes that an average of one third of young trees experience fatal damage; another one third of trees of diameters 20-50 cm diameter at breast height (DBH) experience non fatal damage to crown and bark, while for trees with greater than 50 cm (DBH), the upper limit of damage is 55 per cent. Whitmore (1975) estimates that the area of damage associated with each felling is on average 0.04 hectare. This means that if ten trees are felled per hectare, nearly half of that area will be affected. Referring to the possibility of sustained yield Alan Grainger (1980) writes: 'If there is to be the same number of good sized trees when it is time for the second rotation, the density of young trees before the first felling must be at least 225 per cent that of the original stand. This necessitates the inclusion of very small trees which will take at least 40 years to reach exploitable size'. According to the World Bank (1978): 'There is no documented case of a logged Dipterocarp[2] forest actually reverting to its original climax state'.

In the case of Peninsular Malaysia the 1977/78 Economic Report revealed that: 'Selective logging has also resulted in the wasteful exploitation of the timber resources where the average annual rate of harvesting over the past decade is around half a million acres compared to the potential productive forests of about 12.8 million acres' (Ministry of Finance 1977:108). In West Malaysia, a Colombo Plan silvicultural ecologist who was attached to the Forest Research Institute, Kepong, P.F. Burgess, has reported that in a Hill Dipterocarp forest area of one acre only an average of six trees are felled. 'These exploitable trees are all large emergents with crowns often 50 ft across, and when they fall they smash up a considerable part of the lower stories of the forest'. In fact his study has shown that to extract ten per cent[3] of the standing trees for timber in a hill forest, some 55 per cent of the forest basal area is destroyed during logging operations (Burgess 1971:232). According to Professor Soepadmo of the Botany Department, Universiti Malaya, although the remaining 35 per cent of the forest stand is undamaged, the following silvicultural treatment will virtually reduce the complexity and species diversity of the forest to not more than ten per cent of the original condition. 'This means that even under a careful selective logging operation followed by proper silvicultural treatments, many of the so-called undesirable (from forestry point of view) tree

2.   Dipterocarps are giant trees reaching more than 147½ feet. They are highly prized light hardwoods. In Sarawak the largest logging acreage is from the hill mixed dipterocarp forests.

3.   A tree has to reach at least 4½ feet in basal girth before it is marketable. Of the some 2,500 tree species found in West Malaysia, less than 150 of these are of commercial value (P.F. Burgess 1971:231). On the other hand there are about 1,680 species capable of reaching a minimum girth of 90 cm (Whitmore 1972).

species will disappear'[4]. Moreover, Burgess says there is every reason to stop the uncritical girdling of forest in areas where there is no regeneration of commercial species as 'such a practice results in the systematic elimination of the most valuable family of timber trees the Dipterocarpaceae'. Poison girdling when not carefully controlled does much to increase the loss of species in exploited forest and by the long delayed effects of the falling of poisoned trees it extends the period of disturbance to the ecosystem[5] (Burgess 1971:235).

'Along with this loss of tree genetic resources will go hundreds of other plants which originally characterise the complexity and species diversity of the primary forest. This disappearance of these plants will also mean the loss of habitats for various animals[6] inhabiting the forest' (E. Soepadmo 1979:54). Citing other studies Professor Soepadmo further adds that the disturbance or complete clearance of forest will drive away or greatly reduce the population density of ecologically useful soil fauna, birds and mammals, and increase the population density of undesirable species like pests and disease-vectors (*Ibid*).

Damage Caused by Logging Roads: Referring to Peninsular Malaysia, P.F. Burgess says that road making is probably the greatest damaging factor in hill forest exploitation. This practice generally takes place ahead of felling to enable the fellers to get into the forest easily and also to give the road time to settle before hauling begins. In general, loggers pay little attention to drainage on their roads. The road is usually cleared of trees and undergrowth to a width of one chain on either side to enable the sun to dry out the surface. No attempt is made to ensure proper drainage to prevent it from eroding the exposed outer face of the road and the hill side below, or to reduce its velocity by keeping road

4.   Under the Malayan Uniform Silvicultural (MUS) System, the larger uneconomic species are destroyed by poison girdling after the area has been logged. This is to ensure the young generation of timber species without suppression from the others. Commenting on this method, D.I. Nicholson, an FAO consultant has said: 'It is disappointing to see the way in which a management system can be so completely moulded by economic conditions . . .' (Nicholson 1979:3).

5.   The use of sodium arsenite poison in the peat swamp forest and increasingly in the Hill forest in Sarawak (Tan Yaw Kang 1980:148) will lead to long term contamination of the environment. In Peninsular Malaysia, 2,4,5-T is used. 2,4,5-T is usually contaminated with Dioxin as a by-product. Dioxin is said to be one of the most poisonous synthetic products ever made. The residues of both these poisons can have long term effects on aquatic and wildlife, the soil, the vegetation and the health of man living in these areas.

6.   It has been noted that logged forests are conspicuously lacking in wildlife. Logging drives them away as the noise of heavy machinery particularly the chainsaw is said to be very disturbing to animals. Stevens (1969) records that 48 per cent of mammals move out of exploited forests.

gradients down or by building check dams. The result is that erosion goes on during logging and it often continues for many years until whole sections of the road slip. Deep gullies to a depth of 12 feet have often been found on abandoned logging tracks due to erosion (Burgess 1971:233-4).

According to the Perak Director of Forestry, the lack of proper supervision in the construction of steep forest roads have resulted in serious soil erosion of many forest roads (Othman 1978:199). He also warns that since logging has moved up to the hills, management of water catchment areas is very important as it can affect the water quality (Othman 1978:199). The Secretary General of the Ministry of Agriculture has also stated that large scale clearing of forests in river catchments disrupts water resources, triggers an increase in the surface run-off which causes floods, 'accelerates erosion of the soil and causes serious sedimentation problems in irrigation canals, reservoirs, roadway, fish spawning areas etc' (Arshad 1979:352-3).

In Sabah, researchers have found that over 40 per cent of the forest area was laid bare as a result of damage by tractor tracks and loading areas, which will adversely affect the regeneration of the forest (Nicholson 1979:15). Expressing his grave concern for the Dipterocarp forests in Sabah, D.I. Nicholson, FAO consultant, said that: 'It cannot be too strongly stressed that a well regenerated forest depends on a careful logging operation . . . only extraction has the potential to reduce the regenerating forest to a mass of useless weeds, by destroying existing seedlings and poles. The forest can tolerate a fairly high percentage of its land surface being scraped bare so long as this percentage is scattered and made up of narrow logging roads. The most destructive damage appears to stem from inefficient use of tractor tracks, widening of tractor tracks and large collection points near loading points' (Nicholson 1965). From the above discussion, we can see that logging activities have caused considerable harm to the forest ecosystem.

The Sarawak Experience: In Sarawak, the same environmental destruction caused by logging is taking place. According to a senior Sarawak forester, large scale hill logging operations in Sarawak are already causing floods, siltation of rivers, turbidity of upstream river water, reduction in the aquatic and wildlife population. 'If millions of trees are felled without replacement, Sarawak's climatic condition, its soil condition, and its forest will surely and certainly degrade to the detriment of its inhabitants, flora and fauna' (Tan Yaw Kang 1980:146).

Only a few trees are removed by loggers in each hectare of hill forest, but damage to residual stands is extensive. According to H.S. Lee, of the Sarawak Forest Department, because the demand is for high grade export logs, the number of trees removed per hectare is between four and 20. This has resulted in very high residual stands.

A study of four Forest Reserves between 1974-76 found that the average number of trees felled was 6.1 trees/hectare. The average residual stand was 71 per cent (Lee 1982:6-7). Following Whitmore's

estimates this means that 0.24 or almost one quarter of that area felled
would be damaged. Again using Sastrosumarto's findings, one third
of the residual stand or 24 per cent of the trees would be destroyed.
Lee further implies that the damage to immature trees can be total
(*Idem* 1982:7). Hence the destruction caused by logging operations
poses a serious threat to regeneration. This threat has been made worse
by the increase in illegal felling (Lau 1980).

Moreover, observations by FAO Forestry officials revealed that
current conventional logging methods in Sarawak's Mixed Dipterocarp
Hill Forest inflict extensive damage to the remaining stand even when
harvest is selective and light. According to them the three important
causes of logging damage are felling, extraction and roadbuilding.
During felling operation, damage to the forest is particularly severe
when large trees with wide spreading crowns are felled in the direction
of neighbouring trees which then break and fall against successive stems.
In this way, extensive areas of forest are completely destroyed.
Extraction also results in substantial damage to the residual stand. 'The
heavy crawler tractors are so powerful that almost no effort is required
to push through a stand of small trees and, with little more effort, quite
big trees can easily be uprooted. This power enables the operator to
take his machine almost anywhere in the forest provided the terrain
is not too steep'. They also remarked that without planning and adequate
supervision, even low intensity selective logging can damage the forest
to the extent that the development of the next crop is severely inhibited
(H. Mattsson Marn and W. Jonkers 1982:28).

Roadbuilding in the forest also causes heavy damage. In Sarawak,
hundreds of miles of logging roads, snig tracks (tractor paths) and spur
roads in the forests have resulted in severe soil erosion. According to
H.S. Lee, construction of forest roads have led to the damage of
drainage systems and consequent flooding in hill forest logging in the
State (1982:6). According to the FAO forestry officials, the area
occupied by roads in a normal logging operation in high forest in
Sarawak represents four per cent of the total area being logged. Main
roads used during one felling cycle can be considered areas in the forest
which are removed from forest production permanently, while
regeneration of the forest in secondary and feeder roads develops very
slowly because of the hard compacted surfaces. During road
construction, trees along the edges of the roadway are exposed to
damage from both the road clearing and earth moving operations. Such
damage can be very serious especially on steep side slopes when earth
and broken trees may slide down-hill a long way. In addition, the felling
of trees which shade the road on each side of the carriageway can cause
the same type of damage to the stand as in felling (H. Mattsson Marn
and W. Jonkers 1982:28).

In a logging trial conducted in 1979, a comparison was made between
the extent of logging damage in two areas: a control area using
conventional logging methods, and an experimental area where logging
was carefully planned and efficiently supervised. It was found that under

conventional logging, damage to trees was almost twice as high as that resulting from the experimental block. The logging intensity in the control area was over 13 trees/ha ($53m^3$/ha). In this area some 26 trees per hectare of commercial species were uprooted and an additional 22/ha were broken. This amounted to some two thirds of the total available commercial stems in the forest area. Using data from another experiment which shows that about 35 per cent of the trees with minor damage will not recover, the researchers concluded that the total number of trees of commercial species destroyed due to logging will amount to 60 trees per hectare. This figure represented 40 per cent of the growing stock left after logging. There was also considerable loss of harvested logs due to wastage. The researchers noted that 3.3 trees/ha felled, were left in the forest. A quarter of these (0.8 per ha) showed extensive rot and a further 7.3 trees/ha were hollow and split during the felling operation. Logs from these trees were of such poor quality that their removal from the forest was uneconomic. The remaining 1.3 logs per ha were not damaged and would have contributed a further $11.5m^3$/ha of sound timber to the harvest. It was also found that the extent of open space and bare soil increased dramatically as logging becomes more intensive. When logging reached timber boom intensity, the area cleared was 30 per cent. This means that under intensive logging the area remaining under standing forest never exceeded 60 per cent. This shows that there was a high incidence of open space and bare soil under conventional logging. This is significant because it will have a crucial bearing on the perpetuation of the forest and its capacity to provide a subsequent crop of adequate volume within a period of 25 to 30 years (*Idem* 1982:33-6). Thus traditional logging practices in Sarawak destroy 40 per cent of the residual forest and kills almost half of the young growing stock. The researchers concluded: 'Under these circumstances, silvicultural treatment of the forest is difficult to justify and it will prove impossible to achieve the desired 25 to 30 years cutting cycle' (*Idem* 1982:36).

It can be seen from the above that extensive damage to the residual stand occurs during logging in high forest in Sarawak. The extent of the damage is related to the intensity of logging and to the degree of planning and supervision. According to the researchers, most logging operations in Sarawak are carried out with little planning and without any technical supervision (*Idem* 1982:30). The tractor operator and the feller are the two people solely responsible for the operations of felling and skidding to the loading vamp. In their own words, the system is as follows:

'After arriving with his tractor and mobile living quarters at the logging block, the tractor operator makes a brief reconnaissance to decide where to locate his landing (loading area). Once this decision is made, felling begins at the landing and proceeds into the logging block. After clearing the landing, the tractor follows behind the feller proceeding from log to log and skidding them one at a time, extending his skidtrail as he follows the felling operation.

Trees are felled in the direction convenient to the feller and are thus scattered at random over the block. Extending as they do from log to log, skidtrails are usually long, steep and winding, sometimes completing a full circle; curves are often very sharp. As a result the skidding tends to be slow and damage both to logs and the remaining stand is excessive. The tractor operator has one assistant known as the hookman, who works with the machine at all times, proceeding back and forth between forest and landing. Thus, the tractor operator must spend some time searching for each log or lose valuable tractor time while his assistant searches and locates it. Frequently, however, the tractor driver moves aimlessly around with his tractor until he eventually locates a log, destroying many trees in the remaining stand during his search.

Once a log is located the tractor operator turns his machine and the hookman then attaches the cable. If this operation proves difficult from the initial position, the tractor may be moved again to a better position or the log pushed or lifted to a better position with the dozer blade. During all this activity many more trees of the remaining stand may be destroyed or damaged. At times the tractor may even completely circumnavigate the whole log, this resulting in even greater destruction. Should the log lie at a sharp angle to the intended skidding direction, the log must be turned after the hook is attached and even more trees broken or damaged.

At times, but infrequently under this traditional system, two logs are skidded together. Chokers are not used and the main cable must be pulled around the ends of both logs. This is achieved by pushing the logs together with the tractor. This results in further damage to the remaining stand' (*Idem* 1982:31).

They stressed that there is a need to improve the standard of planning and execution of logging operations in the Mixed Dipterocarp Forest (MDF) in Sarawak. Furthermore 'no improved logging technique, no efficiency, and no reduced logging damage can be achieved in any logging operation unless it is properly supervised by trained operatives' (*Idem*:38). This was imperative not only to reduce the loss of actual and potential raw material but in order to 'ensure the perpetuation of the forest as a viable entity' (*Idem* 1982:27).

Calling for a better surveillance of swiddeners, Lau himself reveals that the Forest Department has been saturated with revenue collection, forest management and forest research. The shortage of personnel has

also led to the poor supervision of logging operations as can be seen
from the above discussion. At present all Stateland Forests below
2,500 feet are not managed under sustained yield[7] (Sarawak Forest
Department 1979:315). Thus logging goes on unchecked in the
Stateland Forests. This will lead to the depletion of the forest in no
time, according to a senior forester, and whatever is left of the
Permanent Forest will only last Sarawak for another 20 years. In
1979, about 250,000 acres (at an average of ten tons per acre) of
hill forests were logged. More than 60 per cent of these were from the
Stateland Forests. This was a two fold increase compared to 1978
(Tan Yaw Kang 1980:146). With the issuing of long term licences,
larger areas of hill forests are now being logged. This is especially
so in the remote hill forests of the Fourth and Seventh Divisons.

Under the 'sustained yield management' concept, the annual quantity
of logs cut should not exceed the annual growth. However, there is
presently no reliable data available on the growth rates of the different
species of trees, their yield and mortality, and information on site
qualities for the various forest types in the tropical forest (Leo Chai
1980:130). In fact knowledge of the tropical forest system and the data
available 'is still too rudimentary, too inconclusive and too ambiguous
to enable successful sustained yield management' (Mok Sian Tuan
1982:48). In other words the Malaysian forest which has existed
essentially undisturbed for some 100 million years is probably the most
complex and least studied in the world (Betterton 1982:92). It is thus
impossible to use any of the traditional methods developed for European
forests for determining the amount to be cut or predicting future yields
(Leo Chai 1980:130). Hence 'without reliable growth and yield
projection tables it is almost impossible to calculate annual growth or
to predict future yields accurately to determine the cutting budget for
natural forests' says a senior forester (*Idem* 1980:132). Thus the present
'sustained yield management' concept remains academic at best and
arbitrary at worst.

Apart from the fact that present attempts to rehabilitate our

---

7.   'Sustained yield' management refers to the selective felling of the natural forest
where only a portion of the trees are harvested. The unfelled stand, that is trees below
a certain girth limit, is conserved for further harvesting operations at some future date.
When these trees mature, the forest is ready for another round of felling. In this way,
timber yield is sustained in a forest area in a perpetual cycle. As long as damage to
the residual stand during logging is kept at an acceptable level, the forest will perpetuate
itself. Every area under 'sustained yield' management has a 'Working Plan' which
describes the area, how it is to be logged, the species removed, cutting limit, prescribed
allowable cut and penalties for poor logging. It is a legal document written for five
to ten years and subject to periodical revision. In the Mixed Swamp Forests in Sarawak,
the logged area is treated under the Malayan Uniform Silvicultural System (MUS).
In the hill Mixed Dipterocarp Forest (MDF), logged areas are treated by the Liberation
Thinning Method developed by the FAO. Liberation Thinning refers to the removal
of selected trees in the logged forests so that these would not compete with the standing
commercially valuable trees for growth.

devastated forests are made in the absence of sound scientific data, the very nature of timber exploitation techniques is so destructive that natural regeneration has very little chance of success. 'Efficiency in the use of bulldozers, power saws and logging lines, all this sophisticated technology has had only one effect biologically — disastrous . . . Using machinery meant for another clime have resulted in severely eroded slopes in hill terrain; churning up of low moist areas, creation of artificial swamps and indiscriminate damage to seedlings and saplings' (G. Dhanarajan 1982:89-90). The other major impediment to regeneration is the lack of control over timber exploitation. Enforcement has been neglected due to the lack of professional foresters. Most foresters devote their time to administration, which means that breaking of the regulations goes unchecked. Thus 'the picture of renewability (of our forests) is therefore bleak' (*Idem* 1982:90). In the words of the Director of the Forest Research Institute: 'The absence of sufficient regenerated or treated forests makes the possibility of sustained production quite remote' (Salleh Mohd Nor 1982:78). Although plantation forest management or reafforestation has been attempted in Sarawak, this has been largely limited to research studies and is still in the experimental stages. Reafforestation by the Forest Department has been confined to shifting cultivation areas within the Permanent Forests. It has 'so far been carried out on an ad hoc basis'. In 1982, 197 hectares of land had been planted. Many of the species were alien species imported from Australia, Philippines and Africa (Lee and Lai 1982:9). In the same year, high mortality rates were encountered. In one area planted over 77 per cent of the plants died (Forest Department 1982:32). It can be seen that forest management has been unsatisfactory and forest research has been minimal.

Logging: A Wasteful Industry

We have seen how conventional logging methods are destroying large tracts of forests. This also results in poor regeneration of the forest and loss of rare animal and plant life. According to many researchers, there is no doubt that under present conditions in forestry where there are no organised and systematic efforts in planning and management, the consequent damage to the forest is never as extensive and rapid as in timber extraction (Y.C. Wee and A.N. Rao 1982:115). Timber exploitation incurs great waste in the destruction of forest flora during logging operations, in incomplete recovery of felled logs from the forest and in silviculture treatment where species which have no commercial value are destroyed by poison girdling after logging has taken place in the area. In cases where the forest areas are marked for development schemes, all the commercially valuable species will be extracted. The rest will then be put to the torch. According to scientists, 'this practice represents the ultimate in wastage, as besides destroying the non-popular timber, many species are totally lost to science especially the rarer species and those yet to be discovered' (*Idem* 1982:116).

This also reflects the poor utilisation of timber. Speaking of the selective nature of logging in Peninsular Malaysia, Salleh Mohd Nor and Ho Kam Seng, Director and Research Officer respectively of the Forest Research Institute, Kepong, have noted that logging is extremely selective and utilisation very low. In fact both have estimated the waste incurred in logging to be as high as 50 per cent. The actual number of felled trees utilised was also very low. In a separate joint paper Salleh Mohd Nor and Francis S.P. Ng noted that 'only an average of 30 per cent of the total standing volume of timber (belonging to the species that are in commercial demand) is extracted during logging. From the timber utilisation point of view, the remaining 70 per cent is "wasted"' (1983:486). Another study has shown that although the total volume of wood present in one hectare of lowland dipterocarp forest may reach 375 tonnes, only about 27.5 tonnes is recovered as sawn logs[8] (Flemmich 1964). The number of trees felled in any given area was also low. In Kalimantan, it was reported that loggers take a mere five to seven trees per hectare but damage some 40 per cent of the other standing timber in the process (*Asiaweek* 1984:41). The lower yields per unit area results in the logger 'exploiting a larger area than necessary, building more roads than necessary, causing more damage to the environment than necessary and wasting more' (Salleh Mohd Nor and Ho Kam Seng 1982:105). Loggers become 'choosy' because the 'economic' value of a particular species is very dependent on the market and particularly the existing orders of the miller and the general economic situation rather than the properties of the timber. Thus 'burning logs in agricultural conversion areas is a common sight' (*Idem* 1982:103, 106). This practice represents valuable timber and an irreplaceable heritage 'going up in smoke'.

The profligate wastage of timber does not only occur at the point of timber extraction. During the conversion and processing stages, wastage is also evident. Referring to Peninsular Malaysia where the timber industry is fairly sophisticated, Salleh Mohd Nor and Ho Kam Seng estimated that waste by processing mills averages 40 per cent. Thus, 'complete utilisation will continue to remain a dream — a myth!' (*Idem* 1982:106). In December 1983, the Director of the Sabah Foundation (which owns about 36 per cent of Sabah's remaining unlogged commercial forest), Tan Sri Ben Stephens, reported that for every cubic metre of timber sold by Sabah, another cubic metre is cut but discarded (*Borneo Bulletin*, December 17, 1983). According to Salleh Mohd Nor and Francis S.P. Ng the real reason for this wastage is the continued and ready availability of forest for 'creaming' at the rate of over 282,800 hectares (700,000 acres) each year (1983:486). In calling

8. In fact the great forest fire in Borneo in 1984 has been attributed to the effects of selective logging. The 'waste' timber in selectively logged districts provided excellent tinder for kindling in what would otherwise have been a moist tropical rainforest (*Asiaweek* 1984:37-8).

for a more concerted effort to reduce the wastage, the Malaysian foresters stated that there 'is a need for political commitment to reduce the opening of forest areas'. Furthermore 'if rational and judicious management of their resources is not practised, it is very likely that Sabah and Sarawak may face the same prospect as Peninsular Malaysia in the not-too-long future' (Salleh Mohd Nor and Ho Kam Seng 1982:102-6).

According to a senior forester, in 1979 when the demand and prices of logs were good, loggers and licensees in Sarawak were known to have felled and extracted trees of all species even down to eight inches in diameter. In the Stateland Forests, where there was no yield control being exercised, logs with hollows were also taken. The forests were exploited to the maximum. On the other hand when the demand and the prices were at its lowest in 1972 and 75, timber operators were creaming their forest areas. Blocks were left opened for months and even years. Extraction was poor as only the best logs were removed which comprised some ten per cent of the available log volume. This occurred in both the Stateland Forests and the Permanent Forests (Tan Yaw Kang 1980:145). He added that because the log industry is export oriented and because it was a buyer's market, only selected species were cut. Others with great utilisation potential were not favoured. This unwanted resource becomes silviculturally undesirable for the next crop. It is therefore destroyed by poisoning. This represents a further waste of financial resources and presents an environmental hazard as well (*Idem* 1980:146). As the logging industry is entirely dependent on the world economy, it is highly volatile. The main aim of most licensees of the hill forest concessions is to log the area fast and get out quickly, before the market becomes unstable again (*Idem* 1980:147).

From the above discussion, it can be seen that the forest resources of Malaysia are facing a critical shortage situation. The rate of timber exploitation due to uncontrolled logging is far exceeding any attempts at rehabilitation. In 1978, the Director of the Forest Research Institute warned that the total loggable forest left in Peninsular Malaysia was a mere 3.8 million hectares (9.3 million acres). Of this, *less than half* are primary forest. 'If current logging rates are allowed to continue within the agri-conversion forests, it is estimated that all these forests would be depleted of timber resources within 12 years' (Salleh Mohd Nor 1982:78).

As pointed out in Chapter Eight, the rate of logging has been reduced in Peninsular Malaysia but logging has tremendously expanded in Sabah and Sarawak to make up for the decline in Peninsular Malaysia. At current rates of logging, the timber resources in East Malaysia will run out very soon as well. In December 1984, Prof. Ismail Salleh, Head of the Department of Analytical Economics, Universiti Kebangsaan, declared that Malaysia's timber resources will be depleted by 1996. This would lead to a collapse of the timber industry and 60,000 people would lose their jobs. On top of this, the country will face balance of payments problems with greater outflow of the ringgit (*New Straits Times*,

December 3, 1984). From this dismal prediction by a leading economist, we see that the headlong and wasteful exploitation of the forests by the timber industry has not only caused severe social and environmentally adverse effects but will soon also lead to a crisis of economic dislocation. The unplanned fast-as-you-can rush to make profits from timber is rapidly destroying the forest and we will have to pay the environmental and economic costs.

Residual stands of a logged forest, with sparse canopy as compared with the thick canopy of a primary forest.

Timber camp with severely damaged forest land around it.

Above: Logging roads stretching for hundreds of miles cause the most damage to the forest ecology, with massive erosion of valuable topsoil.

Below: Erosion of hillsides and river banks caused by uncontrolled logging.

CHAPTER ELEVEN

Dams Flooding Out Native Lands

It is increasingly realised that the construction of large dams can have devastating effect on indigenous societies. By flooding out large areas, dams would mean the total loss of native lands and the disintegration of viable native communities through forced resettlement. This Chapter analyses the socioeconomic and environmental impact of dams on native society in Sarawak.

Plans to Build Dams in Sarawak

Whilst the timber industry has in the past posed the gravest threat to the lands of Sarawak natives, a major new problem has emerged in recent years in the form of hydroelectric dam projects. The Federal Government has accorded high priority to hydro power development as part of its energy diversification programme to reduce the country's dependence on oil. Sarawak has been identified as a region with a rich potential for hydro development, due to the abundance of rivers. Feasibility studies conducted in the 1970s identified at least six locations where hydro dam projects were recommended — Batang Ai (in the Lubok Antu District in the Second Division), Pelagus, Bakun, Murum, Baleh and Belaga (all of them in the Upper Rejang of the Seventh Division).

In 1977, the Batang Ai project was started, and it was officially opened in August 1985. The project, which cost $526 million, is now in operation and provides electricity for Kuching and Sibu areas. Meanwhile, plans were seriously being laid to introduce new dam projects in Pelagus and Bakun. When rich coal deposits were found at the Pelagus area, the project there was cancelled, and attention focused instead on Bakun, where a dam originally costed at $10 billion was proposed. According to the feasibility study recommendations, dams at Murum, Baleh and Belaga on the same river system as Bakun would be built at a later date as part of an integrated hydro development programme.

The hydro projects are a threat to the natives' traditional ways of life and their land rights since large portions of their forests would be flooded and thousands of natives would be forced to resettle to make way for the dams. The Batang Ai dam led to the flooding of 21,000 acres of land and the resettlement of 3,000 natives. The Bakun project, if implemented, would flood almost 700 sq. km. of forests and cause the resettlement of 5,000 natives. The remaining projects — Murum, Baleh, Belaga and Pelagus — would displace an estimated 15,000 other natives from their lands, if carried out. To make way for the dams, the natives would have to surrender their customary rights to land, move from their forests, and be 'resettled' on fixed agricultural lands provided by the government, together with some monetary compensation. Hydro development has already dislocated many natives in the Batang Ai project and will disrupt the lives of many thousands more should the other dams be built. This Chapter examines the impact of the Batang Ai project, the possible effects of the Bakun project, and also looks at the general issues of the social, health and environmental impact of dam projects.

The Batang Ai Hydro Power Project

Work on the concrete-faced rock filled dam began in December 1980. It was officially opened by the Prime Minister in August 1985. The dam is already operational. The Batang Ai dam consists of a main dam across the Batang Ai and three saddle dams to prevent the lake that will result from spilling into other valleys. The main dam is 85 metres high and 810 metres long at its crest. This project was financed by both local sources and foreign loans. The Employees Provident Fund supplied $128 million while the Federal Government provided $100 million, $100 million came from the Overseas Economic Cooperation Fund of Japan, $90.1 million from the Asian Development Bank, $81 million came from Mitsui Trust and Banking Company of Japan, $22 million from the Export Finance and Insurance Corporation of Australia, and $5 million from the Export Credit Guarantee Department in Britain (*Borneo Bulletin*, May 4, 1985). The main contractor was the Japanese joint venture group Maeda-Okumura. The consultants were Snowy Mountains Engineering Corporation, an Australian firm engaged by the Australian Government Assistance Bureau under its development assistance programme to Malaysia. SESCO (Sarawak Electricity Supply Corporation) which owns the Batang Ai project is working on a lifespan of 50 years for the dam (*The Star*, August 27, 1985). The scheme will generate 92 megawatts (mw) of electricity per year. (The energy needs of Sarawak in 1983 was 100 mw).

The people affected by the Batang Ai Dam are Iban. The Batang Ai can well be considered the heartland of Iban tradition and culture. When the first wave of Iban left their homes in the middle reaches of the Kapuas river in East Kalimantan sixteen generations ago (sometime in the middle of the sixteenth century) they entered (what was then not even Sarawak) through the low lying watershed between the Kapuas and the Batang Lupar (Batang Ai), settling first in the Undup and Kumpang river valleys. From the Kumpang valley they moved to the middle reaches of the Batang Ai, between the present day towns of Engkilili and Lubok Antu[1]. From here, the Iban moved further up the Batang Ai into the upper tributaries, the Engkari Debok, Mepi, and Jingin. Thus it was the Batang Ai which was the repository of the oldest and best of Iban oral tradition and folklore.

The Batang Ai project covers some 40,000 acres of land, of which 21,000 acres would eventually be flooded (*Sarawak Tribune*, September 16, 1981). This means that large areas of forest and lands held under customary tenure which include swidden farms, crops and ancestral lands belonging to shifting cultivators have been submerged. This project involved the resettlement of 29 longhouses above the dam and 4 longhouses below the dam site. Out of the 29 longhouses, ten have been inundated. It involved the compulsory transfer of these families to a resettlement site about six kilometres below the dam site (Masing n.d.). Some 3,000 people from 26 longhouses were resettled (*Borneo Bulletin*, May 4, 1985). The longhouses below the dam were also affected as part of their land were acquired by the government as the resettlement area for the displaced communities (Masing n.d.).

The resettlement area comprises 8,000 acres which was acquired from other Iban who were paid $10 million in compensation (*The Star*, August 27, 1985). The Iban will now have to abandon shifting cultivation and grow cash crops instead. SALCRA is the agency primarily responsible for implementing this policy. Each family in the resettlement scheme was promised it would be given 11 acres of land, five for rubber cultivation, three for cocoa, two for padi or general farming land and one acre for fruit trees (*Borneo Bulletin*, September 3, 1983). They were also promised cash compensation for their lost swidden farms, fruit trees and ancestral lands.

An opinion survey conducted by the Sarawak Museum of the longhouses which would be affected by the h.e.p. project between 1978 and 1979, revealed that the majority of the people interviewed did not fully understand the project and its implications. Most of them were hill farmers and over 70 per cent of them had no schooling. Almost half (40-50 per cent) of the male population and 30-35 per cent of the female population were below the age of 15 years. The shifting cultivators expressed the following fears:

i)   the most important was the loss of their property;
ii) loss of income from pepper and rubber;

---

1.   The Batang Lupar is known as the Batang Ai or Ulu Ai beyond Lubok Antu. For further discussion on Iban oral genealogies (*tusut*) and migration see Benedict Sandin, 'The Westward Migration of the Sea Dayaks', *Sarawak Museum Journal*, Vol. 7 No. 7 (1956); *The Sea Dayaks of Borneo Before White Rajah Rule*: Macmillan, London (1967).

iii) loss of traditional heirlooms and assets;
iv) to have to start a new way of life all over again;
v) flooding of sacred land means breaking taboo and the gods would punish them with natural disasters (*kudi*);
vi) the fear that the government would not meet their demands; and
vii) there will be no more place to plant padi.

The survey concluded that the resettlement and flooding would engender many problems concerning *adat* and importance and due recognition should be given to the traditional leadership patterns before they were eroded by administrative leaders in the new resettlement villages. The survey's findings further stated that the dam project 'would mean the displacement of those Iban communities found living in the areas required to be flooded into a lake. Their enforced relocation would likely be difficult and traumatic. Unless proper regard and due consideration are given for their social and economic interests, the evacuated Iban will suffer from the experience of moving; as it would uproot them from their traditional life patterns; upset their productivity and income; and deprive them from their most important assets — land. In short, they may see it as a direct threat to their very existence' (*Sarawak Museum* July 1979).

The resettlement of the affected people began in August 1982 and was completed by the end of 1984. During the construction period, many natives demonstrated their opposition against the dam project and the resettlement plan. In one incident in 1982, 15 Iban stormed the dam worksite and demanded compensation for the land and their burial grounds which had been affected by the project. The Iban men took away the keys of 32 heavy machinery vehicles from the workers and said they would only return them when their demands were met (*New Straits Times*, July 30, 1982). A little more than a week later, two Japanese workers were attacked on their way back to their quarters at the dam site around midnight. One of them died a few weeks later from the injuries (*Borneo Bulletin*, Aug 28, 1982). Clearly these were acts of desperation by the people who felt extremely threatened by the dam project. These protests prompted the Chief Minister to issue a warning that the government would deal firmly with those who hinder the implementation of development projects (*New Straits Times*, August 21, 1982). In August 1985, a demonstration was staged by more than 50 natives who were protesting that they had not been paid their compensation. This assembly was broken up by the police just before the arrival of the Prime Minister who had come to officially open the dam (*Borneo Bulletin*, August 31, 1985).

In January 1984, a newspaper report revealed that the resettled Iban felt that they had been given a raw deal by the authorities. According to the *tuai rumah* Tampa anak Munaung, head of the Kaong Ili longhouse: 'We were told that when we arrived at our new longhouses, we would be given 11 acres of cleared land. The land was also supposed to have been planted with five acres of rubber, three acres of cocoa, and two acres of padi. The remaining acre was to be used for growing fruits or vegetables'. So far, each family had been given only one acre of cleared land. 'At present we have no steady income. The cocoa when planted will take three or four years before it is ready for harvesting, and the rubber trees will take seven or eight years. In the mean time how are we to pay for our homes, our electricity and water supply? The next few years will be hard for us, until the money from our cash crops comes in', he said. The headman of another house added that 'our land has not been cleared or planted yet, and we don't even have the seeds. Right now, all we do is eat and sleep!'. (*New Straits Times*, January 31, 1984).

Another *tuai rumah*, Marajang anak Achang said that they were first told that the houses built by the Housing Development Commission for them in the resettlement area would cost $26,000 and that a deposit of $8,000 would be made in their name as compensation for their old longhouses and *temawai* (previous abandoned longhouses) (*Ibid* January 31, 1984). However they were now charged $27,300 per *bilek*. 'We didn't want to move to the resettlement area, until we were told that the houses would be free' said another longhouse dweller (*Ibid*). This cycle of indebtedness that they find themselves in has deeply troubled the settlers as the *tuai rumah* himself foresees: 'We have no work. What are we going to do when our compensation money is finished?' The *tuai rumah* added that although they have been compensated for their crops, money for their swidden farms and burial grounds (for which they were promised $350 per acre) had not been paid.

According to the Deputy Chairman of SALCRA, Sidi Munan, the compensation for their farm land is being paid in stages 'as each claim is verified' (*Ibid*). SALCRA had to work out the amount of swidden farm land each farmer owned and this would be determined by the amount of rice each farmer obtained in one season (in *gantang*) from his swidden farms (UNESCO/UNEP 1983:223). He added that the land which they were given in the resettlement scheme was free 'and it is good land'. The farmers will be discouraged from planting traditional hill padi and the settlers have been granted titles to their land in perpetuity. However, the housing and development will not be for free. 'We (SALCRA) have given each family a loan of $2,000 per acre, which will be repaid out of their income when the farms are in production. This is the SALCRA method: we finance the projects and they pay us back. The farmers know they are not getting a hand-out, and must work to repay the loan' (*News Straits Times*, January 31, 1984).

SALCRA's policy of giving the farmers one acre of cleared land per family was a deliberate move to coincide with the amount of work at the dam site. 'Most of them are supposed to be working on the dam construction site until 1985. Then as the work tapers off, they will begin to work on the remaining 10 acres' said Sidi Munan (*Ibid*). However according to *tuai rumah* Marajang anak Achang, 'We were told that first preference at the dam site would be given to our people, but most of us have been denied jobs. They are bringing in people from outside to work at the site'. Another settler said that although many people from his longhouse had applied, only ten people were given jobs at the Sarawak Electricity Supply Corporation (SESCO) office, and five others at the dam project. 'They told me I was too old', said the 65 year old man, who claimed that he was still strong enough to work in the farm (*Ibid*).

Apart from the above complaints the settlers said that they were promised free electricity, water, and housing when they moved to their new homes by some politicians. When these promises were disclaimed by SALCRA, the settlers felt cheated. Sidi Munan summed up the reaction of the settlers very aptly when he was quoted as saying, 'I think they are probably in shock ... because the new system is so different' (*Ibid*).

In April 1985, a SESCO official admitted that Iban who had moved from the danger zone of the dam area had not been paid the full compensation. According to him, Iban in the 'partial danger zone' whose lands were not submerged were also resettled. These people had been promised compensation for their fruit trees and crops. However, they were later informed that they would be compensated *only* for their crops which had been submerged. 'These people didn't really want to move where they would each have only 13 acres of land . . . . But they moved, because they were told: "Before you move, the crops at the resettlement area will be full grown and the houses will be ready". But at least 18 families were not paid compensation for their crops, were given uncleared land and were also not paid compensation for their homes as these were considered 'temporary' homes. A SALCRA nursery has been growing cocoa and rubber and about one member of each family has been employed at the nursery. They are not paid very much — I believe it is $8 per day ... And the resettlement houses are giving problems. Some of them have started cracking and leaking'. Pupils from five primary schools which were resettled are all crammed into the Lubok Antu primary school. Even holding two sessions of school has not solved the overcrowding (*New Straits Times*, April 3, 1985). In August 1985, the Member of Parliament for Lubok Antu, Sylvester Langit (whose family was among those resettled as a result of the project), said that many of the longhouses which were resettled in the first phase of resettlement had yet to be fully paid compensation promised to them. Of the $35 million compensation due to them, $10 million had yet to be paid. (*Borneo Bulletin*, August 31, 1985). Mr Langit subsequently was killed in a car accident in June 1986. When the Press visited the late MP's longhouse, Rumah Jarop, for his funeral they were shocked by the deplorable living conditions the resettled families were living in. Rumah Jarop comprising 18 families is presently squatting on someone else's land. They have been living in their makeshift house since 1983 when they left their homes in the Batang Ai. Says one resident, 'no land has been allocated to us for the promised new longhouse.' (*Sarawak Tribune*, June 7, 1986).

The resettled Iban were not the only ones who lost their lands. The resettlement area was acquired from other Iban who were made to surrender their land as a result. In a letter to the press in September 1985 a native complained that he had not received compensation for his land affected by the dam. 'I was told that if I refused to sign the deeds of surrender, there will be no compensation whatsoever. So I signed the deeds and they paid me a dollar per cocoa tree (of about 18 months to 2 years) which I have planted. When they count our seedlings, they did not consider the labour and cost.' He had gone to see the Lands and Surveys officials and they had asked him whether he had a land title for the acquired property. He was paid $60 for every durian tree he lost. 'Losing these durian trees are like losing the tombs of a memorial of our great grandfathers. They grow in strength eating these fruits and now we sacrifice them for somebody, not the soul of the dead grandparents, but the tower (dam), wires and roads. We are the wellknown squatters of native origin.' (*Borneo Post*, September 14, 1985).

For those who had received compensation, the effects were also devastating. Each Iban family were given between $30,000 to $100,000 and many of them did not know how to deal with this new found wealth. They went on a spending spree buying expensive consumer goods like cars, television sets and electrical gadgets. Others were cheated of their money by smooth talking conmen who promised them land and shares. Many squandered thousands of dollars on cockfights. (*The Star*, August 27, 1985). This had happened in the space of 17 months to the first batch of settlers (who moved in August 1982) many of whom had received as much as $100,000 to $150,000 per family. Money was frittered away on TV sets, video, hifi sets, cars and gambling. Those who received $10,000 to $15,000 had already spent it all during the past year. (*New Straits Times*, January 31, 1984).

Below is a pathetic example of what occurred to a resettled Iban family after receiving compensation. This was related to me by a young native man who had made many visits to the new homes of families resettled by the Batang Ai project:

'When the Batang Ai dam was being built, I had gone there to work. I was happy to be there because I thought I would have a chance to see the dam and now I would like to share with you my experience from the very beginning of my visit to Batang Ai. I met an old Iban who happened to be the head of the longhouse so I introduced myself to him. I asked him a question. I called him "Father" as a way of respect.

"Father, how is the life after the dam, how is your life now after you've been resettled?" He said: "It is lovely, it is fantastic. I have a lot of money in the bank. I have a good house. I have a big car, brand new. And we now have roads to go to town". He asked me: "Son, what do you want to drink?" I told him: "I want only a cup of coffee". He was so disappointed with my words. He told me: "I do not drink coffee here. I've only brandy, whisky, Bacardi and the expensive brands of liquor. Why, you want to drink coffee? Why do you look down on me? You are not a good boy and I'm sorry we have no coffee here". So I had to get drunk because I forced myself to drink. And I started to wonder how beautiful their life was because at that time I still had very little knowledge about them.

After ten months in the Batang Ai I came back home. I went again to Batang Ai to visit my old father and his face smiled when he saw me. He said to me: "O you're here again" and I asked him: "Father how is life now, it has been so long since I left you all and we have not seen each other". And he answered me slowly "Son, to say that it is good will be bad, I should say here that the life here is good because I have a house, I have electricity, I have water supply and I have a car, I have roads. But I say it is bad because I have to pay for the water bill, I'm going to pay for the electricity. I'm surprised that I have to pay $27,000 for this house and I'm paying it monthly and last month my electricity bill was very high, because I had opened it for 24 hours: with the refrigerator on, with the TV on, ironing clothes, using the rice cooker and the heater and the lights. I thought it was free at the beginning. So it was a burden to me to have to pay the very high bills last month. And I have to maintain this house with my own money. And I have to buy the petrol for this car and maintain this car. I'm going to buy the vegetables and fish in the town because hardly anything is found around here. No crops are available to us here although the government promised to give crops to us before we came. That's why I tell you it is bad and the life is bad here".

I went back to my own district. After I returned I read about the problems of the Batang Ai people in the newspapers and that the people in the resettlement areas were blaming their politicians for many of the problems they were facing in the resettlement scheme. I wanted to know what had happened to my rich father so I met him again for the third time and I asked him again, "Father I have come, how is life now? After reading a lot of news about you all here, I am anxious to know". With his sad face, I should say, he never smiled again. He spoke to me in a low voice which had no life at all "*Parai tok anak*" — (Son, we are going to die).

But I said "Why? I'm not satisfied with the answer". He said after a long pause, "No money. The money in the bank has finished. I can't afford to pay the electric bill so I cut off the meter, maybe I will cut off the water meter later on if I can't afford to pay that too. The house is leaking, I have to pay for the maintenance". I asked him: "Father, where is the big car?" And he answered me: "I have sold it, son". I said "Why, it is a good car, it is brand new, it is only over a year old". He said: "I have no money". I asked him how much did he sell it for and he answered: "$500". "And how much did you buy it for?" and he told me "$25,000". And that car is a Galant Sigma, a big car. I shook my head. "So what will happen, father?". He told me: "We are going to fight for our rights because we have been cheated. We thought the authorities were sincere, but they are not". I told him: "It is too late to struggle now".

He never answered me and brought me a cup of water. I thought it was expensive brandy which they were offering me again. But it was only plain water and it was not boiled and he gave it to me with a very sad voice: "I have only this, son — *nadai utai ka beri nuan* (I've nothing to offer you) — *Ayer kosong tu aja*" (It is only plain water). I was so sad to drink this. They were laughing at the beginning but now they are crying, and I believe they will cry forever and forever because they have lost their lovely land'.

Even the promises of employment have turned sour. At its peak, the dam project employed 1,500 Iban. By May 1985, this figure had been halved (*Borneo Bulletin*, May 4, 1985). An earlier news report projected that when the scheme was completed some 1,000 workers would be laid off and many of those retrenched would be Iban from the Lubok Antu area (*Ibid* October 13, 1984). In fact when the project is on stream, there will be a permanent on-site work force of only 40-50 people (*Ibid* May 4, 1985). This would mean that many Iban will face unemployment, and an uncertain future.

As can be seen from the above discussion, the farmers have not been provided sufficient land to plant their cash crops, while others who were working at the dam are now retrenched and have no regular income. Cash crops take a few years to mature. This means that they will have no steady source of income for some time to come. Being unfamiliar with the cash economy, many of them have also squandered their compensation money. For those who have not, it will be a matter of time. The 11 acres provided will not be sufficient for each family as it expands and fragmentation occurs. Land hunger and scarcity will be an increasing problem. With no land, no money and no skills, they will ultimately drift to the urban areas in search of employment. This was precisely what happened in 1974 in Mukah, in the Third Division. The Sarawak Land Development Board (SLDB) took over native customary land for its development purposes and compensated the natives. The compensation money ranged from hundreds to thousands of dollars. These natives who had never handled such huge sums of money before, started to spend it on consumer goods like cars, sewing machines, generators and so on. The money quickly disappeared and without any more land or a steady source of income they drifted to nearby towns like Sibu (UNESCO/UNEP) 1983:213, 229) and joined the urban poor becoming landless squatters.

It can be seen that resettlement of the 3,000 natives due to the construction of the Batang Ai dam has meant a total loss of customary tenure to their farm lands. This in effect spells the death of shifting cultivation and *adat* related to swidden farming for these people. With cash crop cultivation under the SALCRA system, they have become indentured labourers who have to work to pay for the houses they now live in, the amenities provided for, and the crops they plant. 'The housing and development will not be free' says SALCRA. This is adding insult to injury as in the first place, they were forced to leave their lands and abandon their traditional way of life. In return they have been told that they would have to pay for the cost of resettlement in terms of the crops, the house and the facilities provided.

But an even greater social cost is the loss of their ancestral lands and customary rights, their sacred burial grounds and the forests which have been a major source of their sustenance. In fact the dam has forced Iban to move higher across its waters to the hills beyond to hunt for food. In November 1985, seven Iban drowned when their boat capsized after returning from a hunting trip (*Borneo Bulletin*, November 23, 1985). The forest and customary rights are part and parcel of the traditional society and *adat* of shifting cultivators. With its passing away, the entire social fabric of swidden society breaks down. The impact of this and the social stress incurred is only beginning to be felt.

To make matters more confusing, the Prime Minister, when he opened the Batang Ai dam in August 1985, announced that the people of Sarawak would have to 'pay the price' in higher rates for electricity generated by the dam. This was because of the millions of dollars paid in compensation, which the Prime Minister described as 'completely ridiculous' (*Ibid* August 31, 1985). This statement revealed that Sarawakians might not be able to benefit from the dam in terms of electricity rates which are cheaper or even similar to pre-Batang Ai levels; and also how political leaders view the compensation paid to natives who are forced out of their lands as a ridiculously excessive burden to the State. This, as expected, generated bitterness among some Sarawakians, as expressed in letters to the press. For instance, a letter-writer calling himself 'Bujang Orang Ulu' (An Unmarried Native) in Balui, wrote: 'After the people have reluctantly sacrificed

their land, properties and moved to restart a completely new life, the
Prime Minister described as "completely ridiculous" the millions of
dollars paid in compensation over the Batang Ai project . . . What does
all this mean to people affected and the state? It is but a realisation
of their fears and what the environmentalists have been saying prior
to the commencement of the Batang Ai hydro project.' (*Borneo Post*,
September 20, 1985).

The Bakun Hydro Power Project

When the Batang Ai project was being constructed, the authorities
were evaluating the possibility of starting two other hydro power
projects. The locations identified were at Pelagus and Bakun in the
Upper Rejang river in the Seventh Division. In 1983, however, the
proposal to build Pelagus dam was put off indefinitely because of
the discovery of large coal deposits (200 million tonnes) in the area
(*Borneo Bulletin*, September 17, 1983).

Meanwhile, the proposed Bakun project was actively pursued,
with feasibility studies commissioned. The dam was proposed to be
located at the Bakun rapids on the Batang Balui (the part of the Upper
Rejang river beyond Belaga bazaar), 37 kilometres from Belaga.
The dam is planned to be 204 metres high, and would have a water
surface of 695 sq. km., flooding forests and farm lands. The dam's
maximum generating capacity is planned at 2,400 mw. Of this,
750 mw will be transmitted by undersea cables to Peninsular Malaysia.
The high voltage direct current (HVDC) cables will be 650 km in
length, making them the longest underwater cables in the world.
This has raised questions about security and technical feasibility
(*Utusan Konsumer*, February 1986). Of the remaining electricity
generated, a large proportion is also planned to be channelled to
Sabah, Singapore and Indonesia, besides other parts of Sarawak.

Although the original cost of the Bakun project was estimated
at $10 billion, the final cost could balloon to $20 billion or more
when increases in costs are taken into account. When the interest
on loans are included, the cost could balloon further to $40 billion.
Half the cost is to build the dam, another half to build transmission
lines to other parts of Sarawak, Sabah and Peninsular Malaysia.
This means that the Bakun dam project if implemented will dominate
a very big chunk of investment funds in the Fifth and Sixth Malaysian
Plans. Economically, this will be risky, because the project will involve
huge foreign loans (M$10-$15 billion) pushing up Malaysia's foreign
debt (already at M$40 billion in 1985). According to the project's
feasibility report, Bakun will be profitable for SESCO, the owner of
the project. However this has been disputed. Dr Ismail Salleh an
economist from Universiti Kebangsaan (Malaysia's National University)
says: 'It all depends on the assumptions in the feasibility study.
Feasibility reports can sometimes be used to serve the interests of a
project. By manipulating assumptions on revenue and cost, a project

can be made to look profitable'. Dr Ismail further added that even if
the project was profitable for the owners, there might not be a net benefit
to society since there are added costs such as displacement of people,
and adverse ecological and health effects (*Utusan Konsumer*, February
1986). So far the government has spent $37 million on a feasibility study
conducted by SAMA[2] Consortium. The government has told
Parliament that it has no intentions of releasing these reports to the
public (*The Star*, December 3, 1985). This report will form the basis
for the government's decision whether to go ahead or not with the giant
dams at the Pelagus and Bakun Rapids. One of the Bakun project site
engineers has estimated that it may take as long as 30 years to recover
the initial expenditure for the dam. The life cycle of the dam is expected
to be between 30 and 50 years. After this, the dam will be rendered
useless by excessive erosion and siltation (*Sunday Star*, March 4, 1984).

The 204 metres high and one kilometre long concrete arch dam will
have a surface area of about 73,000 hectares (which is larger than
Singapore Island). It will be Southeast Asia's largest dam. This dam
will displace more than 5,000 people living in 52 longhouses belonging
to 16 communities. The ethnic groups affected are the Kenyah and
Kenyah Badang (52 per cent), Kayan (38 per cent), Kajang (6 per cent),
Ukit (3 per cent) and Penan (1 per cent) (Lahmeyer International Draft
Report n.d.). Vast areas of primary forests (at least 80 per cent
according to Forest Department estimates), ancestral lands, crops, fruit
trees and burial grounds will be flooded. 'To all these areas, native
customary rights of acquisition and possession laid down in the Sarawak
Land Code, 1958, apply' stated the Lahmeyer International Draft
Report on 'Socio-Economic Aspects and Resettlement: Midi Pelagus and
Balu 073 Hydro-Electric Projects'.[3] The project will also submerge
seven primary schools, four of which are boarding schools, a dispensary
and four sub-dispensaries. To date no particular area has been proposed
as the new settlement site for the displaced communities[4]. In March

2.   SAMA Consortium is a joint venture of four consulting Engineering Companies
namely: Lahmeyer International the leading company from the Federal Republic of
Germany (FRG), Fichtner (FRG), Dorsch Consult (FRG) and Motor Columbus
(Switzerland).

3.   Lahmeyer International (the West German consultants based in Frankfurt)
together with SESCO prepared the Master Plan study in December 1979 under a
German technical aid programme. Lahmeyer's final report was submitted in July 1982.
(*New Straits Times*, November 27, 1983).

4.   Interestingly, Lahmeyer has suggested to resite the people affected by the Bakun
dam in the Usun Apau plateau 'which apparently has fertile soils' and 'should be
considered as a potential resettlement area'. However, the State Government has plans
to turn the plateau into a private country club cum big game hunting park for the
rich with an entrance fee of M$1 million. The Usun Apau is the traditional homeland
of the Kayan and Kenyah. It is part of the Central Borneo plateau and the watershed
of many rivers in Kalimantan and Sarawak.

1982, the Chief Minister announced at a community dinner in Belaga that he had earmarked an area along the Belaga-Bintulu road for the resettlement of the fifty-two villages which will be submerged by the dam. This resettlement area will be called Bandar Orang Ulu (Interior Peoples' Township) (*Sarawak Tribune*, March 20, 1982). Again in November 1985, the State Assembly was told that the people displaced by the Bakun dam will be resettled in 'model villages'. Although these areas have been identified, no mention of their locations were given (*Sarawak Tribune*, November 13, 1985).

According to Lahmeyer's Draft Report, the dam construction and resettlement scheme 'can initiate a process of rapid social disintegration of longhouse communities'. In the absence of alternative social institutions and mechanisms which could provide the people with a sense of social identity, 'this process' can be 'disadvantageous and critical . . . Most people will find it hard to part with a familiar environment, their graveyard and places which are linked to their oral tradition or personal experiences, such as graves of great chiefs, battle-grounds or places of old longhouses. Especially older people with no knowledge of other regions will find it difficult to adopt the idea of moving and adapting to a new environment'. The Report also warns that for these communities 'uprooted from their former homes and familiar surroundings and settled in a new and under unfamiliar conditions could be traumatic and disorienting . . . the first few years will be a critical period. If resettlement is not well-timed and people have to miss one year of padi cultivation, scarcity of food will result. Also the Kajang[5], the original population of the area, will find it hard to move from their inherited places, because they do not have a tradition of migrating like the Iban, Kayan and Kenyah, and the nomadic Penan' (Lahmeyer International Draft Report n.d.:76).

Referring to the nomadic or semi-nomadic groups like the Penan, Ukit (or Bukat), Bukitan, Sihan and some Kajang subgroups, the Report wrote that these 'subgroups will find the settled way of life in the new settlement difficult to adjust to. The allocation of a small plot of land per household will be felt as a severe restriction on their movement. This would be increased if there is no "hinterland" available to provide them with game and jungle produce.' (Lahmeyer International Draft Report n.d.:76). The report (p77) also says: 'Minority groups like the Bukitan, Ukit and Penan will be absorbed, through intermarriage and exposure to the more numerous and culturally dominant groups like the Kayan, Kenyah and Kajang.'

---

5.   Kajang is a collective term for all the subgroups other than the Kenyah and Kayan in the Upper Rejang. They include the Punan Bah, Tanjong, Sekapan, Kejaman and Lahanan. Very little is known about the history of the Kajang group of peoples. The Sekapan, Kejaman, Lahanan, and Punan Bah have a stratified society. So did the Melanau who are believed to belong to the Kajang group of peoples. The Melanau moved to the coastal areas from the interior and were converted to Islam.

In other words, resettlement may lead to the cultural extinction of these minority groups and their way of life.

According to a newspaper report, opposition to the dam is gathering momentum. Both young and old natives have expressed that they do not want to leave their ancestral lands. (*Borneo Bulletin*, August 27, 1983). This concern about the dam construction and its adverse consequences for the natives has been spearheaded by the young educated Kayan and Kenyah. A Kayan representative of *Sahabat Alam Malaysia* (SAM) has questioned the economic viability of the dams. He also cited two Federal Ministers who say that Malaysia already has more than enough electricity-generating capacity to meet demand.

In January 1983, the Deputy Prime Minister Datuk Musa Hitam when announcing the scrapping of plans for the Tembeling dam project in *Taman Negara* (the National park in Peninsular Malaysia) said that it had been 'found that the existing hydro projects and energy expected from Bintulu gas would be sufficient to meet the nation's needs.' Later in July, the Minister of Energy, Telecoms and Posts, Datuk Leo Moggie had said that 'the electricity supply from various power stations in the country has now exceeded the present need. The present sources are producing 2,400 mw compared to our needs of only 1,300 mw' (*Borneo Bulletin*, September 17, 1983). SAM concluded that there appears to be no need for the 'huge and costly' Rejang power projects which would bring 'tremendous problems to our people who will have to be unnecessarily uprooted and displaced' (*Ibid*).

Apart from this, the project can have adverse social, environmental and health consequences. SAM further added that 'this area is rich in folktales, local legends, folk beliefs and medicines, folk songs and dances and games, traditional handicrafts and technologies — these traditions would be endangered if the people are made to move. The cause of scholarship would also suffer, for anthropologists and sociologists would lose their chance to study the history, traditions and activities of these minority groups' (*Ibid*).

Several Kayan residents have told a newspaper that they would agree to resettle only if they could go to the area of their choice. One headman said his people would only move further upriver, as they did not want to go to an area which was unfamiliar or even unfriendly. A Kayan headman feared that resettlement to a place like Sepakau near Bintulu (which was rumoured to be the resettlement site) would encourage the young adults to desert the community to work for timber companies as well as industrial projects. He saw little advantage in working for a daily wage, as unskilled labourers are poorly paid. He said that the main compensation issue is not money, but land. 'If we are not given enough land to farm, what is the use of money and luxuries like television in the new area?' he asked (*Ibid*).

In 1985, the natives in the Balui voiced their fears and disillusionment concerning the Bakun dam project. At a dialogue session, the *Penghulu* said:

'We have been living on this land for as long as we can
remember. We fought the British, the Japanese and the
communists to protect our land. Some of us even died for it.
Now they want to take it away. We heard that the Bakun
Hydro Electric Project is very big and it will make our country
very rich. But who will get the money? . . . Many times we
have applied for timber concession here . . . but each time we
were rejected. That's why we do not understand — isn't this
our land? If it is, how come others, who do not live in this
area, managed to get the concession? That is why we want to
know what we will get out of this project . . . We heard we will
be given compensation as we will be moved far away from this
area. We heard we will be given money. Most of us do not
know the value of money . . . I know my people and I know
some of them will buy two or three cars, even though they do
not know how to drive . . . put us in a town and most of us
would die, or the young ones would get carried away and bring
shame to our people . . .' (*New Straits Times*, May 25, 1985).
The people also expressed disappointment that they were never
consulted regarding their future. 'We are never given the
chance to talk . . . It would be nice if someone had come to tell
us what is going on and inform us about the government's
instructions . . . We only get important visitors when election is
around the corner'.

In June 1985, the local press visited five longhouses above the Bakun
dam site and found that most of the people opposed the project. The
headman of a Kayan longhouse in Long Murum said that he refused
to leave unless he was fairly compensated by the government. He added
that his people would not let the government decide on their lives by
resettling them just anywhere: 'We would rather die here with our
children and our ancestors if we are forced to move to an area we don't
like' (*Sarawak Tribune*, June 23, 1985).

At Long Bulan in the Ulu Balui, the Uma Bakah Kenyah expressed
a deep attachment to their forests, and their simple way of life which
they fear will disappear when the dam forces them to leave. 'We love
our land. We farm on it, plant fruit trees, build our houses, we rear
and hunt animals, get our wood and *rotan*. And beneath it are buried
our grandfathers and their fathers — we just can't flood their graves',
they said. At Long Geng in the Linau River, the Badang Kenyah were
equally adamant against the dam. 'They never consulted us properly'
a 20 year old youth complained. Others said 'We don't want to resettle,
with a few acres somewhere else, where everything is paid for by money,
where we'll lose all the land and things we now get free from nature'.
The old people have said that they would rather die than leave their
land. 'Let the Dam come and flood us. I won't move out, I will stay
and die with the land . . . If they want to move us, *matai ne'mek, matai
ne'mek, matai ne'mek*' (kill us, kill us, kill us). In fact they realise that

the problems will be worse for their children. With only ten acres per family (in the resettlement scheme) the second and succeeding generations will not have enough land (*Utusan Konsumer*, February 1986).

This love for their land, and their way of life is movingly expressed by this young native when he spoke to me in his village:

'First of all when the dam is built all our land will be flooded and we will be resettled in a new house where it is not like this. And they will give us money for compensation and electricity, water supply, roads and other infrastructure. I feel these are the advantages. The disadvantages we can't see.

We Kenyah are living our own way of life. We are not controlled by whoever except our *tuai kampong* who takes care of us, if we quarrel or divorce or do anything in the longhouse. Now we are practising shifting cultivation freely. We search for wild boar freely in the jungle — nobody can stop us and we have a very beautiful river, beautiful mountain, beautiful scenery and beautiful trees.

We use all this without any payment. We enjoy them all from the very old to the young. And with all these, we have our culture that make us Kenyah. We are the new generation because the old one has gone — they are resting forever in the graveyard. My grandfather, my grandmother, our relatives and whoever they are, they are all gone.

And when starvation comes, nobody is worried because we have a lot of hopes, our land is very rich, a lot of vegetables and other foods which we can take to eat and also the wood is available in the jungle. Nobody can say "no" to us if we want to use them. They are for me and my generation. They were even here before us, before we existed and even before the existence of the government.

Now they are going to flood it. The question is: can they replace this type of life of ours with $10 billion? (A long pause). I don't believe when lots of people tell me that the life of the *ulu* is hard otherwise long long ago we would have all died. Remember we have been here for generations to generations with the same way of life.

I should say that they are saying this to persuade us to give them the green light to go ahead with the (dam) project. Now if they fail to give us the type of life we have now in the new resettlement, I'm going to say that what we are going to lose and this will be the disadvantages of the dam.

The Government always say we should not reject development and building the dam is development. We can't deny that it is development. But let the development be acceptable to me and all of us. A good example would be if they were to give me $1 million and ask me to go into business, for sure I will not know what to do and I will not be successful because I do not have any experience.

But the $1 million is also development and giving me the money is also one way of development but in the end I would still not be successful. Why? because I can't manage this $1 million. This means I can't accept this type of development which will end with nothing but a big loss in my life.

But if they give me nothing and yet bring development to me and give me a school to educate myself on how to do business, even if they have not given me a single cent, but they educate me on how to do business I will still be successful and I will survive. So I prefer this type of development because if they are going to block Bakun, we are going to flood and with the money in our hands, and our ignorant minds, the money will be gone and our lives will be miserable.

Remember that the money can finish tomorrow or today but we are going to live for generations to generations. I should say I'm very clear that we are not ready for this type of development. Even for myself I can't imagine what will happen to me. And what more my grandfather, grandmother, my relatives and all of them here. We are illiterate and ignorant and won't know what will happen tomorrow.

(Turning to those sitting around) So how about you all, do you want the dam? Answer with all sincerity, with your hearts. (Those who were present said): "*Entah mek kelo' perintah, kemempeng Bakun*" (No, we don't want the government to build the dam).

The dam is going to be a heavy burden to everyone of us. It will put us to death with a $10 billion debt. So we have to struggle by all means. If we can't compromise with them, what shall we do? Are we afraid to risk our lives to defend our land? If we are afraid why? If we are not why?

I should say that the spirit of our grandfathers and grandmothers, which depended on this land is a good example for us all. They fought the Iban at the time they called them. headhunters, and they fought with the Colony (British) and they fought with the Japanese and some even died, some suffered hunger and lastly they fought the Indonesians during Confrontation. Many of them died.

That is the symbol of their "breathness" (life) they died for this land, for every single wood in this forest, for every single fish in the river, for every single bird in the air. And for this beautiful river and they are now resting forever in the graveyard. So I should say that everyone of us here must realise this and take the spirit and remember the struggle of our grandfathers for this land.

And now another "*Rajah*"[6] is coming. This is what I call the modern *Rajah*. It is coming to kill us, flood us and to flood our ancestors, flood the fish, flood the trees, chase the birds away — all of which our grandfathers have fought for before. Who are we now — we are the *orang ulu*, the children of our grandfather, what shall we do? What is our stand on this position?

If our grandfathers dared to lose their lives just for this land, how about us? Do you agree with me that we fight till the end of our lives to save this land? We are all the heroes. Nobody can be the hero, we cannot depend on one person alone, we are all the heroes. That is why I say we all must be the heroes. To fight for our dignity, to fight for our rights and protect ourselves from this tragedy.

We need all our brothers the Kenyah, the Kayan, the Penan who are affected to come together and unite to save this land. We have every right to fight because if we don't want the dam, nobody can force us. So we must decide and keep all these words in our hearts forever and forever and if we fail and if all the heroes fail, we must remember these words.

In the new resettlement area we are going to live with oil palm, we are going to live with the rubber, we are going to live with the cocoa, we are going to be given 12 acres of land which is not enough for us. Today the price of all these crops may be higher and we may laugh but how if the price were to drop one day? That is the time we will cry and we will all be fooled.

If we don't have money in the resettlement area, nobody can help because everyone will have to live with money, every step we take, every decision will depend on whether we have money. Our electric bill, our water supply bill, our house maintenance will cost us money as the Batang Ai people has shown us. This has made me not to like to live in the resettlement area.

We have been living here for generations to generations. Whatever happens to the prices in the world market it won't affect us. Here, we can plant many things, we plant padi, we plant vegetables, we plant fruits. And we take care of the fish in the river, we are living with the wildboar in the forest and we are mixing with the birds in the forest on this land. We can take them at anytime if we have nothing to eat.

If I were not able to get any, my brothers and my neighbours can still help me. That is the way of our culture that has enabled me to live until today because this land is a rich land. The government always say that we are living in very

---

6.   *Rajah* refers to the former Brooke rulers who controlled Sarawak until 1946 when it became a British colony.

poor conditions. I don't believe it. They also tell us and tell the world outside that we are eating low quality food. I don't believe. I don't agree with this.

Here we can eat the State fish *ikan semah* (*Tor sp*). We can eat very good quality fish, we eat fresh fish, we eat fresh vegetables, we take fresh meat, we use clean water and we breathe fresh air. We are living in beautiful scenery on this land, which the critics do not enjoy. Our life on this land is peaceful, my grandfather, grandmother and all my brothers here, we enjoy the life.

Our life here is peaceful compared to the towns where life is always threatened by robberies and other crimes. Who will benefit from this if not the big companies and the industries, while we will always become the losers.

I dare to speak out because the Iban in the Batang Ai now suffer after being given a lot of hopes, after being given sweet promises that they are going to enjoy a better life, beside their lovely land. But they have only experienced loss. And now they are crying. Nobody can help them now because they did not help themselves. They did not fight. I don't want the Batang Ai story to happen to us.

So this is a good lesson to us. It is better to cry now, and it is better to argue now and it is better to struggle as it would be useless to struggle after it is too late. You remember my words today and believe we are richer than them now. Now we can catch fish freely, and whatever we need daily we are free to get without using any single cent.

Of course, we need energy to search for whatever we want as the Malay proverb says *"Kalau tidak di pecah ruyong, manakah dapat sagonya?"* (If the palm bark is not cleaved, how can one get the sago?) We are richer than them now because for them in the Batang Ai resettlement if they want to eat fish, they have to buy, if they want to get firewood, they have to buy and everything needs money. How long can the compensation money last?

So no matter what life we face, no matter what difficulties we face on our land, we still can survive because we are rich. Economically we are rich. Culturally we are rich. So we must not give up our struggle and we must not face the same luck as they have. They have given us a very good example. And we should accept it.

I tell you this if we are brave to fight for this land, for our people, I will be the first man to die. But if we are cowards, and fail to protect our ancestors, to protect this lovely land, and to protect our *adat* and our way of life, I will be the first man to go away. I hope everyone of us will have the confidence — to be brave to struggle.

It is worth to die, if we are struggling for our people and it is worth to sacrifice our lives for our children who are coming after us. You see the small face of the younger generation here, they may be my relative, they may be my brother, they may be my sister here. They do not know anything. They do not even know what we are fighting for and what we are talking about today.

Who are responsible for them? It is I and all our people. We know what is good, what is bad for them, because we have always lived our way of life, the young and the old together. And my last word, we will keep the spirit forever and forever in our way of life. It will be with us anywhere we are — like our own heart and our own body. Nobody can remove it except God. One heart, one body, one spirit, united in strength to fight the modern *Rajah*.'

The natives in the Bakun dam area had heard about the problems and hardship faced by the Batang Ai Iban when they were resettled for the dam project. Some of them had also visited the Batang Ai settlers. Others had been informed by Iban workers about the plight of their people in the Batang Ai. These accounts of the Batang Ai people have made the Bakun natives very anxious about their future. This has been made worse by the fact that the latter have not been sufficiently informed by the authorities or visiting politicians regarding the Bakun dam project. They do not want to suffer the same fate as the Batang Ai Iban and thus most of them are opposed to the Bakun dam project.

In February 1986, a group of ten Kayan and Kenyah leaders and representatives of various communities from the Upper Rejang held a press conference in Sibu and swore to defend their land from being destroyed by the Government with their lives. The group led by *tua kampong* Uloi Lian and *tuai rumah* Ngaban Kulleh from Long Geng had sent a memorandum bearing 2,000 signatures to the Prime Minister in which they appealed to the Government to scrap the Bakun project. Copies of the letter were also sent to the Chief Minister and other Members of Parliament. According to *tua kampong* Uloi Lian the scrap-the-dam signature campaign began three months ago and is still going on in several communities. They are confident of collecting at least another 1,000 signatures in the next two months. Most of the natives do not wish to see the project implemented because they would lose their lands, culture and have to move elsewhere. Land is their survival kit according to *tua kampong* Uloi Lian: 'We don't want our land destroyed. Money is nothing to us. Even if we were paid millions of dollars, this money cannot guarantee our survival', he said reiterating that 'money can be printed, land cannot be created'. *Tuai rumah* Ngaban added that his people no longer believed in empty promises as 'too many have been made by the Government and have never been fulfilled' (*Sarawak Tribune*, February 5, 1986). The group who call themselves the 'Bakun Residents' Action Communities' urged the Government to instead spend more money on building roads, improving existing educational and medical facilities and assisting them to develop a more efficient method of cultivation of food crops and cash crops and also to ensure a fair price for their farm products. They also appealed to all Malaysians who are concerned about their fate to support their effort in opposing the Bakun dam project by speaking out on their behalf, to collect signatures and write protest letters and send them to the authorities concerned. They also invited interested parties and individuals to visit their longhouses to see for themselves their way of life and their real problems.

Since the middle of 1985, opposition against the Bakun dam project has increased in momentum. Natives as well as various public interest groups have appealed to the Government to cancel the project. In January 1986, the Minister of Science, Technology and Environment, Datuk Amar Stephen Yong, a Sarawakian, urged the Prime Minister to re-assess the proposed Bakun project. He said that this was necessary because the project would affect the environment and the people living there. 'We may think it is good to bring progress to the otherwise backward tribes but they may not be able to cope with the changes. We need to heed their wishes. They might not want to adopt a different lifestyle because they have for years wandered freely in the jungle choosing their own homesite', he said (*The Star*, January 18, 1986). The call to examine all the arguments expressed by various groups on the Bakun project was also made by the State Minister for Infrastructure Development, Datuk Dr. Wong Soon Kai (*Borneo Post*, March 19, 1986).

Needless to say, the implementation of the Pelagus, Bakun and related dam projects would lead to further displacement of natives, the destruction of their ancestral lands and denial of their rights to customary tenure. Resettlement and cash crop cultivation will mean a complete disruption of their traditional way of life as shifting cultivators. It will lead to the breakdown of *adat* and the economic and sociocultural entity of the various communities affected by the dam. In their new resettled areas, the longhouse community will be dispersed and in its place artificial communities will result, displacing traditional or accepted authority structures. With the forest gone, they will be no longer able to depend on the forest for jungle produce for their food and resources to build their homes and material needs.

For the first few years before their cash crops are ready for harvesting, the natives may not have an income. If this results, they may experience a scarcity of food supply and this will depress their standard of living. Cash crop production will only make them more vulnerable to the world economy. If unsuitable and/or insufficient land is given to them, there will be nothing left for the next generation. This can only lead to a worsening of their socioeconomic condition and encourage the landless impoverished second generation to migrate to the towns thus abandoning rural life altogether.

As has been mentioned, it is the expressed policy of the State government to turn the native communities into settled sedentary agriculturalists and fully integrate them into the cash economy. This policy will be a traumatic experience for shifting cultivators. For the nomadic forest dwellers this can only spell disaster. Under the present land laws, there is no protection and recognition accorded to these forest peoples and their rights to land or territories. Many of these groups have hunted, fished and gathered forest products in the areas they are presently found even before other groups came to settle[7]. In fact they know no other home.

Firstly resettlement would mean that these forest folks cannot hunt, gather products and find wild sago which is their staple food. They will be deprived access to their customary areas (that is if these areas are not flooded), and deprived of their only and sole means of livelihood. Secondly and more importantly, these peoples have no knowledge of sedentary agriculture, let alone hill padi cultivation. Where they have attempted the latter, their efforts have not been successful as the experience in the Seventh Division and other areas of Sarawak have shown; and they have always fallen back on the forest to supplement their needs (Nicolaisen 1976:52; Kedit 1982:225-79). Thus if they can no longer collect wild sago, hunt or fish in their traditional lands and being poor farmers the crops they plant will not be enough to feed them or provide them with a source of income, resettlement can likely lead to malnutrition and extreme psychological deprivation and alienation for these people.

Besides proposed hydro power dam projects in Bakun and Pelagus, there have also been proposals in energy master plans and feasibility reports that other dams be built at Murum, Baleh and Belaga within the same Upper Rejang river system. Altogether, these five dams, if implemented, would displace over 20,000 natives.

At the time of writing (July 1986), the Government has not yet given the final approval for the commencement of the Bakun project, although both the Prime Minister and the former Deputy Premier Datuk Musa Hitam announced that in principle the Government has agreed to the project. It is believed that due to the high cost of the project, and the economic recession currently faced by the country, implementation of the project has been postponed. Until a final decision is made — to proceed or to abandon the project — the natives living in the Bakun area will continue to worry about their land and their future.

---

7.   The Penan of the Seventh Division fall into 13 groups, the Penan Long Kupang, Penan Long Urun (Penan Datahdian), Penan Long Jaik, Penan Long Peran, Penan Long Wat, Penan Long Pangah, Penan Long Luar, Penan Long Lusong, Penan Long Kajang, Penan Belangan, Penan Apaw Long Tanyit, Penan Apaw Long Lawan, Penan Long Saboah. The Balui was the original home of the Penan. When the Kayan migrated from the Apo Kayan, they gradually pushed the Penan into the tributaries of the Balui where they became more and more scattered (Urquhart 1951:497). The Penan here are linguistically and culturally closely related to some of the Penan in the Fourth Division. The 13 groups of Penan in the Seventh Division number 1,200-1,300 persons excluding the Punan Busang. Today they live scattered over a vast area in remote and inaccesible areas in Belaga (Nicolaisen 1976:35-42).

Problems of Resettlement Caused by Dams:
The International Experience

We have already seen the unsatisfactory nature of the resettlement of 3,000 natives affected by the Batang Ai dam. Since the impact of dams on Sarawak natives is bound to be a major issue in the present and future, it would be useful to look at the experience of other countries in this regard.

The displacement of local communities by large scale hydro power projects and the problems which have arisen as a result of this development have been documented by many researchers. According to A K Biswas, President of the International Society for Ecological Modelling: 'Resettlement planning for large dams and their implementation have seldom been successful in developing countries. Most of the sites selected for resettlements are not ready when the settlers arrive, and lack of potable water and sanitary facilities force people to use lake or river water which could be contaminated. People often store water near dwellings for convenience, and this could become potential breeding grounds for mosquitoes which are carriers of numerous diseases. Medical facilities are often non-existent, and people, mostly illiterate and often nomadic, are unaware of the basic precautions necessary for health. Theoretically, the health of settlers in the new environments should be better than before they were evacuated, but in reality conditions generally turn out to be worse than before.' (A K Biswas 1982:527-37).

According to Biswas, people are often moved to areas with less desirable soil and sources of water which are not conducive to farming: 'Agricultural yields diminish and become inadequate. Whereas in earlier locations diet could be supplemented with fish, a common and important source of protein, new areas are often far from water bodies and this source disappears. For example, World Food Programme had to step in at the Volta Dam and the Aswan Dam to alleviate widespread sufferings.'

When faced with food shortages, the settlers may experiment with unfamiliar and toxic plants for food items to which they have been accustomed. This was probably what caused the 'Lusitu tragedy' in 1959, when 53 women and children who were resettled due to the construction of the Kariba dam on the Zambesi river, were poisoned (*Idem* 1982:534). Where the staple diet is changed completely as a result of resettlement, malnutrition may arise. In Thailand, for example, the people who were displaced by a rising lake were resettled in a new area where their staple diet was changed to milled rice. Subsequently, the children aged one to three suffered malnutrition (World Bank 1974:45).

When people are relocated to totally unfamiliar environments they suffer considerable psychological stress. For example the construction of the Kariba dam caused the evacuation of 57,000 members of the Tonga tribe. These people suffered great cultural shock when they were thrust into communities as different from their own as theirs from

Great Britain. Two years were required to clear sufficient land to meet even their subsistence needs. The government had to establish grain stores to avert famine and very serious hardships. Ironically the grain distribution centres became transmission sites of the dreaded sleeping sickness disease (A K Biswas 1982:535).

It has also been found that generally the displaced communities were often neglected by both local governments and international organisations. According to Biswas, 'Operation Noah' a much publicised and expensive scheme to resettle only some of the animals threatened with inundation from the rising waters of Lake Kariba, received more international attention and assistance than the people whose sad plight went unnoticed. He added that planning and constructing adequate and appropriate housing, provision of basic services, including health, and preparation of the land for agriculture have seldom been completed in any developing country prior to the arrival of the displaced people. In most cases, the settlers faced worse facilities than they had enjoyed earlier. In the experience of the major African dams, the emphasis has been placed mainly on constructing 'improved' housing, which has too often turned out to be unsuitable for the people being resettled. 'Rarely had the infrastructure been developed to provide facilities like health services or means of earning a living. The psychological trauma of enforced resettlement, lack of the type of food to which the evacuees had been accustomed for generations, local resentment of the newcomers, breakdown of social order, and the exploitation of the settlers by government officials and local people, all ensured that the refugees were under multidimensional stress for a prolonged period, which in certain cases has extended beyond a decade. In such situations, the people were more susceptible to disease, and consequently their health suffered' (*Ibid*).

According to a World Bank Report, in the long term, local peoples suffer the most serious effects of dam development. 'Displaced from their ancestral homes . . . the adverse psychological impact of these migrations, involving the loss of ties to the land and the destruction of long established traditions, are not compensated for simply by building new towns for the displaced. The adverse health experience of these groups cannot be attributed solely to their increased exposure at the new village sites to those communicable diseases that are peculiar to a lakeside environment in the tropics. Change alone may have a harmful effect' (World Bank 1974:44).

The Environmental Impact Of Dams

The Lahmeyer International Draft Report on the proposed Bakun project optimistically predicts the creation of 'new economic opportunities' which include the development of fresh water fisheries, tourism, employment, electricity and other public amenities as a result of the hydropower project. This is questionable as the experience in other areas have shown. Speaking of African dams, B.B. Waddy states that: 'They wreck the existence of the community displaced, for the minimum possible compensation and for no advantage at all. There are no local electricity supplies around manmade lakes, and seldom any water supplies derived from the lakes themselves. The exclusive beneficiaries are cities or industrial centres far away' (Waddy 1975:39-50). Apart from this, the environmental and health consequences of manmade dams have seldom been taken into consideration let alone seriously studied. These environmental and health problems are examined below.

Environmental Problems: According to a newspaper report quoting the team of German consultants engaged in feasibility studies at the Bakun site, the lake that will be created by the dam will be so large that it will cause changes in the weather in the area (*Borneo Bulletin*, August 27, 1983). The immediate effects in the area of impoundment would be the submersion of valuable timber and some rare plant species which will totally disappear. Destruction of wildlife habitats would lead to the deaths of a significant number of wildlife some of which are already on the endangered list. Sites of historic, archaeological and cultural significance will also be lost forever (*Ibid* September 17, 1983).

Sooner or later the reservoir of a dam fills up with silt and sediments. This is especially so in the tropics where erosion is heavy. Given the present rate of deforestation in the tropics (twenty five acres of rainforest are lost throughout the world every minute of the day) it is no surprise that the rivers carry enormous quantities of silt. Dams very often silt up faster than expected. In the Philippines, the Ambuklao reservoir will last only 30 years instead of the expected lifespan of 62 years. The Peligre dam in Haiti has only 30 years instead of the expected 50 years. In India, the Nizamsagar dam experienced a siltation rate of 530 acre-feet a year. The dam's reservoir is said to have lost 60 per cent of its storage capacity. In China, the Sanmenxia reservoir which was completed in 1960 had to be decommissioned in 1964 due to premature siltation (Goldsmith and Hildyard 1984:228-9). In Malaysia, massive silting is causing 11 hydro power plants (with a total capacity of 260 mw) in Cameron Highlands to operate below capacity and even shut down at times. The silt (from bulldozers denuding the forest cover of the hills) clogs up the tunnels of the dams, causing equipment to malfunction. If Bakun's actual lifespan is less than 50 years, it would jeopardize the project's revenue projections (*Utusan Konsumer*, February 1986).

Big dams often cause earthquakes. The heavy weight of the water increases the pressure on the rock structure and can result in tremors. Major earthquakes caused by dams have occurred in China, India, Greece and Zimbabwe, with loss of lives and property. In 1981 the Aswan dam in Egypt experienced an earthquake of magnitude 5.6 on the Richter scale. In 1967, in India, the Koyna dam experienced a tremor causing the dam to fail, resulting in the loss of 177 lives and injuring 2,300 people. In Italy, an earth movement at Vaiont dam in 1963 caused a landslide resulting in a flood which killed 2,000 people (Goldsmith and Hildyard 1984:107-16). In Malaysia, earth tremors occurred around the Kenyir dam area in Trengganu State in 1985 and will continue for two to three years (*Berita Harian*, November 28, 1985). The biggest fear is a dam collapse or failure. The failure of small dams is one per cent a year. Examples of dam failure can be found all over the world. The Johnstown dam in US killed between 2,000-10,000 people while the St. Francis dam saw 300 dead; the Malpasset dam in France took 421 lives; and the Machau dam in India killed 1,500 people (Goldsmith and Hildyard 1984:103-4). In July 1985 a dam burst in Italy burying an Alpine valley and killed more than 200 people (*New Sunday Times*, July 21, 1985). In April 1986, an irrigation dam burst in Sri Lanka inundated dozens of villages and killing at least 100 people. At least 30,000 people were made homeless. Thousands of hectares of rice and crops were destroyed (*New Straits Times*, April 22, 1986). There is no certainty that Bakun will be free from such risks. In fact early in 1985, rumours were rife that the rocks on one side of the hill where the proposed Bakun dam will be built would not be able to withstand the pressure of the water build-up behind the dam. This had sparked fears among people living as far down as Sibu, Kapit and Belaga. It was believed that the rumour originated from workers at the dam site. It was said that if the rocks could not bear the water pressure, the dam will give way and the water would rush downriver flooding all the towns along the Rejang river. A German geologist working at the dam site was quoted as saying that such a disaster had happened in Russia. He had pointed out that if the rocks cannot take the pressure, there might be an earthquake (*Sarawak Tribune*, June 23, 1985).

A study of large dams and their environmental impact by Peter H. Freeman found that in dam areas submersion of river stretches will affect fish spawning and breeding areas. This will reduce fishery resources downstream. Erosion and siltation will also occur at the construction site. When the lake is filled, large quantities of nutrients are released into the water from the soil and vegetation. This will stimulate the growth of algae and water weeds. Moreover, large quantities of decaying plant material will deplete the dissolved oxygen and some fish species will die (especially those found in swift running water). As plants and grasses emerge, the area can be a breeding ground for vectors of diseases such as mosquitoes and snails. The quality of the water will change and increase salinity may result from evaporation in the dam area. The new lake ecosystem can expose the people living around the lake to endemic diseases transmitted by water. The water can be contaminated by human faeces, and urine in the immediate vicinity of the villages. This will lead to an increased risk of diseases like dysentery, typhoid, cholera, hepatitis and parasitic diseases (Peter H. Freeman 1977) which are all communicable.

Human Health Problems: Hydro power projects involve the construction of large structures like dams, spillways and diversion works. These create employment oportunities and large number of workers of different categories move into these areas. This also means that large numbers of unskilled and uneducated labourers arrive to look for jobs. Sometimes this involves large scale imported labour from other regions as in the case of the Aswan dam in Egypt and the Bhakra-Nangal project in India (Biswas 1982:530-31). This also occurred in the Batang Ai project. In 1982, a news report said that 800 skilled, semi-skilled and non-skilled male Bangladesh workers were employed to work in the Batang Ai hydro electric project, Bintulu airport construction and timber concession areas in Sarawak (*Sarawak Tribune*, July 2, 1982).

Since most dams are built in remote interior areas of the country, they often lack suitable housing, sanitation and other infrastructural facilities. While the existing level of sanitation though primitive, may be adequate to meet the needs of a small population, the arrival of many outsiders and the increase in population can have adverse health consequences. According to a World Bank Report, new arrivals introduce new diseases or new strains of locally endemic diseases. Highly mobile workmen who tend to follow new construction projects are a serious source of disease transmission. 'A special problem' it noted 'is an almost certain sharp increase in venereal disease, first among the migrant workmen and then the local population' (World Bank 1974:43).

Improvement of the habitats of disease carrying vectors due to hydro power development can give rise to many serious endemic diseases. These include malaria, schistosomiasis, dengue, viral encephalitis and Bancroftian filariasis (elephantiasis) (*Ibid* 1974:48-50).

Malaria: An increase in the mosquito population often occurs in the early stages of clearing and constructing a project site, as breeding occurs wherever water accumulates, however small. These include ground puddles, vehicle ruts, and trash heaps containing discarded metal containers. According to A.K. Biswas, very few in-depth studies are available on the relationship between water development projects and malaria. However it has been found that in India, Pakistan and Sri Lanka, the incidence of malaria has increased owing to impoundments (A. K. Biswas 1982:527-37). In an environmental impact assessment of the Kamburu-Gtaru dam in Kenya it was indicated that 'increase in transmission in Kamburu will move malaria from the presently low mesoendemic towards hyperendemic level' (Oomen, J.M.V. 1979:134). Malaria was also a problem during the early days of the dams operated by the Tennessee Valley Authority in the US (A.K. Biswas 1982:527-37).

There are over 100 species of mosquitoes all over the world which are capable of carrying malarial or filarial infections like Bancroftian filariasis or arboviruses like dengue, yellow fever, and viral encephalitis. The different species of mosquitoes often have different behavioural patterns and prefer different types of habitat, so it is not easy to control

all disease carrying mosquito populations in a specific area by any one
technique which may have been used successfully elsewhere (*Idem*
1982:533). According to the World Bank Report: 'Experiences in
Vietnam and on construction projects in Africa continue to demonstrate
that even the availability of anti-malarial drugs is not completely
protective. Malaria is almost always underestimated as a cause of
disability in the tropics — as to its very wide geographical distribution,
the high risk of infection, and the severity of the disease in non-immune
subjects' (World Bank 1974:48).

Schistosomiasis: This is the most widespread and serious disease which
occurs only in tropical and semi-tropical countries. The spread of
schistosomiasis is common in most tropical climates owing to the
construction of dams (A.K. Biswas 1982:531-33). The disease is
contracted from water infected by a parasite released by certain species
of snail. A single exposure may be sufficient to contract the disease.
The parasite penetrates the skin of humans and results in the infection
of the urinary tract or the intestinal tract. The disease is markedly
debilitating and exceedingly difficult to treat (World Bank 1974:49,52).
The labour productivity of the victim is reduced by 30-50 per cent.
Victims become progressively more vulnerable to other diseases. They
face difficult and unpleasant treatments, which are often not available,
especially in rural areas of developing countries (A.K. Biswas 1982:532).
The characteristics of snail habitats are described by Malek as follows:

> 'The snail intermediate hosts of *schistosomiasis* are adapted to a
> wide range of environmental conditions. They breed in many
> different sites, the essential conditions being the presence of
> water, relatively solid surfaces for egg deposition, and some
> source of food. These conditions are met by a large variety of
> habitats: streams, irrigation canals, ponds, borrow-pits, flooded
> areas, lakes, water-cress fields, and rice fields. Thus in general
> they inhabit shallow waters with organic content, moderate light
> penetration, little turbidity, a muddy substratum rich in organic
> matter, submergent or emergent aquatic vegetation, and
> abundant micro-flora. The snails may be found in isolated
> habitats quite independent of major drainage systems because
> snails or their eggs are sometimes carried passively to such
> habitats which seem favourable' (E.A. Malek 1972).

Thus water resource developments which impound water behind dams
to serve hydro electric plants, irrigation systems or a fishing industry
are most likely to favour the increase propagation and spread of these
snails (World Bank 1974:52).

The disease is currently endemic in over 70 countries and affects
over 200 million people. Infection rates of 70 per cent or more can
often be observed in certain regions of countries with large irrigation
development like Egypt, Kenya and Sudan. The Lake Victoria area
of Kenya is hyperendemic, and the infection rate in schools is up to

100 per cent in certain areas associated with irrigation schemes (A.K. Biswas 1982:532-33). In Ghana, West Africa, as Lake Volta rose behind a major dam completed in 1964, an infective species of Bulinus snail was identified in the inundated area by 1966. 'The explosive growth of aquatic weeds favoured massive reproduction of the snail ... Outbreaks of the disease were soon observed in new townships along the lake. The rate of infection increased steadily, and within two years nearly all the children in these settlements were affected' (World Bank 1974:52). Recently WHO has warned that schistosomiasis is on the increase in developing countries. It has become the second most important tropical disease in terms of socioeconomic impact after malaria (*Star*, December 5, 1984).

According to Biswas although there are several studies on the overall environmental impact of hydro-dams, not much in-depth work has been conducted on their impacts on the health of both humans and animals. This according to him is due to the erroneous belief that such health risks are minimal and hence can be neglected. 'There has been a tendency to aggregate all the available information on dam failures and then determine the failure risks as if they were all statistically independent events. This is mainly because some of these studies have been conducted by people who have very little knowledge of the design of dams and their behaviour after construction. Such estimates are unreliable and would not even provide "ball-park" estimates of risks' (A.K. Biswas 1982:537).

Despite this, some of the problems related to human health and welfare are commonly acknowledged by social scientists, agriculturalists and medical scientists. The cost of resettling displaced communities, always much greater than expected and the longlasting social distress among them, and the economic loss due to flooding of good farming land, valuable timber and the loss to the scientific community of rare plant life, wildlife and historical sites are all well known. Yet according to B.B. Waddy, a renown UN Consultant on dams: 'Governmental authorities are happily — and fecklessly — planning to add yet another manmade lake to the map of the developing world, in complete and usually misplaced confidence that it will benefit their economy' (Waddy 1975:50).

The Batang Ai hydro-electric dam.

Above: Woman and children of Ulu Belaga who will be affected if the Bakun Dam project is implemented.

Below: View of the Balui river from the site of the Bakun Dam. If constructed, the dam will flood 700 sq. km.

Many squatter settlements have sprung up in towns like Miri, housing natives who have migrated from the longhouses.

CHAPTER TWELVE

Consequences of Modernisation and Development on the Natives

The twin policies of discouraging shifting cultivation and the increased exploitation of timber resources should be analysed in the larger developmental context. The restriction on land and the scarcity created, the forced resettlement, and the policy to convert native customary land into titled farm land growing cash crops, will eventually lead to the demise of swidden agriculture and longhouse society. The expansion of the timber industry has forced groups of natives and communities to migrate away from their existing settlement areas. Logging activities are driving natives from their traditional lands. Many of them work as paid labourers in the logging companies. This will also be the likely scenario as dam construction and agricultural development policies are expanded. Natives are increasingly drawn into and dependent on the market economy as cash crop farmers and paid workers. These developments came about with the introduction of new laws and amended laws on land and forest, and the increased involvement of the State in the daily lives of the natives. Another major development was the introduction of formal education. This led to the development of a new generation of educated urbanised natives who have not integrated themselves into traditional society. This Chapter will discuss the social, cultural and environmental consequences of modernisation and development on traditional swidden society in Sarawak.

Land Scarcity

As discussed earlier, one of the prerequisites of swidden farming as an adaptive agricultural practice was its low population density. The population densities of swiddening societies normally fall between four to 15 persons per square kilometer (sq km) and is usually less than 40 persons per sq km (Grainger 1980:13). Between 1952 to 1954 Conklin found that the Hanunoo swiddeners in the Philippines had an average population density of ten persons per sq km. This figure was as high as 25 to 35 persons per sq km in the heavily populated areas (Conklin 1954:224). Schlegel in his study of the Tiruray has shown that one sq km can support 52.6 people (Schlegel 1979:69). Among the

Baleh Iban of Sarawak, an area which Freeman described as a sparsely populated region in 1949, he estimated that the population density was about 3.6 persons per sq km (1970:64)[1].

Between 1970 to 1980, the annual rate of population growth in Sarawak was 3.5 per cent. In the Baram District, the population per square kilometer in 1970 was 1.8 persons. In 1980, it grew to 2.4 persons per sq km. The population density is thus still very low and hence there is still a basis for shifting agriculture to be ecologically and economically viable. However this average low density of 2.4 persons per sq km does not mean that in reality the native communities have so much access to the land. On the contrary their ability to use land resources for swidden has gradually dwindled. Firstly, the introduction of cash crops has meant that the best swidden lands had to be released to plant these new crops. New lands had to be opened to replace them for swidden subsistence. More important, natives found themselves in a position where they could no longer expand their lands because of restrictions caused by the implementation of land and forest laws. As a result, customary rights which were so crucial to shifting agriculture were restricted. This has now resulted in a very high population pressure on the existing swidden farm lands. Natives found that they were experiencing a shortage of land. Land was not sufficient to meet the subsistence needs of the family and the community.

The inability to be self sufficient was aggravated by the agricultural policy towards natives. Through the introduction of cash crop production and rural development schemes, natives were encouraged to take up sedentary agriculture. This made them more vulnerable to the market economy for their income and increased their dependence on food. Sedentary or settled agriculture also meant that natives forfeited their customary rights to land when cash crops were grown instead. As natives have no protection under customary tenure, the creation of titles to land can result in some natives being dispossessed of their

1.   Shifting cultivation has generally been believed to support only low population densities. However figures of shifting cultivators in New Guinea has shown a population of 500 per square mile supported by a very complex and efficient form of shifting cultivation. This indicates to some extent that most shifting cultivator societies are operating at less than maximum potential as far as their agricultural system is concerned. In most regions of Southern Asia, according to Spencer, shifting cultivators have not been allowed the economic and political freedom over a long period of time, necessary to fully test the issue of the maximum carrying capacity of shifting cultivation as a system. (Carrying capacity refers to the area of land required for each person under the system. This concept does not take into account the other aspects of subsistence in which shifting cultivation is but one part of the total subsistence. This refers to the natural environment, such as forests, lakes, rivers, which are a source of food and subsistence and have an important bearing on the carrying capacity of the land as well). Constant encroachment upon the lands of shifting cultivators coupled with economic exploitation, backed by superior political and economic power, historically has been driving shifting cultivators from their lands, upsetting the stability of their cultures, and promoting the decline of whole societies (Spencer 1966:15).

lands. There is thus a danger of the development of a group of landless natives without the means to earn a livelihood.

Timber exploitation further exerted pressure on the land. Natives found that they had to compete with logging companies for access to the forests. More often than not, it was a losing battle. They found themselves hemmed in with no place for expansion while the timber companies were encroaching on their traditional areas. This was made worse when their protests against this invasion on their territory went unheeded. They were told by logging companies and government officials that they have no legal right to the land and forests, which belong to the State. Further pleas to the loggers to stop damaging their rice farms, water supplies and fruit trees were unsuccessful. Appeals to the government authorities did not elicit any favourable response either. The plight and helplessness of the natives only increased further, as shown in earlier Chapters.

With the continuation of present policies — restrictions on customary land and forests, rapid timber exploitation and agricultural development, and dam construction — we can only expect even greater population pressure on the customary lands of the natives. The native communities will therefore face increasing land scarcity, with serious consequences on the swidden cycle, the productivity of land and food output per family. These consequences are described in the following section.

Reduced Food Output and Malnutrition

As swidden land size became stagnant, natives found that the only recourse open to them was to shorten the fallow on the swidden fields. This led to a general shortening of the swidden cycle. In the past a swidden field would be left to regenerate for ten or twenty years (depending on the soil conditions) before it is again cultivated. According to S.C. Chin (1984:476), the 'preferred' fallow period for the Kenyah is at least 20 years, whilst the minimum satisfactory fallow period is 15 years. Presently because of the shortage of land, these fields are cultivated earlier than before (say, three to seven years). Hence regeneration is not complete and the productivity of the land is not at its maximum. When rice is planted on such lands, productivity falls. In the last ten years or so, swidden cycles have been shortened because of the scarcity of land. According to a SAM field staff, the cultivation of secondary plots is the trend among many natives in the Baram today. In the 1969-70 season, the average yield of hill padi for the Baram District was 190 *gantang* per acre (Department of Agriculture 1980:46). The fall in output means that swiddeners find it increasingly harder to meet their subsistence requirements. This is in contrast to the situation in traditional Sarawak swidden society which has produced a surplus of rice in most years, as shown in Chapter Three. The decline in food production has now forced many able bodied members of the community to look for paid employment to buy food or to collect forest products like *rotan*, *damar* and camphor for sale. The latter activity, as we have seen, has also been hampered as logging has led to the destruction of these forest resources.

In 1978 Dr Alec Anderson of the Sarawak Medical Services reported that for the 1977 and 1978 harvests, Kayan and Kenyah swiddeners in the Baram had a rice output sufficient for only 7.4 months in the year. The District Office reported that for 1978, several longhouses in the district were suffering from rice shortages, namely Long Palai, Long Seridan and some Penan settlements in the Akah river (Baram District 1978:18). The situation was even worse for the Iban. Between 1975 and 1977 the average yield for the Sut, Mujong, Lemanak and Ulu Mukah Iban was sufficient for only 4.9 months' food in the year. (Anderson 1978:241-48).

The fall in rice output has led to malnutrition among the natives. A detailed study published by Anderson in 1979 revealed very serious levels of protein calorie malnutrition (PCM) among native children below the age of nine. As shown in Table 9A, out of a total of 4,106 children in the survey (Penan, Melanau, Mukah Iban, Lemanak Iban, Sut and Mujong Iban, Land Dayak, Malay and Kayan and Kenyah communities), 81 per cent suffered Moderate or Severe Malnutrition. This means that 81 per cent of the children were underweight by twenty per cent or more (using the WHO Standard Weight for Age). Of this, 72.6 per cent of the children were moderately malnourished

Table 9A
Protein-Calorie Malnutrition among 4,106
Sarawak Children under 9 Years Old by %
WHO Standard Weight for Age

Communities	Children	Severe 60% or less	Moderate 61–80%	Mod + Severe 80% or less
Penan	130	7.7	84.6	92.3
Melanau	485	6.6	67.6	74.3
Mukah Iban	562	11.0	71.5	82.5
Lemanak Iban	505	13.5	76.5	89.7
Sut & Mujong Iban	502	9.6	76.5	86.1
Land Dayak	696	8.3	76.9	85.2
Malay	516	8.7	75.2	83.9
Kayan & Kenyah	710	3.1	63.5	66.6
Total:	4,106	8.4	72.6	81.0

Table 9B
Child Malnutrition Rates (in %) in Developing Areas
by Gomez Weight Categories

Regions	Severe 60% or less	Moderate 61–75% St. Wt.	Mod. + Severe 75% or less
Latin America	1.6	18.9	20.5
Africa	4.4	26.5	30.9
Asia	3.2	31.2	34.4
Total (173,000)	2.4	22.8	25.2
Sarawak (4,106)	8.4	55.1	63.5

Source: A.J.U. Anderson, 'Subsistence of the Penan in the Mulu Area of Sarawak' in *The Sarawak Gazette*, November 30, 1979 pp208-9.

(which means that this group of children were 20-39 per cent underweight) while 8.4 per cent were severely malnourished (underweight by 40 per cent or more). Anderson also compared the results of his Sarawak study with other child malnutrition studies conducted in Latin America, Africa and other areas of Asia which are quoted by the WHO. His disturbing conclusion was that the level of malnutrition of children in Sarawak was far worse than any other country or region (See Table 9B).

The level of malnutrition in Sarawak was 3½ times higher in the severely malnourished group of children and almost 2½ times higher in the moderately malnourished group compared to the average malnutrition rate in the surveys in Latin America, Africa and Asia. Although Kayan and Kenyah children fared better compared with the other natives, they still suffered a far higher malnutrition rate than the children in other countries under the moderate malnourished group. The incidence of moderate and severe malnutrition among Sarawak children is two to three times higher than those found in the poorest nations in the world (*Idem*1978:243).

Malnutrition among the swiddeners according to Dr Anderson was largely due to insufficient energy foods — carbohydrates or fats which are usually obtained from rice. Insufficient rice production has led to continuing food deficiency among them. Referring to Kayan and Kenyah communities in the Baram, Dr Anderson has called for more government assistance to be given for food production for natives. Up to now the only agricultural aid given to natives is for cash crop production of rubber and pepper. 'This policy is short-sighted and benefit others more than the farmers' he wrote. 'The first necessity for

undernourished people is more food — moreover, plain food which
is easiest to grow — and the most efficient and cheapest way is for
them to produce it themselves, not buy it from shops . . . . it is quite
essential to devote considerable resources and effort to more efficient
hill padi growing, as well as other hill food crops, and not to foster
wet padi only; there is not nearly enough wet padi land to supply
Sarawak, and in any case there are far more hill padi farmers — who
should share in food development also. The State will be unable to
achieve real advance while the greater part of the population farms
so poorly that there is large-scale malnutrition, despite the great
advantage of abundant land. Food production must come first . . .' (*Idem*
1978:247).

It is significant to note that 81 per cent of the population are rural
based comprising subsistence farmers and fisher folk along the coast.
Between 1977 and 1980 Sarawak imported 45 per cent of its rice needs.
In 1977, the State imported 50,806 tons which accounted for half of
its total consumption. In 1980, rice imports totalled 51,262 tons (*New
Straits Times*, April 8, 1981). It can be seen that the State's dependence
on rice imports is becoming critical. In ten years, the production of
hill padi had fallen from 59,973 tons in 1970-71 to 47,554 tons in

Table 10
Incidence of Malnutrition-by-Weight
in Sarawak Divisions, 1980

| | | Number and (Percent) | |
Divisions	Tot. Children Weighed (0-6 years)	Moderate and Severe Malnutrition	Severe Malnutrition
State of Sarawak	186,124	48,060 (25.8%)	3,123 (1.7%)
First Division	90,172	15,732 (17.4%)	653 (0.72%)
Second Division	19,865	6,752 (34.0%)	419 (2.1%)
Third Division	14,310	4,578 (32.0%)	685 (4.8%)
Fourth Division	25,360	7,667 (30.2%)	343 (1.4%)
Fifth Division	6,788	1,964 (28.9%)	78 (1.2%)
Sixth Division	14,095	4,960 (35.2%)	378 (2.7%)
Seventh Division	8,302	3,131 (37.7%)	280 (3.4%)

Source: Zainab Bt Tambi, 'The Nutritional Status of Children under seven years
in Sarawak' in *The Sarawak Gazette*, November 1982 p24.

Table 11
Incidence of Malnutrition-by-Weight
in Sarawak: Age-Groups

Table 11A: Malnutrition within 0 - 1 year (INFANT) group

	Number of 0 - 1 yr	Percent of Tot. Attendences	Number and (Percent)	
			Moderate and Severe Malnutrition	Severe Malnutrition
State of Sarawak	59,886	32.2%	8,098 (13.5%)	545 (0.9%)
1. Urban Clinics	18,818	40.3%	665 (3.5%)	32 (0.2%)
2. Suburban/rural Permanent Clinics	37,366	30.0%	6,562 (17.6%)	450 (1.2%)
3. Mobile Clinics	1,961	26.0%	397 (20.2%)	31 (1.6%)
4. Flying Doctor Service	1,741	24.1%	474 (27.2%)	32 (1.8%)

Table 11B: Malnutrition within 1 - 4 years (TODDLER) group

State of Sarawak	102,430	55.0%	32,624 (31.9%)	1,959 (1.9%)
1. Urban Clinics	18,917	40.5%	1,405 (7.4%)	33 (0.2%)
2. Suburban/rural Permanent Clinics	74,167	59.5%	26,922 (36.3%)	1,640 (2.2%)
3. Mobile Clinics	4,654	61.6%	2,096 (27.8%)	102 (2.2%)
4. Flying Doctor Service	4,692	64.9%	2,201 (46.9%)	184 (3.9%)

Table 11C: Malnutrition within 5 - 6 years (PRESCHOOLER) group

State of Sarawak	23,808	12.8%	7,338 (30.8%)	619 (2.6%)
1. Urban Clinics	8,962	19.2%	277 (3.1%)	9 (0.1%)
2. Suburban/rural Permanent Clinics	13,112	10.5%	6,010 (45.8%)	494 (3.8%)
3. Mobile Clinics	935	12.4%	455 (48.7%)	37 (3.95%)
4. Flying Doctor Service	799	11.0%	596 (74.6%)	79 (9.9%)

Source: Zainab Bt Tambi, 'The Nutritional Status of Children under seven years in Sarawak' in *The Sarawak Gazatte*, November 1982 p25.

1979-80 (Department of Agriculture 1980:43). In his call for a State Food and Nutrition Policy Dr Anderson states that: 'Rising food supply must become the first priority for development. The primary need and right of every person is to have enough food. Any State where there are large numbers of chronically undernourished must be regarded as backward, however wealthy or technically advanced some sectors may be' (Anderson 1978:248).

In October 1982, Malaysians were informed that 25 per cent to 80 per cent of the natives in the interior of Sarawak were facing a shortage of food (*Sarawak Tribune*, Oct 21, 1982). In 1980 a survey of the nutritional status of 186,124 children below the age of six years in Sarawak was carried out. The results revealed that about a quarter (25.8 per cent) were suffering from moderate and severe malnutrition. The highest rates within this category were as follows: Seventh Division (37.7 per cent); Sixth Division (35.2 per cent); Second Division (34.0 per cent); Third Division (32.0 per cent); Fourth Division (30.2 per cent); Fifth Division (28.9 per cent) and the First Division (17.4 per cent) which had the lowest. Except for the latter, the average rate recorded in all the other Divisions was 33 per cent. This means that almost one third of the children in Sarawak (with the exception of the First Division) are suffering from moderate to severe malnutrition. According to the study even higher figures ranging from 40 per cent-45 per cent were recorded by the mobile services in the remote interior areas. When the age groups were broken down, the average figures for malnutrition in the State were 13.5 per cent between 0-1 year (infant group); 32 per cent between the 1-4 years (toddler group) and 31 per cent between 5-6 years (preschooler group). Again the rates for the three categories were much higher in the remote interior areas. The Flying Doctor Services (FDS) recorded malnutrition in nearly one third of the infants (27.2 per cent); nearly half the toddlers (46.9 per cent) and three quarters of the preschoolers (74.6 per cent). The study also revealed that malnutrition is a major problem in the rural and remote areas (Zainab Bt Tambi 1982:21-29).

In terms of petroleum, liquified natural gas and timber resources, Sarawak ranks as the richest state in Malaysia. In contributes more to the country's export earnings than other states. Yet for all these contributions to national wealth, the standard of living of the majority of Sarawakian natives remains very poor. A study published by the Ministry of Finance revealed that in 1976, the incidence of rural poverty in Sarawak was 55 per cent; and 72 per cent of all poor households in the State were engaged in agriculture, forestry and fishing. The poorest ethnic groups in Sarawak were the Iban and Land Dayak for which the incidence of poverty exceeded 70 per cent (Ministry of Finance 1982:169). In August 1984, Datuk Leo Moggie, President of the Parti Bansa Dayak Sarawak (PBDS) stated that the Dayak are still the poorest and most backward community in the country. Figures show that the majority of them only earn a monthly income of between $40 and $50 (*New Straits Times*, July 23, 1984).

Calling for more allocations to fight rural poverty, a Member of Parliament Mr Mutang Tagal told the House of the misery and suffering of his people in the interiors of Sarawak even after 27 years of independence. 'The rural dwellers do not want pure charity, but just aid to improve their own lives' he said. 'How can the poor shifting cultivator hope to buy the basic necessities of life if he cannot even sell his produce?' (*Ibid* Mar 23, 1984). The shift to cash crop cultivation has meant firstly that the native cannot grow enough food for his own needs. Secondly it has made him and his family heavily dependent on his cash crop to earn him enough cash to buy his food. Moreover, cultivation of cash crops such as rubber and pepper exposes him to the vulnerability of the world market. When prices of these commodities are low he will not be able to get enough cash to buy food. With no income and no food, he may well abandon the rubber and pepper gardens, and be forced to seek income elsewhere to feed himself and his family.

Migration to the Towns

If the trend of high incidence of poverty, reduced productivity from shifting cultivation and the inability to open new land continues, the hardships faced by natives will increase even further. As the general population increases and land scarcity becomes more acute with further impingement on native lands by timber exploitation and environmental damage, one can predict that more and more natives will move out of their lands. Outward migration of landless natives towards urban centres is already taking place, as can be seen in the booming squatter settlements and shanty towns on the outskirts of Kuching, Bintulu and Miri. According to a newspaper report, the typical squatter was once a subsistence farmer. Many of the farmers who became urban squatters did not have enough good land and were forced to look for jobs as unskilled labourers or factory workers to earn a living. Even if they managed to get unskilled jobs they found they could barely scrape by because of the high cost of living in the city. They ended up building shacks in squalid squatter settlements (*Borneo Bulletin*, Oct 9, 1982). The fortunate Dayak, according to an educated native, will be employed as clerks and office boys. 'But the luckless ones will continue to idle in the streets. Dayak women who are not able to get jobs become prostitutes and the men turn to violence and crime'. He adds that it is a desperate choice to make but it is a matter of survival in the town (Harrison Ngau 1983:10). Speaking of Iban women who work in Sibu as waitresses, bargirls and 'self-employed females', Sutlive says that some three hundred such women work as prostitutes. 'The role of the prostitute . . . . providing gainful employment not available otherwise to Iban women, has become that of several hundred such young women' (Sutlive 1978:163, 186).

I am told in recent years, some 20 families have left the Baram to join the Miri-Bintulu Land Development Scheme to grow oil palm.

They have been told that after six years they would be given ownership of their plots of three to four acres. This trend towards settled agriculture would in future also contribute to the abandoning of shifting cultivation or traditional agriculture and the loss of customary rights to land.

Cultural Alienation and the Passing Away of Traditional Swidden Society

Apart from the economic forces that work against the viable continuance of shifting agriculture and customary land tenure, formal education has helped to remove many young able-bodied natives from their rural communities. Farms are neglected because there is no one to help the old parents at home. The greater tragedy is that education alienates the young from their traditional culture and way of life. According to Harrison Ngau, himself a Kayan youth: 'The introduction of formal western education has led to the emergence of a new lifestyle and culture among the younger generation Dayak. They are now trained in a new system with its different set of values and patterns of behaviour to fit into a new economic system very different from their traditional system .... Because the students were not given the opportunity to learn and appreciate their traditional values, cultures, lifestyle and skills and knowledge needed in their community's survival, the inevitable result is they would not be able to go back to their traditional roots. They will see no purpose in village life neither will they know how to adapt to life and tradition in the longhouse' (Harrison Ngau 1983:1-5).

A similar view was expressed by a Kenyah headmaster of a secondary school in the Baram who wrote in the *Sarawak Gazette* some years ago: 'No longer did he (the native schoolboy) soil his hand on the farm or lift a finger to aid his aged parents in fetching fire-wood or water. Worst of all, he looked down on our traditional forms of entertainment'. According to him, the education system nurtures in natives a mentality that 'all menial work is not only to be shunned but despised as well. This present aversion of the educated towards their own customs is the culmination of a long process which has its beginning in the primary school system' (Joachim Ulok 1974:187). Hence modern education does not equip the young to integrate into traditional society. 'Schooling the old folks say robs them of their sons and daughters who they need badly on the farms' (*Idem* 1974:50).

According to Sutlive, of the 143 Iban from longhouse communities who studied in secondary schools between 1960-70, none of them has returned to take up residence in his longhouse. 'Secondary schools in urban centers led to a radical disorientation of young people to their culture and disengagement from their society, so that many have refused to return to the longhouse' (Sultive 1978:161-162). '... Education ... is regarded by parents, children, teachers, and all concerned, not as preparation for life in an Iban community, but as a means of escaping it' (*Sarawak Gazatte* Dec 31 1962 c.f. Sultive 1978:162).

Modern education enables young natives to fit into the modern economy as teachers, lawyers, nurses, doctors, and civil servants. 'No doubt few Dayak from the longhouse become professionals. These are the people who become the administrators and officers in the public service and the private companies. It is this cream of the Dayak community that become big businessmen, and politicians in the State', says Harrison Ngau.

'Because of their closeness with the business community and those who hold power, they can get what they want and dreamed of in the classrooms. And because of this proximity, a few Dayak professionals are becoming overnight millionaires particularly from the timber around their longhouses in the interior' (Harrison Ngau 1983:9). Others who have not succeeded in school become paid labourers in the towns or logging camps. When the younger generation leave the rural areas to work elsewhere, the old will not be able to teach the skills and knowledge to them. There will be no one left to carry on the work in the farms and to observe the *adat* of the community. When this happens traditional society will fail to reproduce itself, and thus fades away.

Conclusion

We have seen how development policies have led to the underdevelopment of the natives and the erosion of the basis for their traditional way of life. Natives have been increasingly deprived of their land and the ability to grow food for themselves. This has led to a drop in food production and serious malnutrition among their communities. The encroachment of the timber industry and the construction of dams on their traditional lands have further eroded their rights to these lands. Worse still, the logging activities have caused a further deterioration in their environment and depressed their socioeconomic conditions. Food is the most basic need of human beings. The first function of any economy is to produce food to feed its populace. For most of the rural natives, their ability to be self-sufficient in food depends on their access to land and their ability to continue their method of agricultural production which is shifting cultivation.Shifting cultivation is integral to their way of life and the only form of cultivation suited to their physical environment. According to the Department of Agriculture, 'a very high proportion of the land area of Sarawak is totally incapable of supporting any commercial agricultural crop at all and even more is of a very marginal nature' (Hatch & Lim 1978:3). In fact almost 80 per cent of the land area is unsuitable for commercial or settled agriculture. Most of these lands are hilly with infertile soils. Most of them are in the interior where shifting cultivation is practised. Thus, as discussed earlier, shifting agriculture appears to be the most viable form of agriculture under the circumstances. Given this reality, the important question would then be how shifting cultivators can increase their food production and standard of living. There is a general tendency to compare shifting agriculture with modern intensive agriculture. As a result, shifting agriculture is evaluated in terms of optimal land use, deep ploughing, clean weeding, fertilisers, and application of modern capital-intensive technology, which is more suitable to European soil conditions and intensive farming methods. These types of agriculture are not favourable in tropical forest soils. In fact it can be highly disastrous as the Colonial experience has shown in some African countries. It would be more appropriate, then, to devise policies and assistance which work to make shifting cultivation more economically and ecologically viable instead of starting with *a priori* assumptions that this form of agriculture must be replaced by permanent and settled agriculture. Only then can a more serious commitment and an efficient programme be drawn to tackle the problems related to shifting cultivators.

Lau

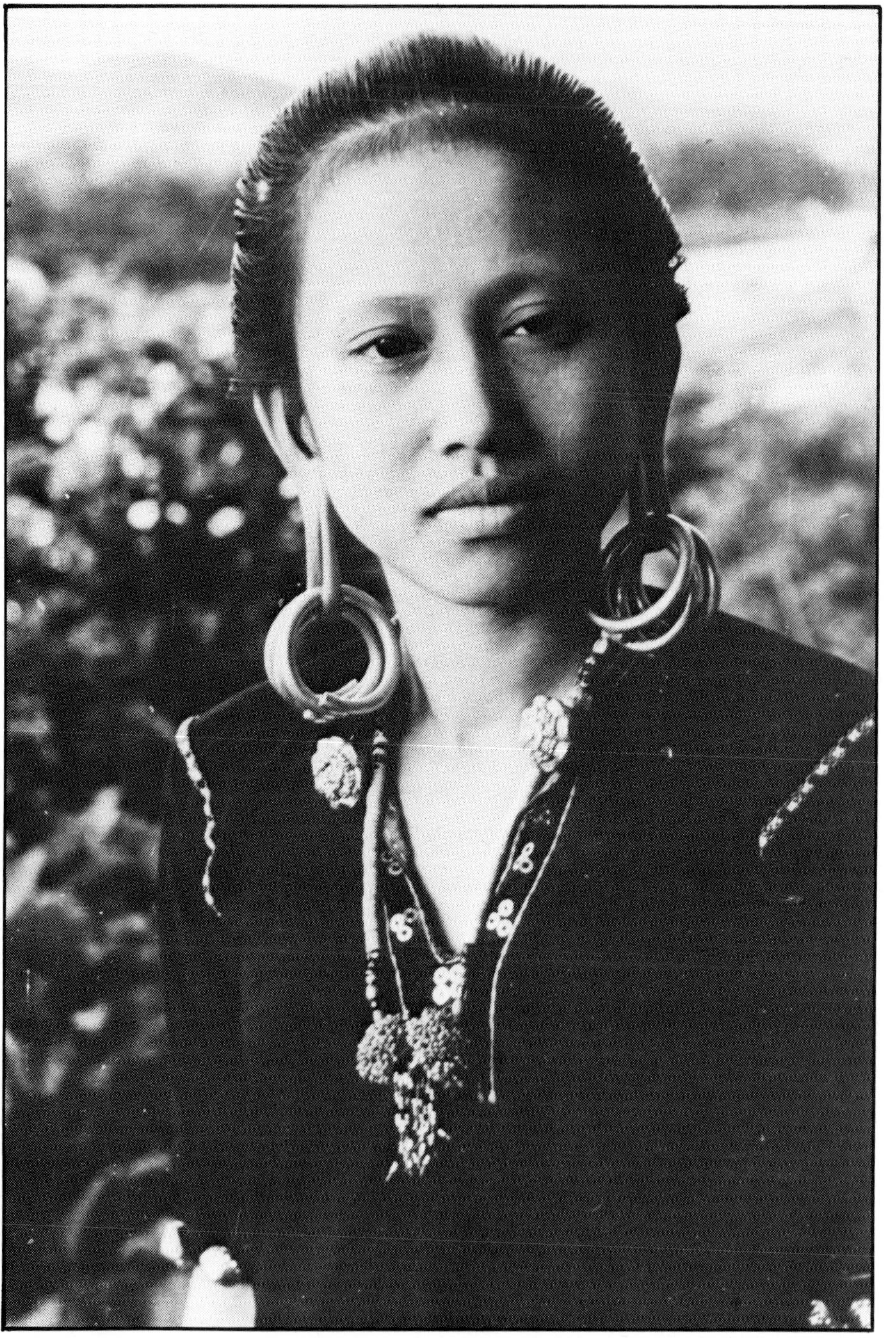

Kon. Inst. v.d. Tropen

CHAPTER THIRTEEN

The Cultural and Development Rights of Natives

It is becoming increasingly realised that the rights of cultural minorities are violated worldwide and that there is an urgent need to address this issue. These peoples who have lived their way of life even before the birth of the nation state have found that the latter has posed the greatest threat to their survival and existence. In many ways this is linked to the worldwide expansion of the market economy. In Third World countries this has led to the transformation of societies which has been unprecedented in their history. Now, in the closing decades of this century, the cultural minorities or the 'tribal peoples' are at the last frontier, facing the march of modern capital. Many of these societies will not be able to withstand the onslaught and the demands of the modern economic forces. Thus, many groups and international agencies involved in human and social rights are seeking recognition of the rights of cultural minorities, and legal mechanisms to protect these rights. This Chapter examines the efforts of these groups and agencies in protecting the interests of cultural minorities.

International Conventions Protecting Cultural Minorities

In recent years, several international agencies have adopted declarations or positions recognising the rights of indigenous peoples.

Since the early 1980s, the United Nations Sub-Commission on the Prevention of Discrimination and Protection of Minorities has been working towards an International Declaration on the rights of indigenous peoples. In August 1984 a report on the 'Study of the Problem of Discrimination against Indigenous Populations' (otherwise known as the Cobo Report) was submitted to the UN Sub-Commission by its working group. The key conclusions of this report was as follows:

- It must be recognized that indigenous peoples have a natural and inalienable right to retain the territories they possess, to call for the return of land of which they have been deprived and to be free to decide as to their use and development.

- Genuine guarantee should be provided and full effect given to the right of indigenous populations to the land which they and their ancestors have worked since time immemorial and to the resources which such land contains, as well as to traditional forms of land tenure and resource exploitation.

- Recognition must be given to the right of all indigenous nations or peoples, as a minimum, to the return and control of sufficient and suitable land to enable them to live an economically viable existence in accordance with their own customs and traditions, and to develop fully at their own pace . . .

- Millenary or immemorial possession and economic occupation should suffice to establish indigenous title to land . . .

- . . . Land occupied and controlled by indigenous populations should be presumed to be indigenous land. In case of doubt or dispute the *onus probandi* (the burden of proof) of the ownership of land should fall . . . on the non-indigenous populations who claim to have acquired a right to part of the land.

- All indigenous reserved areas should be immediately handed over to the respective indigenous groups . . .

- Public land which is sacred or of religious significance to the indigenous populations should be attributed to them in perpetuity.

- . . . No intermediary institution of any kind should be created or appointed to hold the lands of indigenous peoples on their behalf.

- A protective regime should cover indigenous land . . . This regime should at least include restrictions on alienation, encumbrance, attachment and proscription . . .

- All illegal acquisition of indigenous land should be null and void *ab initio* (from the beginning) and no rights should be vested in subsequent purchasers or acquirers of the land . . .

- Indigenous populations should be compensated for the loss of all . . . lands that have been or may be taken.

- . . . The resources of the subsoil of indigenous land also must be regarded as the exclusive property of indigenous communities. Where this is rendered impossible by the fact that the deposits in the subsoil are the preserve of the State, the State must . . . allow full participation by indigenous communities in respect of:
  - i)   the granting of exploration and exploitation licences;
  - ii) the profits generated by such operations, and
  - iii) procedures for determining damage caused and compensation payable.

These recommendations recognise the rights of indigenous peoples over their land and all resources found on it; to compensation of lands of which they have been dispossessed and protection against future dispossession and to manage their land free of interference (Lucas 1984:63).

In 1957, the Indigenous and Tribal Populations Covention (No 107) adopted by the International Labour Organisation (ILO) had recognised the rights of tribal populations over their lands. These are expressed in various articles, among which are the following:

- *Article 11*: The right of ownership, collective or individual, of the members of the populations concerned over the lands which these populations traditionally occupy shall be recognized.

- *Article 12*: The populations concerned shall not be removed without their free consent from their habitual territories except in accordance with national laws and regulations for reasons relating to national security, or in the interest of national economic development or of the health of the said populations.

  When in such cases removal of these populations is necessary as an exceptional measure, they shall be provided with lands of quality at least equal to that of the lands previously occupied by them, suitable to provide for their present needs and future development. . . .

- *Article 13*: Procedures for the transmission of rights of ownership and use of land which are established by the customs of the populations concerned shall be respected, within the framework of national laws and regulations, in so far as they satisfy the needs of these populations and do not hinder their economic and social development.

  Arrangements shall be made to prevent persons who are not members of the populations concerned from taking advantages of these customs or of lack of understanding of the laws on the part of the members of these populations to secure the ownership or use of the lands belonging to such members.

The ILO also adopted a Recommendation which states:

- The populations concerned should be assured of a land reserve adequate for the needs of shifting cultivation so long as no better system of cultivation can be introduced . . .

Article 17 of the Universal Declaration of Human Rights provides that: 'Everyone has the right to own property along as well as in association with others' and that: 'No one shall be arbitrarily deprived of his property'. According to the International Commission of Jurists (ICJ):

'This is a far wider guarantee of land rights than is commonly recognised . . . In the first place, it recognises common as well as individual rights of property, and calls for both to be respected.

It is commonplace that fundamental guarantees such
as this do not depend upon the idiosyncracies of municipal
law. It would be quite inappropriate therefore if Article 17
were so interpreted that a State could escape its obligations
simply because under the law of that State, its indigenous
inhabitants had never had property in their land.

Article 17 imposes a universal standard. If an indigenous
person or group ever enjoyed property rights in land, and was
arbitrarily deprived of them, their rights have been infringed.
They will have had property in their land if, before the State to
which they are now subject imposed its laws, certain conditions
were met.

If a previous State, which would include an indigenous State,
had recognised their property in land, they cannot be arbitrarily
deprived of it. If there was no such central authority to
determine the validity of their claims, it does not follow that
they did not have rights of property. In such societies groups
often reached mutually accepted views as to hunting or
cultivation rights, and other matters of concern with respect
to land. Provided the result was to exclude others from
these rights, they constituted a form of property. The
Universal Declaration of Human Rights was not meant to
enshrine narrow values, fixed in a particular culture. It is not
necessary to point to title deeds, if there were rights over land
recognised and enforced by the communities which inhabited
those lands.

. . . If the damage is irreparable, then, at the very least, the
peoples concerned have a moral claim to compensation. And
where indigenous people have been arbitrarily deprived of land,
and it is now vested in a State, the State in many cases should
recognise the right of that people to its return. It should be
noted that in many legal systems, lapse of time does not affect
the claims of the rightful owner of property. This is so
irrespective of the innocence of a person who has purchased it
in good faith.

. . . Many of the seizures of land from indigenous peoples
have been in breach of the principle in Article 17 of the
Universal Declaration of Human Rights. It follows that, even if
a State has not acceded to the ILO Conventions guaranteeing
land rights, it may be in breach of its international obligations
if it does not return land which was arbitrarily seized' (Lucas
1984:63-5).

It can be seen that the rights of indigenous minorities and guarantees
against the dispossession of their lands are already supported by several
sets of international laws and conventions.

In December 1983, the Regional Council On Human Rights In Asia
drafted a 'Declaration of the Basic Duties of Asean Peoples and

Governments'. Article VIII of this document which concerns Cultural Minorities, reads as follows:

> 'It is the duty of government to recognize that members of cultural communities have the same rights as other citizens including the right to participate on an equal basis in public life, and to take affirmative action to ensure such equality. Where equality had been denied in the past, it is the duty of government to provide special representation of cultural communities in order to obtain true equality. It is moreover the duty of government to enforce respect for the right of such peoples to preserve their identity, traditions, language, cultural heritage and customary laws, and enforce protection of their ancestral domains, providing them, if they do so desire, with all care and facilities to develop, but respecting their right to determine for themselves the manner and extent of their relationship with the larger society . . .
>
> It is further the duty of government to review its land policies with a view to restoring all ancestral lands belonging to cultural communities to the tribe, bearing in mind the changes that have taken or are taking place in those communities'.

It is thus the fundamental duty of the State to protect and safeguard the rights of all cultural minorities living in the country. Indeed it is the mark of an enlightened and democratic government to do so. Governments must ensure the protection and the continued freedom of these natives to carry on their way of life if they so wish.

The Case of Sarawak Natives

Unfortunately, in the case of Sarawak, as we have seen, the natives have not been adequately consulted on policies and laws which adversely affect their position. Not only are their views not sought, but policies and projects are thrust upon them which force them to give up their land rights, their cultural identity and their human dignity. For instance, in relation to the proposed dam projects in Sarawak, according to the Lahmeyer International Report, 'no information is available on the wishes of the communities' which will be affected by the dams (p92). This reveals that the affected peoples have not been provided adequate information regarding the hydro power projects, the prospects of resettlement as a result of it and the loss of their lands and crops.

Similarly, when the forests and lands of natives are leased to timber concessionaires or mining interests, the natives affected are often not even informed. In recent years, land development policies, as we have seen, have also deprived them of their lands. Natives are not aware of the full impact of the market economy on their way of life and culture. They are not sufficiently trained or prepared to protect their interests.

These peoples must be consulted about their lands and their future. They should be given an informed choice and allowed to decide what they want for themselves as well as to participate in the decisions affecting them.

When moves were made in the early 1960s for Sarawak to become independent from British rule and to join the Federation of Malaysia, the natives expressed concern about the status of their customary rights. In 1962, a Commission of Enquiry was instituted under Lord Cobbold of England to determine the feelings of Sarawak people towards the idea of joining Malaysia and to provide recommendations. The Cobbold Commission Report in many places noted the fears and aspirations of the natives on the eve of Sarawak's entry into Malaysia. It observed a 'genuine fear' among the natives 'that their customary laws and practices would be affected' after joining Malaysia (Cobbold 1962:12). Groups from all the native population expressed a general desire that special privileges should be given to the natives and that 'land, forestry and agriculture should be subjects to be controlled by the State Government. Great emphasis was also laid on the need to safeguard customary rights and practices' (Cobbold 1962:13). The report found considerable reservation among a number of native groups about the Malaysia concept; the Land Dayak were particularly concerned about the 'safeguarding of customary land rights', for instance (Cobbold 1962:21). Among its recommendations, the Commission suggested that 'land, agriculture and forestry, and native customs and usage should be under the sole control of the State Government'. Subsequently, when the Malaysian Constitution was drawn up, land and forest came under the jurisdiction of the State Government, with the Federal Government having very limited powers in these matters.

Despite the natives' wishes being fulfilled that the State Government retains powers related to land and forests, their most precious resources, many longhouse natives I met are saddened and disillusioned because of the gradual erosion of their land rights and their access to forests. Their hopes that they would not lose their lands, their way of life and their *adat* appear to have dimmed over the years. A number of government policies have increasingly restricted their customary practices and rights, especially in relation to land and forests. Some of the elder natives even feel they had enjoyed a greater measure of protection in pre-Independence days compared to the present, although of course they too prefer self determination to Colonial rule. They presently yearn for State policies and a legal system that will truly protect their customary rights, their lands and the resources on it. The existing legislation lacks such protection, as we have seen in our analyses of land and forest laws of Sarawak. Since the Sarawak State laws on land do not give adequate protection to native rights (since such rights where they exist can be 'extinguished'), some protection should be afforded by the Federal Constitution. Article 13 of Malaysia's Federal Constitution states that:

(1) No person shall be deprived of property save in accordance with law.

(2) No law shall provide for the compulsory acquisition or use of property without adequate compensation.

This law should be interpreted in a broader context to incorporate the rights of native peoples and recognition of their 'customary law'. Under customary tenure, natives did not 'own' property. They merely had rights to use the land and waters for hunting, fishing and growing hill padi. Thus this right to the use of their lands should be recognised as rights to property. This is of fundamental importance because presently, nowhere in the Federal Constitution is the right to customary tenure and customary land of the natives guaranteed. Similarly, although the Federal Constitution guarantees the fundamental civil liberties, the freedom and protection for natives to practise their culture and traditions on their customary lands are not guaranteed. In this regard, the recognition and the preservation of native *adat* law and rights to land is a duty and responsibility of the State.

The issue of land is so central and crucial to the Sarawak natives because land lies at the heart of their cultural, spiritual and economic life. The very identity of the natives is defined in many-faceted ways through their relationship to the land, their use of it and their rights to it.

Moreover, the erosion of land rights has also affected the basic human needs of the natives: their food supply has in many instances been reduced, and their access to forest produce very much curbed. Most disturbing is the recent reported high incidence of malnutrition, which researchers have at least partly attributed to the natives' diminishing access to land.

The Right to Development

In this regard, it is also pertinent to relate the plight of the natives to the emerging concept of the 'right to development'. The right to development has been recognised by the United Nations as one of the fundamental human rights of all peoples and individuals. In February 1982, a working group of the UN Commission on Human Rights declared that:

'The right to development is an inalienable human right and it concerns individuals, peoples and States. The realization of the right of development requires, at the national level, the full exercise of the fundamental rights and freedoms of individuals, as well as the granting of equality of opportunity for all in the access to basic resources and services. It was considered that this requires in particular the participation of all in the process of taking decisions that concern them and in the implementation of those decisions. It was noted that it is important to encourage local development initiatives and to permit equitable distribution of the resources and advantages resulting from development' (United Nations 1982).

The International Commission of Jurists (ICJ) has concluded that every person has the right to participate in, and benefit from, development in the sense of a progressive improvement in the standard and quality of life (ICJ 1981).

Thus the right to development incorporates the right of all individuals to have their basic needs (especially food, proper nutrition, health facilities, clean water and sanitation, education and adequate employment) fulfilled to participate in decisions which determine the development process and to enjoy a fair and equitable share of the fruits of development. Thus if every person is entitled to the right of development, and if development incorporates the satisfaction of basic needs and participation in the development decision-making process, then there is development justice if the broadest segments of society are able to exercise their rights to genuine development (Khor 1982).

Of all these rights, the right to food remains one of the most fundamental. This would include the right to be free from hunger and malnutrition. This right is expressed in several international instruments like Article 11 of the International Covenant on Economic, Social and Cultural Rights which reads: 'The right of everyone to an adequate standard of living for himself and his family including adequate food ... (and) the fundamental right of everyone to be free from hunger ...'; and Article 25 of the Universal Declaration of Human Rights and Article 1 of the Universal Declaration on the Eradication of Hunger and Malnutrition which states: 'Every man, woman and child has the inalienable right to be free from hunger and malnutrition in order to develop fully and maintain their physical and mental faculties' (Eide 1984:152).

Given that 'development' in the genuine sense of the term should improve the condition of life of the poorer sections of society, it would be an ironic travesty if 'development projects' themselves actually deprive poor communities of their sources of livelihood, particularly land. Unfortunately this has been happening to many indigenous communities around the world, including Sarawak, whose natives in many cases have become victims rather than beneficiaries of 'development projects' such as logging activities and the construction of dams. If the interests of natives are to be enhanced and if their right to development is to become a reality, and if development is to serve the needs of the people rather than oppress them, a thorough rethinking is required in the government's policy towards natives and their lands.

From the above, we can see that the rights of indigenous peoples to preserving and enhancing their cultural identity, traditional economic resources and their capacity to fulfill basic and human needs are covered under several international covenants and declarations.

The Right to Cultural Identity

It is universally recognised that indigenous people have a right to their way of life. As such they have a right to be different and have a claim to be treated as such. Many of these peoples have lived on their lands as separate entities long before they were colonised or subjugated, in fact long before the existence of the modern State. If their self respect and separate identity are to be respected and honoured, they must be given control over their own lives. Most vital, their rights to land have to be protected and safeguarded. Without their lands, and the freedom to practise shifting cultivation, they will never be able to grow food and survive and practise their culture.

Malaysia has been fortunately endowed with a rich and diverse cultural heritage. In Sarawak alone there are some 27 recognised ethnic groups. And the greatest strength and wealth of our nation, lies in this rich cultural diversity. The *Rukunnegara* (National Creed) is dedicated to 'ensuring a liberal approach to the nation's rich and diverse cultural traditions, creating a just society in which the wealth of the nation shall be equitably shared, maintaining a democratic way of life and achieving a greater unity of all her peoples'. However, greater unity of our peoples does not mean conformity. Unity can emerge through the respect and preservation accorded to the culture, customs, tradition, language, and religious beliefs of the ethnic communities in our nation. It would be a great tragedy if this unique heritage of ours is eroded and eventually lost forever. To respect cultural rights is to respect and honour the native peoples' rights to their land and its resources. Unfortunately this right has been increasingly denied to them in the name of 'development'.

Earlier Chapters have shown that government land and forest policies, reflected in the many modifications to legislation and in various 'development schemes', have led to the rapid erosion of the natives' rights over land, forest and resources. The natives are also facing grave threats from private companies, mainly involved in logging, which encroach on their lands or destroy it through ecologically damaging practices. The State should reexamine its land and forest policies to avoid discrimination against the natives, and thus pull back from its present leading role of interfering with the resources and ways of life of the natives.

However, it is simply not enough for the State to refrain from interfering with their resource base, their freedom, and cultural identity. It is also the duty of the State to give special protection to these vulnerable and disadvantaged cultural minorities, in this case the indigenous peoples of Sarawak. This would have to include primarily the protection of their lands and resources. Natives should not be deprived of their lands through State policies and laws, through sheer political and economic dominance or through brute force. They must be adequately protected against outsiders and non-natives who destroy their lands, forests, waters and crops, thus subjecting them to extreme physical deprivation. They must be protected against policies, enterprises and people who cheat and deceive them of their lands and resources.

Only then would the natives' rights to cultural identity, human dignity and to genuine development be recognised in practice.

CHAPTER FOURTEEN

Towards the Restoration of Native Rights

In this book, we have tried to trace the evolution of the present position of the Sarawak natives. In particular, we looked at how the natives' land rights and swidden system were systematically eroded by land and forest policies, and by logging and other projects such as dam construction and agricultural settlement schemes.

The current plight and problems of the Sarawak natives are deep-seated and complex, and solutions will be very difficult to come by. What is vital is for the plight of the natives to be openly recognised for what it is, and for frank and honest discussion to be generated, most of all by the natives themselves. Indeed, natives in increasing numbers and increasing effectiveness are already voicing out their problems and suggesting ways in which the erosion of their rights should be checked and reversed. This can be seen not only in their protests against logging and dam projects, or against the violation of their land rights, but also in their appeals to the authorities for the creation of more Communal Forests and for their customary rights to be recognised.

After 23 years of Independence and 16 years of the New Economic Policy, most Sarawak natives (who are also classified officially as *Bumiputra* or 'sons of the soil') have still not seen their full share of the benefits of development. Poverty levels are the highest among Dayak communities, whilst health and nutritional levels remain low. High drop out rates are the norm among native school goers. Those who succeed in the school system leave the longhouses for greener pastures in the towns. Those living in the longhouse also leave to seek employment elsewhere, forced by low commodity prices and diminishing returns from shifting cultivation on shortened fallow lands. Only the women, the children and the old are left to tend the farms and eke out a living in the harsh environment. Employment opportunities available to most natives remain mainly at the manual level. In the timber industry, they are exposed to the most hazardous jobs. In the land schemes they are alike indentured labourers on their own lands. And they had expected their elected representatives to protect their lands and support them in their suffering and plight. But the irony is that these modern educated native sons who now live in the urban centres would like to see their people give up shifting cultivation, leave the longhouse and become modern farmers integrated into the mainstream of development.

Clearly, if the various Dayak communities in the State are resettled and integrated into the larger society and market economy, they will lose their social and cultural identity. Many of these peoples are not equipped with the skills, knowledge and understanding that will enable them to adapt to a lifestyle and social system so alien from theirs.

However, this book would be incomplete without some suggestions on what can be done to improve the position, status and situation of Sarawak natives. The following recommendations are thus presented in the hope that they can contribute to the process of discussion on the future of Sarawak and its natives.

Royal Commission of Enquiry

The Federal Government should institute a Royal Commission of Enquiry into the state of the native communities of Sarawak: The protection and the safeguards relating to their interests and rights; rights to customary lands and their socioeconomic position should be reviewed as 23 years have passed since Independence. Although the natives of Sarawak are specially protected under Article 161A of the Federal Constitution, and their special status is equivalent to the Malays in Peninsular Malaysia, many of the indigenous groups especially in the remote interior, have not attained the same level of material development. Hence special protection should be afforded to these natives (and their lands) along similar provisions for the protection, well-being and advancement of the aboriginal peoples of the Malay Peninsula.

In 1973, a Joint Ministerial Committee was set up to review the special status of the States of Sabah and Sarawak. This review was to look into the various issues raised in the early 1960s by the Inter-Governmental Committee (which was established on the recommendations of the Cobbold Commission in 1962). The duty of the Inter-Governmental Committee comprising representatives of the Governments of the United Kingdom, Malaya, North Borneo (Sabah) and Sarawak was to prepare the future constitutional arrangements for Malaysia and the special safeguards for North Borneo and Sarawak. This 1973 review of the Inter-Governmental Committee was never published or made available to the public.

Now, more than a decade after, a Royal Commission should be instituted, which should offer proposals on how native identity, interests and welfare can be further protected and enhanced.

A New Forest Policy

The State of Sarawak should set up a new Forest Policy. This Forest Policy should incorporate the following elements:

The forest ecosystem, its resources, and watersheds should be protected and preserved. The forest has been regarded mainly in terms of its commercial value as an abundant supplier of raw materials for export. This thinking should change. The forest is and should be regarded as a renewable resource, which is held in perpetuity by the Government for the good and welfare of its people.

Since knowledge of the tropical forests is still sadly lacking, the Forest Department should make it a top priority to concentrate its efforts and resources on research into the various species of trees and plants, their ecology, pharmaceutical potential, reproduction and so on, with the view of preserving the genetic resources of the tropical forests. In this connection it should work very closely with the forest peoples whose knowledge of the forest and its resources is unsurpassed.

In line with the above, logging activities in the State should be rapidly phased out. If the current rate of logging continues, less than half of the State's forests will be left in ten years from now. For a start, logging operations should be cut down so that it can be phased out within a stipulated time limit. All timber concessions which have not started operating should be cancelled.

The welfare and interests of the natives who depend on the forests and its resources for their survival must be safeguarded. In this regard, the area of Communal Forests should be increased. Recognition of the natives' rights to their lands and reserves must be given. These rights of natives to the forests must be made publicly known and guaranteed by the law.

It must be realised that to the natives, the forest is their life, it provides them with their daily needs, and its products are a source of income for them. Hence forests play a decisive role in the life and economy of these peoples. The forest peoples are the rightful custodians of the forests because they know only too well that the forests and its resources are crucial to their well-being and survival. As such, the protection of the forests should be assigned to the natives themselves. All this while, the forest has been regarded as a source of revenue and profits, and the people who live in it have ironically been seen as 'intruders'. This can be seen in the forest and land laws which actually protect these resources not for the people but from them.

To enable it to carry out its duties, the Forest Department must be expanded to include more natives in forest conservation and protection. This will strengthen the Forest Department which is highly lacking in personnel. It will also give meaningful employment to young natives and cut down corruption in the bureaucracy.

Presently unlike the shifting cultivators, the Penan rights to their customary lands are not legally recognised. Their rights to territories must be legally protected. These nomadic groups have a right to claim the use of the forests, to collect produce and to look for *sago* which they have been doing since time immemorial. Their traditional areas have to be protected against the encroachment of other groups and outsiders who may hunt and fish in their territories thus threatening their resource base. The problem is especially imminent among the Penan in the Mulu National Park which is opened to the public. Elsewhere in the Baram, logging activities have already destroyed their resources and caused great hardship to these nomadic groups.

All areas which have been destroyed by logging activities should be rehabilitated as far as possible. Replanting should be carried out on these devastated lands, bearing in mind the careful selection of sites, species and under proper management. Natives must actively participate in these programmes where tropical rainforest trees, plants and fruit trees (and not exotic species) can be grown.

In drafting the Forest Policy, natives should be consulted. Very often laws, decisions and policies which directly affect natives have been drafted and implemented without prior consultation with these peoples. Consultation is part and parcel of the democratic process, and peoples whose interests are affected by any Government policy have a right to be consulted. To carry this out, committees which will have the responsibility of liaising with the people can be created. These committees should hold meetings, make frequent and long trips upriver to discuss with the people and effectively engage in dialogues with them.

Due protection to natives to prevent further erosion of their communal and customary lands from timber exploitation must be provided immediately. Timber concessionaires should be prosecuted for the wanton destruction of lands, water catchment areas, river systems, the forest environment, farmlands, communal property, and causing hardship to natives with their roads, bridges, and timber camps, thus depriving them of a livelihood. Existing laws and constitutional remedies should be effectively used and enforced against the misdeeds of loggers and to give ample protection to shifting cultivators and forest dwellers.

Each village should be empowered to set up vigilante committees to monitor the activities of the timber companies and report to the Forest authorities, the District Officer and the Police.

A special Legal Aid Committee should be set up to assist natives. This can be done by the Legal Aid Bureau. Natives should be informed of their legal rights and free legal services should be provided to natives so that justice would not be denied to them and their constitutional rights will be protected. The Legal Aid Committee should also train para-legals among members of the community who will inform natives of their rights and what recourse they can take under the law.

Equitable and just compensation must be given to natives whose lands and resources have been destroyed by logging activities both by timber concessionaires and the State. The Government should compensate natives from timber revenue. These monies should be equitably and fairly distributed among the various communities. This money should be held in trust by the village council, who should be properly advised on how best they can invest it and what best use can be put to it. Apart from this, timber concessionaires should be made to give just compensation to natives whose fields, communal properties and waters have already been destroyed by logging activities. A Complaints Bureau should be set up in each District by the Forest Department working with the District Officer to receive representation from natives.

Adequate protection must be given to timber workers. The Government should set up a Commission of Inquiry to look into the shocking state of affairs in the timber industry. The Ministry of Labour and Manpower, and the Forest Department must draw up laws, regulations, and safety standards to ensure that maximum precaution is taken during logging activities. Presently, there is no incentive for timber companies to protect their workers as they are covered under the Social Security (SOCSO) Act 1969. This has led to the shameful neglect of the health and safety of timber workers. Thus the onus of responsibility must be placed squarely on the timber concessionaires and they should be promptly prosecuted if they flout the law.

Laws are useless if they are not enforced. To ensure this, it must be made mandatory for safety officials to carry out frequent and regular checks at factory, camp and logging sites to assess and check that safety and health standards are adhered to. The Government should also institute a rehabilitation programme for injured workers so that the latter will be given suitable vocational training and be better prepared psychologically to return to society.

A New Land Policy

The Forest Policy can only be effective if there are changes in the land policy to complement it. In this regard there is a need for a new Land Policy in the State.

A thorough review of the existing land laws, land policies and the land system in Sarawak should be carried out. This review should be carried out by a Parliamentary Committee with powers to draft native community representatives and experts from the social sciences, law, native customary law, foresters, soil scientists and ecologists. The review and new Land Policy should take the following into consideration.

Firstly, the special position of customary land tenure and the need for its protection should be recognised. Under the present land laws, native customary lands can be extinguished without natives even realising it. On top of this, adequate compensation for the loss of their lands is often denied. There is thus in effect no real security of tenure for natives who practise customary rights. *Adat* law should not be integrated or unified with municipal law. It should instead be given constitutional protection. Those sections of the land (and forest) laws which deny natives the rights of control and ownership of their property should be reviewed and removed if possible.

Laws should be formulated to grant natives legal communal (or collective) rights and tenure under communal land titles to enable them to plant food crops. Each community should be given sufficient reserves of land to cultivate, hunt, roam and gather, and farm for all its members.

Following from the above, adequate land must be set aside to natives to expand swidden farming activities. In established swidden agriculture, the area of land used is eventually stabilised in the sense that no or little new primary forest is cleared as farmers rotate the use of previously cultivated secondary forest. This process has been hindered in recent times because a large part of secondary forests is denied to the farmers or damaged due to logging and land development policies. The authorities should now seriously plan with the farmers the amount of new primary forest land that is required and the geographical locality and timing of land rotation. Thus a plan can be worked out for the whole swidden cycle, with land areas to be used being stabilised. The land to be used for swidden should be earmarked and strictly protected against all encroachments from timber activities or development projects.

In relation to this, native courts must be upgraded and vested with more powers to facilitate this process. Presently, the power of native courts has been reduced to only hearing cases concerning personal law in the Native Officer's or Chief's Court and the Headman's Court.

The Native Courts Ordinance should be amended to allow *all* matters pertaining to native customary land and tenure to be heard and tried *by* natives. Only natives who are well versed in *adat* should sit in these courts which should preside over Appeals as well. At present, the District Native Court and the Native Court of Appeal is presided by a Magistrate, and a Judge or Magistrate respectively. These officers of the court are Western trained and unfamiliar with native customary law. These officials tend to disregard native procedures and observe rules of evidence which are diametrically opposed to native principles of equity and justice.

It is recognised that the land review suggested is no easy task. To facilitate the successful implementation of the project would require the combined efforts of the following:

- A high powered team of technical experts on swidden agriculture, soil sciences and the social sciences, drawn from the universities and Government agencies. The members must have knowledge of and sympathy with the native communities.

- The expansion of the Agriculture and Forestry Department in terms of manpower and infrastructural resources.

- The coordination of the various State Departments especially the Forestry Department and the Agriculture Department.

- The resources of the Federal Government, especially the Ministry of Agriculture, Ministry of Land and Rural Development and the Socio-Economic Research Unit in the Prime Minister's Department should also be used to draw up a new Land Policy.

- Most important of all, the participation of representatives of native communities must be ensured at all stages of review, planning and implementation.

In terms of criteria for future policy on land use, attempts to improve the efficiency and organisation of swidden must be given first priority. For example, participation of natives in reafforestation policies must have as its main purpose the maximising of swidden yields and not timber yields.

A New Agricultural Policy

In line with some of the proposals on Land Policy, a sound Agricultural Policy is also required, since agriculture plays a major role in the natives' well-being. Urgent attention must be given to the cultivation of food crops for their daily subsistence. As this study has attempted to show, compared to modern technologically advanced systems of mono-agriculture (or monoculture), shifting agriculture has been proven to be ecologically sound, dynamic and highly adaptable to the tropical forest ecosystem. It allows the farmer to grow a variety of food crops with minimal effort. Given the fragile tropical forest ecosystem, efforts to improve shifting agriculture would be ecologically and economically sound. Any other alternative would only incur tremendous social, economic and environmental costs. Thus food production and the improvement of swidden productivity must be assigned as top priority in any agricultural programme to improve the living standard and general welfare of the shifting cultivators and to enable them to be self-sufficient in food.

The Government should undertake serious research into the nature and practice of shifting cultivation. At present very little is known about it. Detailed studies should be carried out on the relationship between soil use, fallow systems, felling and clearing practices, site selection, types of crops and varieties of hill rice grown in relation to soil conservation, weeding practices, and agricultural productivity. Only with a clearer understanding can any attempts be made to stabilise and improve swidden as a viable system of agriculture. More funds and resources should be channelled in this direction.

Similarly, very thorough studies must be conducted on the effects of pesticides, fertilisers, new crops, mono-agriculture regimes on soil fertility and yields in the long run. Experiences from swidden communities in other countries should be used for comparative studies as well.

The Agriculture Department should set up a marketing service to enable natives to market their jungle produce, meat and fish products so that they can obtain a fair price for them.

All land and agricultural development projects should undergo environmental and socioeconomic impact assessment studies before they are approved.

An examination of rural-urban migration must be conducted to find out the extent and nature of the problem and steps must be taken to prevent this problem from growing.

Hydro Electric Dam Projects

At present the Government has in principle agreed to build the Bakun dam and is looking into the possibility of constructing another four dams in the Seventh Division. As shown in this book, this series of dams would cause massive dislocation to several thousands of natives and damage the forest ecosystem. It is suggested that the plans for these dams be seriously re-considered and that the losses to be endured by the natives as well as the destruction of the forest ecosystem and the loss of land be taken into account by any cost-benefit analysis or evaluation of such projects. Such human, social and ecological costs are usually under-weighted (and in some cases ignored) in such evaluations. Moreover, the loss of cultural identity and way of life to affected native communities would be too great to be reflected in any monetary evaluation of costs. It is therefore suggested that big hydro electric dam projects should not be planned for Sarawak and other energy sources (including small dam projects which have less social and environmental consequences) be considered instead.

Regarding the already functioning Batang Ai dam, the authorities should look into the problems of the natives who had been resettled and settle all outstanding compensation and claims.

Health, Food and Nutrition Policy For Natives

Adequate food and proper nutrition is a necessary condition for good health. If both these requirements are fulfilled in the community, health is easily ensured. And a State with healthy people is a wealthy State; because there is no better investment than the better health of its citizens and its future generations. However, good health depends on various other factors like a clean environment, adequate sanitation, good personal hygiene and sound eating habits. Thus health education and preventive health remains an important component of the health services. In Sarawak, the health services are still beyond the reach of many, especially natives who live in the remote areas.

According to a survey conducted by the Sarawak Medical Department in 1979, the State has the highest percentage of villages and population 'underserved' by the Government's health care and delivery system. Nearly 5,000 Sarawak villages with a population of some 830,000 people or 74 per cent of the State's villages and 68 per cent of the population are underserved, compared to Peninsular Malaysia where 24 per cent of the villages and 12 per cent of the population are underserved. The most underserved Districts include Sri Aman (Simanggang), Kapit, Sibu and Baram. This means that Sarawak's health services is in dire need of improvement.

However, with the current economic slow-down the health budget has suffered severe cutbacks. For instance, the Deputy Health Minister Datuk K. Pathmanaban informed Parliament in March 1984 that there will be no increase in the mobile dispensaries' service and doctors' service to rural areas in Sarawak. This cutback in the health budget will seriously affect the State's health programme. This will have adverse effects especially among the native communities. Many of them live far in the remote interior. For them to go to the nearest District hospital or clinic entails a few days of travelling, often across dangerous rapids. This is a long, tiring, risky and expensive journey. Natives find it almost impossible to carry out this undertaking on their own.

The Health Ministry must upgrade and improve its services to these rural communities. Indeed rural health should be an urgent priority of the Ministry. For a start the Ministry should give food aid to the most deprived communities. This should be done together with the State Department of Agriculture. The Health Department should frequently monitor the nutritional status of the people especially children and expectant mothers. This food aid should be extended to schools in the rural areas. Native children should be provided with a simple nutritious meal in school.

There should also be an expansion of public health services to the native communities especially those living in the more inaccessible areas of the State. More mobile clinics, and doctors' visits should be initiated to serve their needs.

Preventive health education should also be emphasised. Natives should be educated on the use of boiled water for drinking, proper sanitation and hygiene. Animals should be penned or put into enclosures some distance from the longhouse. Wherever possible they should be assisted on the proper construction and location of toilets. Balanced nutrition, proper cooking and food storage, the dangers of junk food consumption, and the importance of breast feeding should be stressed.

The Ministry should also train health workers or medical auxiliaries in each community to carry out its health education and health care programme. This training should combine modern health care with traditional health care. For instance, natives have a very sound and sophisticated knowledge of herbal medicine which should be incorporated into the health care system. Scientific research should be conducted on the medicinal plants used by the natives.

To cut down costs, a boat doctor service should be introduced. This service should make upriver visits at least four times a year. It should include both medical, dental and nursing professionals.

However, a flying doctor service should still be maintained to deal with emergencies. This is also crucial especially for the remote forest dwellers like the Penan who cannot be easily reached.

More clinics which will provide maternity and child care services should be introduced. Dispensaries or clinics should be increased in the interior to provide a given area, serving a few longhouse communities and Penan areas. These centres should be manned by local natives who have been given sufficient training. The District Medical Officer responsible for these centres should maintain frequent communication and visits to see their problems and monitor their progress. A radio service should be installed in these clinics to facilitate prompt communication in case of emergencies.

Goitre remains a major problem with these communities. The Health Ministry must take effective steps to overcome this problem. Iodized salt properly treated and packaged should be given free to natives. There have been cases in the past where unsightly huge pieces of iodized salt were given to natives who refused to use them.

Malaria should be monitored constantly especially in areas where logging activities and forest clearing is taking place.

The Health Ministry should set up a special unit to deal specifically with native health care. This unit will be responsible for all health care programmes upriver. Hospitals should be set up under this unit in each Division for natives who require medical attention. These native hospitals should be modelled along the Orang Asli Gombak Hospital in Peninsular Malaysia to cater to their special needs. Natives do not like leaving their families and homes to live in an alien and impersonal hospital environment and be subjected to its strict routines. Hence, they are reluctant to seek proper medical attention even when they need to. These hospitals should be located upriver where families can accompany the patients and stay with them.

Other Services

The Government should provide a subsidised river transport service for natives. This can be done together with the marketing service. These boats must be equipped with sufficient life jackets and safety and emergency measures. Presently, natives have to rely on commercial boats which are grossly overcrowded with no life jackets and safety measures.

Government personnel should make frequent and regular upriver visits to have dialogues with the people and discuss their problems. The oft heard complaint is that Government officials only pay lightning visits during elections or when a VIP was upriver. In this connection, frequent meetings should be held with representatives and headmen of the various communities in their longhouses. These dialogue sessions should be held at least six times a year.

For the Penan communities the *Tamu* should be revived. The *Tamu* was an important and auspicious occasion for the Penan to trade their jungle products and to meet Government officials who were present to ensure fair trading took place so that they will not be exploited. These meetings (or *Tamu*) were the only occasions when the Penan came into contact with the outside world. The Government was represented by the District Officer, the Medical Department, the Agriculture Department and any other relevant authorities when so required. These were the only opportunities available to the Penan to present their problems to the Government. In the past, *Tamu* in the Baram was held four times a year lasting two to three days at each centre. The *Tamu* has a long and illustrious history. It started during the reign of Charles Brooke, the Second Rajah of Sarawak and was seriously pursued under the Colonial Government up until the 1970s. The last *Tamu* was held in the Baram District in 1976. After that it mysteriously died. No official explanation has been given for its demise. From various reports by Government officials, Penan have been appealing for their revival. Without the *Tamu*, Penan have lost the protection of the Government which in the past ensured fair trading took place between the Penan and their Kayan, Kenyah and Berawan neighbours. Penan have also lost an avenue to meet Government officials and seek medical health care. Thus renewing the *Tamu* would prevent further exploitation of the Penan and allow them access to the authorities.

Native Autonomy

It must be realised that in the final analysis the success of any programme to uplift swidden farmers and forest peoples would depend on their genuine participation and their ability to articulate their problems and views. To ensure this, a native consultative council comprising rural natives elected by the people themselves should be formed to enable them to be adequately represented. This council will be consulted on all matters affecting their interests. Special efforts must be made to ensure that the Penan are adequately represented on this council.

Similarly, representatives of the longhouse communities or headmen should be freely elected by the members of their community and regular elections should be held. As much as possible, the least interference should be made so that natives can run their affairs at the village level, and have faith and confidence in their own elected leaders.

Finally, some kind of regional autonomy could be considered for the various native groups in relation to certain issues such as the rights and use of customary land, the practice of *adat* and its regulation through native courts.

Conclusion

The above are only some suggestions for changes or improvements to better the situation of Sarawak natives. It is obvious that these are very crucial and complex issues that should be thoroughly examined and studied in-depth, with the full participation of the native communities themselves. It is hoped that a Commission of Inquiry could fulfil such a task. The natives of Sarawak have been rapidly losing their land, with diminishing access to their forest and its resources; their culture is fast being eroded and their identity as a community is also being threatened. An urgent review of their situation is thus imperative.

Only when the rights, interests and welfare of these natives have been fully recognised and restored, can we proudly acclaim the reality of a balanced, just and integrated nation. All Malaysians should strive towards that ideal.

BIBLIOGRAPHY

Abang Naruddin Zainorin, 'The Status of Logging Safety and Accident Prevention in Sarawak', paper presented at Seminar on *Occupational Safety in Logging Industry In Sarawak* 19-20 August, 1985, Kuching, The Sarawak Timber Industry Development Corporation.

Abdul Razak Tready, 'The Compulsory Acquisition of Land Under The Sarawak Land Code'. Project Paper (LL.B.). University of Malaya 1977.

Aiken, S.R. & Moss, M.R. 'Man's impact on the tropical rainforest of Peninsular Malaysia: A review', *Biological Conservation* 1975 Vol 8 pp 213-29.

Anderson, A.J.U., 'Nutrition of Kayan and Kenyah Children of the Middle Baram River', *The Sarawak Gazette* 1978 November 30 pp 241-48.

____. 'Subsistence of the Penan in the Mulu Area of Sarawak', *The Sarawak Gazette* 1979 November 30 pp 204-16.

Andriesse, J.P., 'Nutrient level changes during a 20 year shifting cultivation cycle in Sarawak (Malaysia)' in *International Society of Soil Science Conference on Classification and Management of Tropical Soils* 1977 Kuala Lumpur pp 479-91.

Arshad Ayub, 'National Agricultural Policy and its Implications on Forest Development in the Country', *The Malaysian Forester* 1979 Vol 42 No 4 pp 348-53.

Bahrin Adeng, 'Native Customary Land Rights in Sarawak'. Project Paper (LL.B). University of Malaya 1975.

Baram District Office, 'Baram District Annual Report 1978'.

Baram District Office, 'Baram District Annual Report 1981'.

Betterton, Christine, 'Endau-Rompin: A Case for Conservation' in Consumers' Association of Penang, *Development And The Environmental Crisis*. Proceedings of the symposium 'The Malaysian Environment In Crisis' organised by The Consumers' Association of Penang, The School of Biological Sciences, Universiti Sains Malaysia and Sahabat Alam Malaysia held at Recsam Complex, Penang, 16-20 Sept. 1978. Penang: Consumers' Association of Penang 1982 pp 91-93.

Biswas A.K., 'Health Implications of Hydropower Development'. Vienna: International Atomic Energy Agency 1982 pp 527-37.

Burgess, P.F., 'The Effect of Logging on Hill Dipterocarp Forests', *Malayan Nature Journal* 1971 Vol 24 pp 231-37.

Caufield, Catherine, *In The Rainforest*. London: Heinemann 1984.

Chai, Leo, 'Sustained yield management in Sarawak', *The Sarawak Gazette* 1980 July pp 130-33.

Chandrasekharan, C., 'Sarawak: Role of Forestry in Ameliorating Rural Poverty'. Preliminary Mission on Rural Poverty Study in Sarawak, FAO Regional Office Bangkok n.d.

Chin, S.C., 'Towards a Better Understanding of Shifting Cultivation', paper presented at Seminar on *Appropriate Technology, Culture and Lifestyle in Development* 3-7 November, 1981, Penang, Consumers' Association of Penang.

Chin See Chung, 'Agriculture And Subsistence In A Lowland Rainforest Kenyah Community'. 2 volumes. Ph.D. Dissertation. Yale University 1984.

Conklin, C. Harold, 'An Ethnoecological Approach to Shifting Agriculture' in Andrew P Vayda (ed.), *Environment & Cultural Behaviour.* Austin: University of Texas 1969 pp 221-33.

Das Murthy, 'The Administration of Forest in Sarawak: A Study of the Forest Ordinance (CAP. 126). Sarawak and Related Legislation'. Project Paper (LL.B). University of Malaya 1980.

Dasmann, Raymond F., John P. Milton, and Peter H. Freeman, *Ecological Principles for Economic Development.* London: John Wiley & Sons 1973 c.f. Terry Grandstaff, *Shifting Cultivation in Northern Thailand: Possibilities for Development.* Resource Systems Theory and Methodology Series No 3. Tokyo: United Nations University 1980.

G. Dhanarajan, 'Forest Resources: The Renewability Gap' in Consumers' Association of Penang, *Op Cit* pp 88-93.

Dove, Michael Roger, *'Swidden Agriculture in Indonesia: The Subsistence Strategies of the Kalimantan Kantu'.* Berlin: Mouton Publishers 1985.

Eckholm, Erik P., *Losing Ground.* World Watch Institute and UN Environment Programme. New York: W.W. Norton 1976.

Eide, Asbjorn, 'The International Human Rights System' in Asbjorn Eide *et al* (eds.), *Food As a Human Right.* Tokyo: The United Nations University 1984 pp 152-161.

ESCAP, *Regional Overview Of Environmental and Socio-Economic Aspects of Tropical Deforestation In The ESCAP Region.* Expert Group Meeting on the Environmental and Socio-Economic Aspects of Tropical Deforestation 28 January - 3 February 1986 Bangkok. ECU/ESATD/2 dated 8 Jan 1986.

Fao and unep, *Tropical Forest Resources Assessment Project (in the framework of the Global Environment Monitoring System) Forest Resources of Tropical Asia.* UN 32/6.1301-78-04 Technical Report 3 FAO and UNEP 1981: Rome.

Francis Jana Wan Lian, 'Aspect of Land Development Programme in Sarawak', *Journal Geographica,* Geographical Society University of Malaya, 1980 Vol 14 pp 1-9.

Peter H. Freeman, *Large Dams and the Environment.* International Institute for Environment and Development, March 1977 c.f. V.B. Pantulu, 'A Case-Study of the Pa Mong Project: Environmental Aspects' in *The Environmental Dimension in Development.* Bangkok: UN Asian and Pacific Development Institute 1979 May pp 145-59.

Freeman, Derek, *Report on the Iban.* London: Athlone Press 1970.

Gabriel Gumis Humen, 'Native Land Tenure Protection in Sarawak'. Project Paper (LL.B). University of Malaya 1981.

Geddes, W.R., *The Land Dayaks of Sarawak.* HMSO 1954.

Gillis, M., *Tropical Hardwood Concessions: The Main Fiscal and Financial Issues.* Bangkok: UNCTC/ESCAP Joint Unit 1980 c.f. Y. Sudhakara Rao, Forest Exploitation in Southeast Asia' in P.B.L. Srivastava *et al* (eds.), *Tropical Forests: Source of Energy through Optimisation and Diversification.* Proceedings International Forestry Seminar, 11-15 November, 1980, Serdang, Malaysia. Serdang: Penerbit Universiti Pertanian Malaysia 1982 pp 13-26.

Goldsmith, E. and Hildyard N., *The Social and Environmental Effects of Large Dams Volume 1: Overview.* Wadebridge: Wadebridge Ecological Centre 1984.

Grainger, Alan, 'The State of the World's Tropical Forests', *The Ecologist* 1980 Vol 10 No 1 pp 6-54.

Grandstaff, Terry B., *Shifting Cultivation in Northern Thailand: Possibilities for Development.*

Resource Systems Theory and Methodology Series No 3. Tokyo: United Nations University 1980.

Gregory S.C. Hii and S.S. Tay, 'An Assessment of Sawmill Pollution in Sarawak', *The Malaysian Forester* 1980 Vol 43 No 2 pp 238-43.

Haji Sulaiman bin Sebli, 'Shifting Cultivation And Forestry', n.d., mimeo.

Hanbury-Tenison, Robin, *Mulu the Rain Forest*. London: Weidenfeld and Nicolson 1980.

Harris, David R., 'Agricultural systems, ecosystems and the origins of agriculture' in Peter J. Ucko and G.W. Dimbleby (eds.), *The Domestication and Exploitation of Plants and Animals*. Chicago: Aldine Publishing Co 1969 pp 3-15 c.f. Karl J. Pelzer, 'Swidden Cultivation in Southeast Asia: Historical, Ecological, and Economic Perspectives' in Peter Kunstadter, E.C. Chapman and Sanga Sabhasri (eds.), *Farmers in the Forest: Economic Development and Marginal Agriculture in Northern Thailand*. Honolulu: East-West Center 1978.

Harrison Ngau, 'Education and Cultural Domination: The Sarawak Dayak Experience', paper presented at *Seminar on Education and Development* 18-22 November, 1983, Penang, Consumers' Association of Penang.

Hatch, T. and C.P. Lim (ed.), *Shifting Cultivation in Sarawak*. A report based upon the workshop on shifting cultivation held in Kuching on 7-8 December, 1978, mimeo, Department of Agriculture, Sarawak.

Hatch, T. and Y.L. Tie, 'Shifting Cultivation in Sarawak and its effect on soil fertility' in Henry T.L. Liau *et al* (eds.), *The Fertility and Management of Deforested Land in Malaysia*. The Proceedings of The Malaysian Seminar on the Fertility and Management of Deforested Land and The Sixth Meeting on the Standardisation of Soil and Plant Analyses in Malaysia, Kota Kinabalu, Sabah, Malaysia May 1979. Kota Kinabalu: Society of Agricultural Scientists Sabah 1979 pp 9-16.

Hatch, T., 'Shifting Cultivation in Sarawak: Past, Present and Future' in J.I. Furtado (ed.), *Tropical Ecology & Development*. Proceedings of the Vth International Symposium of Tropical Ecology 16-21 April, 1979, Kuala Lumpur, Malaysia. The International Society of Tropical Ecology 1980 pp 483-96.

Hinton, Peter 'Swidden Cultivation among the PWD Karen of Northern Thailand: Present Practices and Future Prospects' in *International Seminar on Shifting Cultivation and Economic Development in Northern Thailand*. Bangkok: Land Development Department, Royal Thai Government 1970 c.f. Terry B Grandstaff *Op Cit* p 8.

Hong, Evelyne, 'Kenyah Society in Transition: A Baram case study'. M. Soc. Sc. Thesis. Universiti Sains Malaysia 1977.

Howes, Peter, 'Why some of the best people aren't Christian?', *Sarawak Museum Journal* 1960 Vol IX No 15-16 pp 488-95.

International Commission of Jurists, *Development, Human Rights and the Rule of Law*. Geneva: ICJ August 1981.

Jamaluddin Md Jahi, 'Development Process and Environmental Deterioration: The Need for a Comprehensive Coastal Zone Management', paper presented at Seminar on *Environment and the Natural Resource Crisis in Asia and the Pacific* 22-25 October, 1983, Penang, Sahabat Alam Malaysia.

James J. Masing, 'Hydro-Electric Projects in Sarawak' in Sesco Features n.d.

Janang Ensiring, 'Hill Padi Farming', *The Sarawak Gazette* 1975 October 31 pp 239-41.

Jensen, E.H., *Money for Rice*. Copenhagen: Monograph of the Danish Board for Technical Cooperation with Developing countries c.f. S.C. Chin (1981) *Op Cit* p 10.

Joachim Ulok Laeng, 'The Inexorable Exodus', *The Sarawak Gazette* 1974 March 31 pp 49-50.

_____. 'The "Whys" of Cultural Alienation in the Ulu', *The Sarawak Gazette* 1974 September 30 pp 187-88.

Khor Kok Peng, 'The Human Right to Development: Operationalising the Concept in the Malaysian Context', 1982, mimeo.

Knudsen, A. Bruce, 'The silent jungle transmission cycle of dengue virus and its tenable relationship to endemic dengue in Malaysia', *Malayan Nature Journal* 1977 Vol 31 No 1 pp 41-47.

Kunstadter, Peter, 'Alternatives for the Development of Upland Areas' in Peter Kunstadter, E.C. Chapman and Sanga Sabhasri (eds.), *Farmers in the Forest: Economic Development and Marginal Agriculture in Northern Thailand*. Honolulu: East-West Center 1978 pp 289-308.

_____. 'Subsistence Agricultural Economics of Lua' and Karen Hill Farmers, Mae Seriang District, Northwestern Thailand' in Peter Kunstadter, E.C. Chapman and Sanga Sabhasri (eds.), *Op Cit* pp 74-131.

_____. 'The Lua' (Lawa) and Skaw Karen of Maehongson Province, Northwestern Thailand' in Peter Kunstadter, (ed.), *Southeast Asian Tribes, Minorities, and Nations*. 2 vols. Princeton: Princeton University Press 1967.

Lahmeyer International, 'Socio-Economic Aspects and Resettlement: Midi Pelagus and Balu 037 Hydro-Electric Projects'. Draft Report n.d.

Lau Buong Tiing, 'The Effects of Shifting Cultivation on Sustained Yield Management for Sarawak National Forests', *The Malaysian Forester* 1979 Vol 42 No 4 pp 418-22.

_____. 'Illegal Felling and Encroachment'. Paper presented at the 1980 *Annual Forest Department Conference* 7-12 July, 1980, Miri, Sarawak.

Leach, Edmund, 'Land And Custom', *The Sarawak Gazette* 1947 August 1 pp 151-2 letter to the Editor.

Leach, E.R., *Social Science Research in Sarawak: A Report on the Possibilities of a Social Economic Survey of Sarawak*. Colonial Research Studies No 1. London: His Majesty's Stationery Office 1950.

Lee Hua Seng and Lai Khim Kuet, 'Reafforestation in Sarawak', *The Sarawak Gazette* 1982 November pp 5-11.

Lee, H.S., 'The Development of Silvicultural Systems in the Hill Forests of Malaysia', *The Malaysian Forester* 1982 Vol 45 No 1 pp 1-9.

Leigh, Michael, 'Ethnicity and Regional Planning', *The Sarawak Gazette* 1975 October 31 pp 255-63.

Ling, A.H., Tan K.Y. and S. Sofie Syed Omar, 'Preliminary observations on some possible post-clearing changes (in soil) properties' in Henry T.L. Liau *et al* (eds.), *Op Cit* pp 17-25.

Lucas, Eric, 'Towards an International Declaration on Land Rights' in *The Review*, International Commission of Jurists 1984 December No 33 pp 61-8.

Malaysia, *Bank Negara Malaysia Annual Report 1985*. Kuala Lumpur: Bank Negara Malaysia March 29, 1986.

Malaysia, Department of Statistics, *Annual Statistical Bulletin Sarawak 1977*. Kuching: Department of Statistics Malaysia (Sarawak Branch) August 1978.

Malaysia, Department of Statistics, *Annual Statistical Bulletin Sarawak 1981*. Kuching: Department of Statistics Malaysia (Sarawak Branch) December 1982.

Malaysia, Department of Statistics, *Annual Statistical Bulletin Sarawak 1983*. Kuching: Department of Statistics Malaysia (Sarawak Branch) December 1984.

Malaysia, Department of Statistics, *Population And Housing Census of Malaysia: State Population Report Sarawak Part II*. Kuala Lumpur: Department of Statistics Malaysia October 1983.

Malaysia, *Federal Constitution* (As At 5th April 1986). Kuala Lumpur: International Law Book Services 1986.

Malaysia, *Mid Term Review of The Fourth Malaysia Plan 1981-1985*. Kuala Lumpur: Jabatan Percetakan Negara 1984.

Malaysia, Ministry of Finance, *Economic Report 1977/78*. Kuala Lumpur: The Director General of Printing 1977.

Malaysia, Ministry of Finance, *Economic Report 1982-83*. Kuala Lumpur: National Printing Department 1982.

Malaysia, Ministry of Primary Industries, *Profile of the Primary Commodity Sector in Malaysia*. Kuala Lumpur: Ministry of Primary Industries March 1986.

Malaysia, Ministry of Primary Industries, *Statistics On Commodities*. Kuala Lumpur: Ministry of Primary Industries April 1986a.

Malaysia, *Report of the Commission of Enquiry, North Borneo and Sarawak* (Cobbold Commission). Kuala Lumpur: Government Printer 1962.

Malaysia, *Third Malaysia Plan 1976-1980*. Kuala Lumpur: The Government Press 1981.

Malaysia, *Fourth Malaysia Plan 1981-1985*. Kuala Lumpur: The Government Press 1981.

Malaysia, *Fifth Malaysia Plan 1986-1990*. Kuala Lumpur: National Printing Department 1986.

Malaysia, *Workmen's Compensation Act 1952 (Revised — 1982)*. Kuala Lumpur: Percetakan Negara Julai 1982.

Malek, E.A., 'Snail Ecology and Man-Made Habitats' in M.J. Muller (ed.), *Schistosomiasis*. New Orleans: Tulane University Press 1972.

Maria Perpetua Kana, 'Native Land System in Sarawak'. Project Paper (LL.B.). University of Malaya 1975.

Marn, H. Mattsson and W. Jonkers, 'Logging damage in tropical high forest' in P.B.L. Srivastava *et al* (eds.), *Tropical Forests: Source of Energy Through Optimisation and Diversification*, Proceedings International Forestry Seminar, 11-15 November, 1980, Serdang, Selangor, Malaysia. Serdang: Universiti Pertanian Malaysia 1982 pp 27-38.

Mok Sian Tuan, 'Forest Resource Exploitation and Wastage in Malaysia' in P.B.L. Srivastava *et al* (eds.), *Op Cit* pp 39-50.

Mundy, R., *A Narrative of Events in Borneo and Celebes from the Journals of James Brooke Esquire*. 2 Vols. London: John Murray 1848.

Nicholson, D.I., 'A review of natural regeneration in the Dipterocarp forests of Sabah', *Malayan Forester* 1965 Vol XXVIII No 1 pp 4-26.

_____. 'The Effects of Logging and Treatment on the Mixed Dipterocarp Forests of South East Asia'. (FO:MISC/79/8) FAO, Rome 1979.

Nicolaisen, Johannes, 'The Penan of the Seventh Division of Sarawak: Past, Present, and Future', *Sarawak Museum Journal* 1976 Vol XXIV No 45 (New Series) pp 35-61.

Nye, P.H. and Greenland, D.J., *The Soil Under Shifting Cultivation*. Technical communication No 51 Commonwealth Bureau of Soils. Harpenden: Commonwealth Agricultural Bureau, Bucks, England 1960. c.f. Chin (1981) *Op Cit* p 3.

Oomen, J.M.V., 'Specific Diseases of the Kamburu Population' in R.S. Odingo (ed.), *An African Dam*. Ecological Bulletin 29. Stockholm: Swedish Natural Science Research Council 1979 pp 134 c.f. A.K. Biswas, 'Health Implications of Hydropower Development'. Vienna: International Atomic Energy Agency 1982 pp 527-37.

Othman Abdul Manan, 'Practical Problems in Forest Management', *The Malaysian Forester* 1978 Vol 41 No 2 pp 197-200.

Padoch, C., 'The Environmental and Demographic Effects of Alternative Cash Producing Activities among Shifting Cultivators in Sarawak' in J.I. Furtado (ed.), *Op Cit* pp 475-81.

Padoch, Christine, 'Land Use in New And Old Areas of Iban Settlement', *Borneo Research Bulletin* 1982 Vol 14 No 1 pp 3-14.

Pelzer, Karl J., 'Swidden Cultivation in Southeast Asia: Historical, Ecological, and Economic Perspectives' in Peter Kunstadter, E.C. Chapman and Sanga Sabhasri (eds.), *Op Cit* pp 271-86.

Peter M. Kedit, 'An Ecological Survey of the Penan', *Sarawak Museum Journal* 1982 July Vol XXX No 51 pp 225-79.

Porter, A.F., *Land Administration in Sarawak*. Kuching: Government Printing Office 1967.

Radzuan A. Rahman, 'Economic Utilization of Forestry Resources: Its Impact on the Environment' in Consumers' Association of Penang, *Op Cit* pp 82-90.

Regional Council on Human Rights in Asia, *Declaration of the Basic Duties of Asean Peoples And Governments*. Manila 1984.

Richards, A.J.N., *Sarawak Land Law and Adat*. Kuching: Government Printing Office 1961.

Sahabat Alam Malaysia (SAM), *State of The Malaysian Environment 1983/84: Towards Greater Environmental Awareness*. Penang: SAM 1983.

_____. Memorandum On 'Communal Forest Reserved For Longhouse Communities'. To: The Chief Minister, Sarawak; Minister of Resource Planning, Sarawak; and Minister of Forest, Sarawak. Kuching 1985.

Salleh Mohd Nor and Ho Kam Seng, 'The Myth of complete utilization of tropical forests' in P.B.L. Srivastava *et al*, *Op Cit* pp 101-6.

Salleh Mohd Nor, 'Forestry in Peninsular Malaysia and its role in Environmental Conservation', in *Development and The Environmental Crisis*, *Op Cit* pp 75-81.

Salleh Mohd Nor and Francis S.P. Ng, 'Conservation in Malaysia', *The Planter* 1983 November Vol 59 No 692 pp 483-90.

Sanga Sabhasri, 'Effects of Forest Fallow Cultivation on Forest Production and Soil', in Peter Kunstadter, E.C. Chapman and Sanga Sabhasri (eds.), *Op Cit* pp. 160-84.

Sarawak, *Agricultural Statistics of Sarawak 1970*. Kuching: Government Printing Office.

Sarawak Department of Agriculture, *Agricultural Statistics of Sarawak 1980*. Kuching: National Printing Department 1981.

Sarawak Department of Agriculture, Research Branch, 'Some Research Findings on Wet and Hill Padi', 1982 April 27, mimeo.

Sarawak Forest Department, *Annual Report of The Forest Department 1968*. Kuching.

_____. *Annual Report of The Forest Department Sarawak 1980*. Kuching.

_____. *Annual Report of The Forest Department Sarawak 1982*. Kuching.

_____. *Annual Report of The Forest Department Sarawak 1983*. Kuching.

_____. *Annual Report of The Forest Department Sarawak 1984*. Kuching.

Sarawak Forest Department, 'Forest Resource Base, Policy and Legislation of Sarawak', *The Malaysian Forester* 1979 Vol 42 No 4 pp 311-27.

Sarawak Land Code (Sarawak Cap. 81). Government Printing Office: Kuching 1972.

Sarawak, Ministry for Forestry, the Forest Department and Sarawak Timber Industry Development Corporation, 'Special Article on the Safety Promotion Campaign for the Logging Industry' in *Kempen Galakan Keselamatan Dalam Industri Pembalakan* jointly organised by the Ministry for Forestry, the Forest Department and the Sarawak Timber Industry Development Corporation March 21, 1982, Holiday Inn, Kuching, pp 7-13.

Sarawak Museum, *Batang Ai Hydro-Electric Project*. Batang Ai Report No 1 July 1979.

Sarawak, *Noter-Up Service for the Laws of Sarawak Issue No 2 of 1979*, complied in the State Attorney-General's Chambers, Kuching. National Printing Department: Kuching 1979.

Sarawak, *Report of The Land Committee 1962*. Kuching: Government Printing Office.

Sarawak, *Sarawak Year Book 1963*. Kuching: Government Printing Office.

Sarawak Study Group, *Logging In Sarawak: The Belaga Experience*. Petaling Jaya: INSAN 1986.

Sarawak Timber Industry Development Corporation (STIDC), 'Notes on Forest Industrial Safety and Accident Prevention in Sarawak', April 15, 1981.

Sastrapradja S., Kartawinata K., Adi Soemarts S., Tarmunkeng R.C., 1980, 'The Conservation of Forest Animal and Plant Genetic Resources' in *FAO* 1980 c f. Alan Grainger *Op Cit* p 30.

Schlegel, Stuart A., *Tiruray Subsistence: From Shifting Cultivation to Plow Agriculture*. Quezon City: Ateneo de Manila University Press 1979.

Sen Gupta, ' Post-mortem Report on Fatal Cases due to Logging Accidents', paper presented at Seminar on *Occupational Safety in Logging Industry In Sarawak* 19-20 August, 1985, Kuching, The Sarawak Timber Industry Development Corporation.

Senada, D.A., 'Role of Forestry in the Socio-Economic Development of Rural Populations in Sarawak'. Proceedings of the Sixth Malaysian Forestry Conference 11-17 October, 1976, Kuching, Sarawak, Working Papers Vol 1 pp 123-48.

Setyono Sastrosumarto (1978) 'The Effect of Selective Logging as Applied to The Tropical Rain Forest in the conditions of Residual Stands in Indonesia' in *FAO* 1980 c.f. Alan Grainger *Op Cit* p 30.

Soepadmo, E., 'Ecological changes arising from deforestation' in Henry T.L. Liau *et al* (eds.), *Op Cit* pp 49-60.

Spencer, J.E., *Shifting Cultivation in Southeastern Asia*. Berkeley: University of California Press 1966.

Spurway, B.J.C., 'Shifting Cultivation in Sarawak', *The Malayan Forester* 1937 Vol 1 pp 243-46.

Srivastava, P.B.L. *et al* (eds.) *Tropical Forests: Source of Energy through Optimisation and Diversification*. Proceedings International Forestry Seminar 11-15 November, 1980, Serdang, Selangor, Malaysia. Serdang: Universiti Pertanian Malaysia 1982.

Stevens, W., *Report to the Government of Malaysia on Game Conservation*. 1969 c.f. P.F. Burgess *Op Cit*.

Sudhakara Rao Y., 'Forest exploitation in Southeast Asia' in P.B.L. Srivastava *et al* (eds.), *Tropical Forest: Source of Energy through Optimisation and Diversification*. Proceedings International Forestry Seminar 11-15 November, 1980, Serdang, Selangor, Malaysia. Serdang: Penerbit Universiti Pertanian Malaysia 1982 pp 13-26.

Sutlive Jr., Vinson H., *The Iban of Sarawak*. Illinois: AHM Publishing Corporation 1978.

Tan Yaw Kang, 'Review of log export and processing activities in Sarawak', *Sarawak Gazette* 1980 August 31 pp 145-50.

Ter Haar, B., *Adat Law In Indonesia*. Edited with an Introduction by E. Adamson Hoebel and A. Arthur Schiller. Djakarta: Bharatara 1962.

Umali, D.L., 1980. Keynote address at FAO/SIDA Seminar on Forestry in Rural Community Development, Chiang Mai, Thailand. FOR: GCP INT/313 (SWE). FAO, Rome c.f. Y. Sudhakara Rao, 'Forest Exploitation in Southeast Asia' in P.B.L. Srivastava *et al* (eds.) *Op Cit* pp 13-26.

UNESCO/UNEP/FAO, *State of Knowledge Report on Tropical Forest Ecosystems*. Paris: UNESCO 1978.

UNESCO/UNEP, *Swidden Cultivation in Asia*. Volume Two. Country Profiles: India, Indonesia, Malaysia, Philippines, Thailand. Bangkok: UNESCO 1983 pp 159-238.

United Nations Economic and Social Council, Commission on Human Rights Report of the Working Group of governmental experts on the rights to development'. Document E/CN.4/1489 dated February 11, 1982.

Urquhart, I.A.N., 'Some Notes on the Jungle Punans in the Kapit District', *Sarawak Museum Journal* 1951 Vol 5 No 5 pp 495-533.

Waddy, B.B., 'Research into the Health Problems of Manmade Lakes, with special reference to Africa', *Transactions of the Royal Society of Tropical Medicine and Hygiene* 1975 Vol 69 No 1 pp 39-51.

Watters, R.F., 'The Nature of Shifting Cultivation', *Pacific Viewpoint* 1960 1:59-99 c.f. Terry B. Grandstaff, *Op Cit* p 24.

Wee, Y.C., and A.N. Rao, 'Current and potential plant resources of the tropical rainforest' in P.B.L. Srivastava *et al* (eds.) *Op Cit* pp 115-25.

Whitmore, T.C., 'Introduction' in T.C. Whitmore (ed.), *Tree Flora of Malaya*. Vol I. London: Longmans 1972 pp vii-viii.

_____. *Tropical Rain Forests in the Far East*. Oxford: Oxford University Press 1975 c.f. Alan Grainger, *Op Cit* p 30.

Wong Leong Do, 'Floods in the Fourth Division of Sarawak', *Sarawak Gazette* 1981 April pp 12-16.

World Bank, *Environmental Health and Human Ecologic Considerations in Economic Development Projects*. World Bank Report: Washington D.C. 1974 May pp 43-53.

World Bank, *Forestry Sector Policy Paper*. Washington 1978 c.f. Alan Grainger, *Op Cit* p 30.

Zaidi Khaldin Zainie, 'Land Tenure System in Sarawak', *Sarawak Gazette* 1985 July pp 14-17.

Zainab bt Tambi, 'The Nutritional Status of Children under seven years in Sarawak', *Sarawak Gazette* 1982 November pp 21-9.

Zinke, Paul J., Sanga Sabhasri and Peter Kunstadter, 'Soil Fertility Aspects of the Lua' Forest Fallow System of Shifting Cultivation' in Peter Kunstadter, E.C. Chapman and Sanga Sabhasri (eds.) *Op Cit* pp 134-59.

Newspapers:

Berita Harian, 'LLN jamin gegaran kenyir tiada bahaya', November 28, 1985.

Borneo Bulletin, 'Trying to understand the longhouse view', April 4, 1981.
_____. 'Loggers broke water pipes, villagers claim', October 17, 1981.
_____. 'Big ulu group sought logging compensation', December 26, 1981.
_____. 'Ulu anger over lost forest', June 26, 1982.
_____. 'Ulu folk plea for their forest', August 28, 1982.
_____. 'Japanese Dam Man Dies', August 28, 1982.
_____. 'Plea over logging', September 11, 1982.
_____. 'Ulu folk drift to shanty towns', October 9, 1982.
_____. 'Logging operations threaten ulu survival', November 6, 1982.
_____. 'Sarawak's undeclared logging war flares up', November 6, 1982.
_____. 'Spokesman in armed timber protest freed', March 19, 1983.
_____. 'Two drought deaths', April 2, 1983.
_____. 'Hanging toilet of the ulu', April 16, 1983.
_____. 'Drought hits ulu lifeline', April 16, 1983.
_____. 'Limestone helps a longhouse prosper', August 13, 1983.

_____. 'Trouble for Power Dam', August 27, 1983.

_____. 'Backwater enjoys economic upswing', September 3, 1983.

_____. 'SAM campaigns against huge Rajang River dams', September 17, 1983.

_____. 'Report sees big future for basin', December 17, 1983.

_____. 'Timber waste deplored', December 17, 1983.

_____. 'Police action over timber protestors', January 28, 1984.

_____. 'Concern over dam workers future', October 13, 1984.

_____. 'Loggers are killing rivers', March 30, 1985.

_____. 'Orang Ulu wants rivers protected', April 19, 1985.

_____. 'Batang Ai puts out a rain prayer', May 4, 1985.

_____. 'Kenyahs accuse logging company', August 10, 1985.

_____. 'Chiefs duck Mahathir outburst', August 31, 1985.

_____. 'Goldminers fight farmers for land', October 5, 1985.

_____. 'Five Batang Ai bodies elude police', November 23, 1985.

Borneo Post, '40,000 hectares for estate development', February 24, 1985.

_____. 'Land compensation not received', September 14, 1985.

_____. 'CM raps those who reject power project', September 20, 1985.

_____. 'Foreign tech to develop Sarawak estates', February 12, 1986.

_____. '300 squatters to receive land titles from government', February 25, 1986.

_____. 'Wong: Bakun should be examined in depth', March 19, 1986.

_____. 'Power for devt panels to implement quick, suitable projects', April 16, 1986.

_____. 'Mayang Tea-Project to be expanded', May 31, 1986.

Business Times, 'Plan to boost use of idle land', November 30, 1985.

Daily Express, 'Close Land Board, Sarawak urged', November 11, 1985.

New Straits Times, 'No timber in 12 years if ...', August 30, 1977.

_____. 'Sarawak imported 45 percent rice needs in 1977-80', April 8, 1981.

_____. 'Ibans Storm Hydro Project Site, Three Detained by Police', July 30, 1982.

_____. 'Warning to those who hinder projects', August 21, 1982.

_____. 'Malaria on the rise in Sarawak', October 27, 1982.

_____. 'Resettled Ibans complain of empty promises', January 31, 1984.

_____. 'MPs speak up for poor constituents', March 23, 1984.

_____. 'Dayaks shed their timid, meek images', July 23, 1984.

_____. 'Isis studying alternative use for forest land', December 3, 1984.

_____. 'Batang Ai revisited', April 3, 1985.

_____. 'How native land should be developed', May 17, 1985.

_____. 'Longhouse living — the way it is', May 25, 1985.

_____. 'Sri Lankan dam burst kills 100 villagers', April 22, 1986.

New Sunday Times, 'A Slice of the Profit Cake', November 27, 1983.

_____. '260 killed as river of mud levels resort', July 21, 1985.

Sarawak Tribune, 'World Forestry Day Message', March 21, 1981.

_____. 'Land Custody and Development Authority to be set up', June 25, 1981.

_____. 'Work on Dam Construction to Start in June next year', September 16, 1981.

_____. 'Bau Earmarked For First Project', December 4, 1981.

_____. 'Bandar Orang Ulu coming up', March 20, 1982.

_____. 'CM advises Orang Ulu to regroup for own benefit', March 25, 1982.

_____. 'Coming — 800 Bangladesh Workers', July 2, 1982.

_____. 'Ulu folks in Sarawak hit by food shortage', October 21, 1982.

_____. 'Call for rural help', May 28, 1983.

_____. 'Don't take law into own hands', November 22, 1983.

_____. 'From Our Files: 10 Years Ago August 12, 1974', August 12, 1984.

_____. 'Growth and diversification: The problems and prospects — by Moggie', September 15, 1984.

_____. 'Major thrust of development', November 12, 1984.

_____. 'FELCRA to develop land in Third Division', February 11, 1985.

_____. 'Rural folk do not benefit from timber exploitation — MP', April 11, 1985.

_____. 'FELCRA Act will be amended', May 3, 1985.

_____. 'Most Sibu malarial cases are "imported" ', May 9, 1985.

_____. ' "Forest Concession Area (Rehabilitation and Development) Fund Bill 1985" ', June 8, 1985.

_____. 'Bakun Dam: Fears Run High', June 23, 1985.

_____. 'New Land Policy', October 1, 1985.

_____. 'Unfair for Yong to blame the natives', Letter to the editor, October 24, 1985.

_____. 'Model Villages for folk displaced by dam project', November 13, 1985.

_____. 'Balai Ringin land dispute', Letter to the editor, November 16, 1985.

_____. 'Land set aside for development by FELDA in Sarawak', December 16, 1985.

_____. 'Group to defend land with lives', February 5, 1986.

_____. 'Government to help several prominent firms in Sarawak', February 12, 1986.

_____. 'Another 5MP priority is agriculture — Taib', February 19, 1986.

_____. 'Why the double standard', April 23, 1986.

_____. 'Soon — Salcra's first cocoa scheme in Bau', May 24, 1986.

_____. 'Sylvester Langit's unaccomplished mission', June 7, 1986.

The Star, 'River lives changed by the log rush', September 12, 1982.

_____. 'WHO warning on water-borne disease', December 5, 1984.

_____. 'Sarawak To Save $12m A Year With HEP Project', August 27, 1985.

_____. 'Moggie: Report on Bakun project won't be released', December 3, 1985.

_____. 'Assess Bakun Dam Site First: Yong', January 18, 1986.

Sunday Mail, 'Health Ministry "taken aback" by Malaria threat' by Ainul Zaharah, October 17, 1982.

Sunday Star, '10 Villagers bound over for threatening logging camp', March 6, 1983.

_____. 'Sarawak's Dams: Narrow in perspective and empty in promises', March 4, 1984.

_____. 'Tearing the heart of a tribe', June 17, 1984.

Sunday Tribune, 'Resettling Tringgos farmers', March 18, 1984.

_____. '6,800 hectares to be developed', August 5, 1984.

_____. 'SALCRA — Taking the land scheme to the people', August 26, 1984.

_____. 'Punans more positive now towards changes', May 5, 1985.

Periodicals

Asiaweek, 'Wound in the World', July 13, 1984.

Suara Sam, 'Natives cheated out of tribal land', October 1985.

Utusan Konsumer, 'Horrors At Timber Camps', November 1985.

Utusan Konsumer, 'Bakun: Between Energy and Tragedy', February 1986.

APPENDIX ONE

Shifting Cultivation — Comparative Data on Labour Expenditure and Yield among Shifting Cultivators in Southeast Asia

Feature	Swidden community				
	Iban[1] Sarawak	Kantu[2] Kalimantan	Hanunoo[3] Philippines	Lamet[4] N. Laos	Kenyah[5] Sarawak
Swidden (rice) area farmed per adult worker, ha/year	0.53	0.97	0.35	0.46	0.55
Swidden (rice) area farmed per adult consumer, ha/year	0.32	0.59	0.18	0.31	0.32
Yield of unhusked rice, litres/ha	1325	1213	4000	2153	1456
Labour requirements for (rice), in old secondary or primary forest swiddens, man-days/ha	138-175	88.2	261	—	101.2

1. Freeman (1970)
2. Dove (1981)
3. Conklin (1957)
4. Izikowitz (1951)
5. Chin (1984)

Source: Chin See Chung, 'Agriculture And Subsistence In A Lowland Rainforest Kenyah Community', Ph. D Dissertation, Yale University, 1984: Table 40.

APPENDIX TWO

Principal Forest Types and Other Land Use, 1970
(Area in square kilometres)

Forest Type and Land Use	Division							Land	Land Area
	I	II	III	IV	V	VI	VII		
Forested Land									
A. Swamp Forest									
Mangrove & Nipah Swamp	523.2	103.6	51.8	28.5	155.4	875.4	—	1,737.9	1.4
Mixed Swamp Forest	1,528.1	2,198.9	3,672.6	3,222.0	207.2	911.7	—	11,740.5	9.5
Alan Forest	57.0	577.6	935.0	282.3	—	82.9	—	1,934.7	1.6
Padang Paya Forest	—	5.2	77.7	935.0	—	44.0	—	1,061.9	0.9
B. Hill Forest									
Mixed Dipterocarp Forest	1,678.3	1,085.2	3,325.6	27,845.1	6,192.7	805.5	33,258.2	74,190.6	60.2
Kerangas Forest	790.0	31.1	41.4	891.0	51.8	7.8	1,846.7	3,659.7	2.9
Sub-Total	4,576.6	4,001.6	8,104.1	33,203.9	6,607.1	2,727.3	35,104.9	94,325.3	76.5

Non Forested Land

Settled and Associated non-

Agriculture Land	46.6	20.7	23.3	23.3	5.2	10.4	2.6	132.1	0.1
Settled Cultivation	1,515.2	852.1	893.6	626.8	103.6	549.1	57.0	4,597.3	3.7
Shifting Cultivation	2,375.0	4,791.5	3,763.3	4,356.4	725.2	2,662.5	3,833.2	22,507.1	18.3
Unused Land	116.6	310.8	—	279.7	292.7	—	691.5	1,691.3	1.4
Sub-Total	4,053.4	5,975.1	4,680.2	5,286.2	1,126.7	322.0	4,584.3	28,927.8	23.5
Total Land Area	8,630.0	9,967.7	12,784.3	38,490.1	7,733.8	5,949.3	39,689.2	123,253.1	100
Water	—	—	—	—	—	—	—	1,196.6	—

Total Area of Sarawak = 124,450 sq. kilometres

Source: Land & Survey Department 1970.
c.f. *Annual Report of the*
Forest Department Sarawak 1984, Appendix F, Form 2.

APPENDIX THREE

| Species | All Sections | | |
| | Hill Logs | Swamp Logs | Hewn Timber |

Production of Logs and Hewn Timber 1984
(cu. metre)

Species	Hill Logs	Swamp Logs	Hewn Timber
Belian M'gai	4,627	—	12,001
Ramin	—	454,762	—
Bindang/Sempilor	11,039	—	8
Meranti	4,208,142	167,087	228
Penyau	5,493	—	—
Jongkong	—	222,563	9
Kapur	1,417,738	64,592	894
Kerukup	—	6,386	39
Keruing	1,194,414	7,641	268
Semayur	—	2,586	—
Sepetir/T. Hantu	53,566	122,589	26
Selangan Batu	384,886	—	26
Alan	—	1,333,022	3,755
Nyatoh	83,998	—	26
Other Species	879,323	777,374	376
Total	8,243,226	3,158,602	17,716

Source: *Annual Report of the Forest Department Sarawak 1984, Appendix F, Form 8A.*

APPENDIX FOUR

Letter to the Prime Minister from Baram Natives

*Appeal letter to the Prime Minister from the **orang ulu** of the Baram District for the recognition of their rights to land, request for timber licences, Communal Forests Reserves and an investigation of the issue of timber licences in the Baram. This letter was sent circa 1980.*

Y.A.B. Perdana Mentri Datuk Hussein Onn,
Pejabat Perdana Mentri,
Kuala Lumpur

Dear Datuk Hussein Onn,

Per: A Fair Share In All The Natural Resources.

We the undersigned *Bumiputera kaum*[1] Kenyah, Kayan and Punan in Sungai Apoh and the Berawan of Batu Belah in Sungai Tutoh, Baram, Fourth Division, Sarawak wish to inform you to solve our grievances, consider our requests and to recognize our rights on the following matters.

1) *Historical Rights*

We the above races had lived on our land Sungai Apoh and in Batu Belah, Sungai Tutoh since our forefathers. Each longhouse community always have its own area (*Kawasan* or *Sempadan*)[2] for the purpose of administration with a *Ketua Kampung* or *Penghulu*.

During the Second World War the people in the area fought voluntarily against the Japanese to defend the land. Many died during the battle and many of our warriors are still alive with their medals (*Bintang Berani*)[3] as proof. During the Brooke and Colonial Government our rights on our land were never denied thus we prevailed in our areas. One clear example was the Liddel Brothers Timber Company or locally called by Natives as 'Kompeni Tuan Young'. Before the Liddel Brothers Company established a logging camp at Lubok Bendera within the Batu Belah *Kawasan* (*Sempadan*), Sungai Tutoh in 1952, the Whites and the then District Officer F.B.K. Drake held three meetings and negotiations with the Natives of the area (many of whom are still alive as witnesses). The community leaders and natives were consulted. Since Sarawak joined Malaysia we feel our rights on our soil has been taken away by the Sarawak Government.

1.   *Bumiputera* means 'Sons of the Soil'; *kaum* refers to community.

2.   Territory or Boundary.

3.   Star for Valour.

We felt and always feel that we are still the rightful owners of the land in our area, and we will stand firm and sacrifice ourselves to defend our rights.

2)   *Masharakat Adil*[4]

We the *Bumiputera* in the area have a vast area of land where timber and other natural resources are found. We are now aware of the economic value, profitability and importance of the natural resources in our area such as timber business in particular. It would be unreasonable for us in the area to fell the trees and make farms in this big area of Jungle as our ancestors did. Furthermore we the *Bumiputera* in the area almost have no regular monetary income because we are farmers and rubber tappers. Since Sarawak joined Malaysia we the *Bumiputera* in the area had applied for a licence to extract timber in our own area but our applications were not entertained and were rejected by the Sarawak Government. Instead licences were given to someone else which has no historial rights and no historical backgrounds whatsoever on our beloved land Sungai Apoh and Batu Belah, Tutoh. The issuing of licences has been greatly practised since Sarawak joined Malaysia. We the *Bumiputera* in the area would like to draw your attention that we are not happy at the present condition and situation. We the *Bumiputera* in the area want the Government to withdraw all the licences already issued in our area. Further timber commissions should be given to us since the time the companies operated in our area. Should there be licences of any form given to someone else in future in our area, the *Bumiputera* in the area should be given certain percentage of shares and or commissions or else the licences should be issued to us so as all the natives in the area have an equal share in the wealth of this area. We are weak and poor but by sharing the natural resources that *Allah*[5] had endowed on and in our land, we hope our standard of living will be improved and part of our poverty eradicated as stated in the *RUKUNEGARA*[6].

3)   *Communal Forest Reserves*

Farming is a mean of living, and all sorts of communication and transportation in our area depend on boats which are made from timbers. Since licences were being issued, we the *Bumiputera* in the area are running out of timbers for making boats. Such act of issuing licences means giving away our lands and timbers without giving any percentage share and commissions to us who are living in the area. Due to this fact, this practice of issuing licences in our area means destroying our livelihood and harming our health of which we now realised. To show our unhappiness, we did stop the operation of certain timber companies in our area, after letting our intention known by the Government. We are hoping that by sending you this petition you may stop the issuing of all forms of licences to someone else affecting the natural resources in Sungai Apoh and Batu Belah, Tutoh immediately. Please, solve this serious problem. In addition to this we would like you to consider our request to reserve certain acreage of land for Communal Forest Reserve to enable us to get timbers for making boats and housing purposes.

4)   *Investigation Of Timber Licences In Our Area*

As we have stated earlier, we the *Bumiputera* in the area had applied for a

4.   *Masharakat Adil* means Just Society.

5.   *Allah* is the Muslim reference to God.

6.   *Rukunegara* is the national ideology.

licence to extract timbers in our area since Sarawak joined Malaysia. All our applications were rejected. As *Perdana Mentri*[7] Of Malaysia we the undersigned *Bumiputera* has great hope and request you to investigate to whom the licences in our area were given? Who actually sign and issue the licences? Who are the share holders? Give reasons why our applications were rejected? Why are we the *Bumiputera* in the area not consulted and not given any percentage share and commission? How many and who are the lucky *Bumiputera* in our area who has been given the shares and commissions? We the *Bumiputera* in the area want you and your good office to expose this matter to us.

Once again we the undersigned *Bumiputera* in the area seek your attention and to exercise your power as *Perdana Mentri* Of Malaysia to consider this issue seriously as usual. If you don't take the issue seriously, we on our part will find ways and means to bring this matter to the attention of Foreign Bodies. We will stand firm and we will sacrifice ourselves to defend our human rights and our rights over our beloved land. We the undersigned *Bumiputera kaum* Kenyah, Kayan and Punan in Sungai Apoh and Berawan of Batu Belah in Sungai Tutoh hoping for the best, and waiting for your answer and action towards this issue soonest possible.

Thank you. May *Allah* bless you.

---

7.   *Perdana Mentri* means Prime Minister.

APPENDIX FIVE

Native Account of Native-Timber Company Conflict, Baram

A native account of the 'incident' at the timber camp in the Apoh river, Baram; the negotiations between natives and the company officials; and the court case in Marudi, 1980.

'At eight in the morning, five hundred people from five longhouses took our boats and went to the camp. We asked the camp manager to call the licensee and the contractor who were based in Kuching and Miri to come to the camp in the Apoh as we wanted to talk to them. The camp manager told us that they will both be coming in the afternoon so we waited. But they didn't turn up. Then he told us that they would come the next morning instead. So the people asked the camp manager for some petrol and they returned to their longhouses. The next morning we all went to the Camp again. The Camp Manager told us that they will come that afternoon. We waited but they didn't turn up. The people were getting impatient. We told the Camp Manager: "Why didn't they come? If they are going to treat us like this, how are we going to negotiate with them? We have written many letters already, asking them to come on this day, why didn't they come?" Then the Manager said they were busy and was giving a lot of excuses for them. Then the people said: "We will stop you from logging." The Manager made a radio call again. Then he said to us that they both cannot come. This made some of us angry. Then we asked for the ignition keys to the tractor from the mechanic. But he refused to give it to us. So we went to the workshop and got some pliers and we removed the starters from the tractors. We asked the Manager to radio back to Miri to tell the contractor to come. He radioed again. Then he told us that they are coming. We told him: "What if they don't turn up again?" He said to us "You can burn the camp." We were really very angry with his words. The Manager was made to sign what he said. We gave him a carbon copy of the letter which he signed. Some of us left for the longhouse. The rest of us stayed behind. We waited in the camp till the next morning. But they still didn't come. Then around two o'clock, twenty to thirty police field force personnel came. They took statements from the representatives of all the longhouses. They told us to go home. They said: "Come to Marudi on the 6th." The police assured us that the contractor and the licensee will be there to meet us. They said: "We *polis* (police) shall witness your negotiations."

On 6th February 1980, some 300 people from the affected longhouses went to the *kubu*[1] at Marudi and waited for them. We waited for about three to four hours, but they didn't come. We then went to the police station and met the OCPD (Officer in Charge of the Police District).

---

1.   The *kubu* is the old fort which houses the District Office. It was completed in 1902.

We asked him: "Why did you assure us that they would be here? Where are they?" He made a call to Miri to ask why the contractor had failed to come as the people had been waiting. An hour or so later, company officials from Miri arrived at Marudi. Two of them came but the boss didn't turn up. Then we all went to the *kubu*. We were not allowed in. Only the *ketua kampung* were allowed inside. The police inspector stood at the door of the *kubu* and refused to let us in. Sixteen longhouse elders went inside the *kubu*. After that, six or seven of the policemen and the company representatives told our elders: "We can't give you one cent. We are making a loss. There's no government policy which says that the company must share timber profits with the *orang ulu*. There's no such law". Our old people (elders) told them: "During the Japanese Occupation, we left our longhouses, our children and our wives to come to Marudi to defend Marudi for the government. Now our government and our people are robbing us of our land and trees". The Company officials told our elders: "Very sorry but we can't give you a cent". After this meeting, four of our people — all young men received summons to appear in court in Marudi for:

1.   criminal intimidation
2.   theft
3.   retention of stolen property

The hearing was fixed for 23 March 1980. One to two thousand *ulu* people from all over the Baram came to Marudi to lend their support. It was like during Regatta[2] time. The people were everywhere even sleeping along the river bank and Marudi bazaar was filled with *ulu* people. Twenty police fieldforce men from Miri arrived at the *kubu*. They carried stink bombs. The hearing started and lasted for three days. One of our people a 22 year old farmer was convicted for theft and sentenced to two months imprisonment. He had worked in the same logging camp before. The District Officer who was the magistrate refused bail. The hearing of the other three was adjourned. Then in May 1980, two of them were acquitted. The fourth one, an Apo Kayan, was convicted of criminal intimidation. He is 38 years old and is married. He was given two months imprisonment but he pleaded for bail because his wife was five months pregnant and he had an uncle dying of cancer and there was no one to look after the farm and the family. The court allowed him bail. The bail was $3,000. All our people helped to raise the money for him. He also appealed.'

---

2.   The Baram Regatta, which was held once every two years was the most famous and colourful
      sporting carnival in Sarawak. It was initiated in 1899 to commemorate the Peace Making between
      the various warring 'tribes' in the Baram which was held in Marudi. It has an unbroken tradition
      until 1977 when it ceased but was revived again in 1982. For further details see Hose and
      McDougall (1966), *The Pagan Tribes of Borneo*, Frank Cass: London; and Alfred G. Haddon, *The
      Sarawak Gazette*, May 1st, 1899.

APPENDIX SIX

Letter to Member of Parliament from Baram Natives
Invitation letter to a Member of Parliament in Peninsular Malaysia to Witness A Court Case
At Marudi from the orang ulu, in the Baram District, Fourth Division, Sarawak.

10th March, 1981.

Dear Sir

Invitation To Witness A Court Case At Marudi

We, the people of various races — Kayan, Kenyah, Punan and Berawan
(*Orang Ulus*) of Sungai Apoh, Tutoh would like to invite you to witness a court
case between us and Wan Abdul Rahman Timber Company on Monday 23rd
March, 1981 (Twenty-third March, 1981) at Marudi, Baram, Fourth Division,
Sarawak. The time will be at 9.00 A.M. (nine o'clock in the morning).

The below mentioned points will give you an idea as to how and why this
court case comes to light.

1. We the above races or minority groups have lived and defended the land
    and soil of Sungai Apoh, Tutoh, Baram since our forefather, including
    voluntarily fighting the Japanese during the Second World War.

    Because of the above fact, we know and feel that we have the right to
    have an equal fair share in the land's (Apoh, Tutoh) natural resources
    including timber.

    Due to the above reasons, we did apply and continually applied for a
    licence to extract the timber in our area Sungai Apoh, Tutoh as early as
    1967. However, our applications were rejected without any reason given.

2. A few years later, the licence to extract timber in our area was given to
    Wan Abdul Rahman Timber Company.

3. *First Letter*: After that we in the area asked for timber commission at $40.00
    per ton from Wan Abdul Rahman Timber Company, but our request was
    rejected. The carbon copies of the above application for commission were
    extended to the Minister Of Forestry, and to ten other appropriate
    ministries and departments concerned.

4. *Second Letter*: Two weeks after the above letter, we sent a letter to inform the
    government — original copy to the District Officer of Baram, requesting
    him (D.O.) to call for the Managing Director of the timber company
    concerned, to meet and negotiate with us, within two weeks. The carbon
    copies were extended to all appropriate ministries and departments
    concerned. In his reply the District Officer, said that he had no power to
    deal with the matter. The matter remained unsettled.

5. *Third Letter*: Two weeks after the date of the second letter, we sent another letter to Wan Abdul Rahman Timber Company (all the carbon copies extended to all the appropriate persons above) asking for negotiation once more, of which failure to this last request we in the area would stop the logging operation of the Wan Abdul Rahman Company in our area, Sungai Apoh.

6. Failing to meet and negotiate, we did actually stopped the logging camp from operating. There was no physical injury or damage done by us. Only after stopping the company's operation, then soldiers and police were sent to our area.

We are accused of being wrong, but we do not admit.

Thus the Court Case will be held at 9.00 A.M. on the 23rd March, (Twenty-third of March), 1981, at Marudi, Baram. We will be the defendants and the accused.

Because of the above facts, we sincerely invite you to come, to attend and to witness the court procedures and details from beginning to end.

Please come to Sarawak seven to ten days before the court opens because we want to publicize this issue in the press.

In replying to this letter, please use our address above.

Sir, your attention to this matter and your presence for this particular court hearing, are very much appreciated.

Thank you.

Yours faithfully,

From the Representatives and the
Kayan, Kenyah, Punan and Berawan races of
Sungai Apoh, Tutoh, Baram,
Fourth Division, Sarawak.

INDEX